David Lamp

Dec. '82

JOSEPH CONRAD: Gia...

Joseph Conrad
GIANT IN EXILE

Leo Gurko

WITH A NEW INTRODUCTION

COLLIER BOOKS
A Division of Macmillan Publishing Co., Inc.
New York
COLLIER MACMILLAN PUBLISHERS
London

FOR

Sir Evelyn Howell

Macmillan Publishing Co., Inc.
866 Third Avenue, New York, N.Y. 10022
Collier Macmillan Canada, Ltd.

Library of Congress Cataloging in Publication Data
Gurko, Leo, 1914-
Joseph Conrad, giant in exile.
Bibliography p.
1. Conrad, Joseph, 1857-1924.   2. Novelists,
English—20th century—Biography.   I. Title.
PR6005.04Z7417   1979b   823'.9'12   79-1416
ISBN 0-02-546700-X
ISBN 0-02-003360-5 pbk.

First Collier Books Edition 1979

Joseph Conrad: *Giant in Exile* is also published in a hardcover edition
by Macmillan Publishing Co., Inc.

Printed in the United States of America

Contents

Introduction

WHEN *Joseph Conrad: Giant in Exile* first appeared in 1962, my purpose, as stated in the original foreword, was:

. . . to throw light on Joseph Conrad as an artist by a systematic exploration of his work against the background of his life and personality. My object was not to write a detailed biography or an exhaustive criticism of everything Conrad ever wrote, but to extract from his experiences as a man and his procedures as a writer those strategic points of intersection which, when brought together, may enable us to see the whole of his achievement in a new way.

In the seventeen years since the book was issued, mountains of minutiae about Conrad have been amassed but my purpose remains unchanged: to concentrate on the mysterious connections that exist, as they do with every writer, between the life of Conrad and his work.

What has changed in the meantime is the general interest in Conrad, which has accelerated visibly during the 1960's and 70's. The student ferment of the late 60's, with its animus against culture, its hostility to the past, its devastating assault on the traditional aspects of education, slowed this acceleration. But with the return in the 70's to a more normal temper, the sale of Conrad's books began once again to escalate steadily. Scholars and critics have been pursuing him with mounting zeal. An increasing number of master's and doctor's theses, of full-scale studies from the academic presses, have been devoted to him, accompanied by his expanding presence in course curriculums. New biographies, of blockbuster size, are threatened. Whatever letters by him—and to him—that remain unpublished are being hunted, literally, to the ends of the earth.

A rage for Conrad has assumed the proportions of a small but growing industry. Every aspect of his life and work, of the influences upon him, has by this date been minutely examined. Even nineteenth-century Poland, anatomized to the last detail, down to the very stones of Cracow itself, has been summoned to shed its light on the soul of its self-exiled son. And Conrad himself has been posthumously paid a kind of final accolade by being subjected in a very

long book to a full-length psychoanalysis at the hands of a practicing psychiatrist, a result that has left him fragmented and shredded
almost beyond recognition. In this respect, Freudianism—that faded
darling of our world of intellectual fashion—has been no kinder or
more "humanizing" to Conrad than it has been to other celebrated
writers it has one by one devoured.

In other regions of popular culture, Conrad's name has bobbed up
in widening frames of reference. The highly publicized troubles of
the emergent African states can scarcely be referred to without
quotations from and allusions to Conrad's African stories. A huge
new movie called *Apocalypse Now*, plagued with cost overruns of
epic size, has been announced by its producer Francis Ford Coppola
as a rewrite of *Heart of Darkness*, with the jungles of Vietnam substituting for the jungles of the Belgian Congo. A number of Conrad's other fictions, including the gigantic *Nostromo*, are up for
transmutation into film. Conrad has indeed become a focal point,
a guide to contemporary sensibility. When invoked, as it has been
invoked with ever-growing frequency, his name, and certainly his
art, suggests a certain adventurous fatalism, a plunging into the
more exotic reaches of the globe, and an acute awareness of the
demons lying in wait under the surface of our civilized selves.

We are also becoming aware more than ever before of Conrad as
a force in modern literature. One of the more persistent dogmas of
modern criticism is that the literary titans of the age are Joyce,
Proust, Kafka, and Mann. I have serious reservations about each of
these four. But even if I had not, I should argue that Conrad's stature and significance and influence have grown to an equivalent
point. Certainly the shape of American writing in our century
vividly reflects his influence and bears an intimately Conradian
stamp. Beginning with the early sea plays of Eugene O'Neill, his
presence is pervasive. And nowhere more so than in the work of the
century's three greatest American novelists: Fitzgerald, Hemingway,
and Faulkner.

Fitzgerald, for one, made no bones about his debt to Conrad. *The
Great Gatsby* can indeed be read as an Americanized update of *Lord
Jim*: both are stories of naive young men of obscure background
who rise in the world, and then fall, pursuing ideals well beyond

their power to achieve, their careers all the while being scrutinized by a pair of ironic narrators whose own lives are shaken up morally by the ambivalent young protagonists. Hemingway, while still a newspaperman, used to ration his reading of Conrad so as not to use him up too quickly. At the same time he embraced Conrad's Manichean view of the world as a remorseless struggle between darkness and light. "A Clean, Well-Lighted Place" is only one of numerous expressions by Hemingway of the small circle of human light holding off the immense circumambient pressure of the darkness of *nada*. As for Faulkner, he ran through the works of Conrad as a youth and grew up to write conjectural novels remarkably in the vein of *Lord Jim* and *Chance*.

Similar points can be made, but need not be labored, about Conrad's impact on his successors in England. In a period relatively bare of great English writers, there is nevertheless the example of Graham Greene, who has been said to be incapable of writing a bad sentence. Greene, wrestling strenuously with the ambiguous dilemmas of conduct inherited wholesale from Conrad, stands as a lofty testament to the hold of his predecessor. The same can be said of the recently (and all too slowly) discovered masterpiece *The Raj Quartet*. This spellbinding account of India by the late Paul Scott recalls in every section Conrad's particular preoccupation with those complex moral tugs-of-war for which he is famous.

To read Conrad again more than a half-century after his death is a bracing experience. We are perhaps more conscious than before of how *mature* a writer he is: how measured and controlled his tone, how unwaveringly complex his point of view. Perhaps there is something to be said for a writer living first and writing later. Conrad did not start writing until his late thirties. By the time he began his first novel, he was not only well past his first youth but was a fully seasoned man.

While reading Trollope, Tolstoy is reported to have exclaimed: "His excellence is killing me." Trollope was another novelist who did not begin until his thirties. Like Conrad, he served a short apprenticeship before getting to his masterpieces. Conrad's excellence, on its own ground, moves us deeply, not alone by the cadences of his voluptuous prose, but by the penetrating psychology, the arresting judgments earned, and thereby made convincing, by hard experience. It is this that gives even such baroque tales as *The End of the Tether* and *The Secret Sharer* their "bitter plausibility," to borrow one of Conrad's telling phrases.

With writers who touch us at the heart, there are always compelling moments of special appeal. My own private list of such moments in Conrad would include the following: the extendedly brilliant opening paragraph of *An Outcast of the Islands*; the eleventh and twelfth chapters of *The Secret Agent*, pulse-pounding examples of melodrama carried to the highest level of art; Decoud's suicide in *Nostromo*, creating as he disappears into "the immense indifference of things" one of the arresting death scenes in modern literature; the image of Jim, mired ankle-deep in guano, on an empty island in the middle of a desolate ocean; the supremely credible irony of Razumov in *Under Western Eyes* being taken—and mistaken—for a revolutionary idealist because of his deliberate silence on all political questions; the feat in *Heart of Darkness* of making Europe and Africa humanly indistinguishable after dramatizing in remorseless detail their multitude of self-evident differences. Of special appeal, too are the minor villains—among them Massy in *The End of the Tether*, Sotillo in *Nostromo*, Schomberg in *Victory*, creatures amazingly sensitive to the demands of their own personalities, burning, indeed burning up, with hatred of the world. One could go on at length. Conrad's fiction teems with plummy morsels, masterful stratagems, resonant variations on the psycho-moral themes that magnetized him and continue to magnetize us, and an unerring sense of place aroused by an unfailingly sensuous descriptive power.

Conrad belonged to a generation of writers, perhaps the last such generation, who continue to impress us with the unexpected range of their accomplishments, justifying their collective rubric as men-of-letters. Kipling, Shaw, Galsworthy, Henry James, H. G. Wells, Arnold Bennett—like Conrad—were adept practitioners of numerous literary genres. Conrad was not only a novelist but a writer of memoirs, of essays on literature, politics, and history, even of splendid letters running into the thousands. In fiction he not only turned out numbers of short stories and full-length novels, but also cultivated with consummate skill the art of the novella, producing in *The Nigger of the "Narcissus," Heart of Darkness*, and *The Shadow-Line* exquisite illustrations of that demanding form. So that though he began writing relatively late in life, he fashioned a body of work that is singularly rich not only in the abundance of its individual achievements but in its conspicuous versatility.

Moreover, as with most great writers, the subjects to which he addressed himself are more or less roughly balanced between the timely and the timeless. The timely ones, drawn from the issues and concerns of the day, engaged Conrad's imagination throughout his career, and they continue to engage ours. His early novels, introducing characters like Almayer and Willems, white men married to or sexually involved with Malay women, dealt with race relations, a theme as burningly consequential toward the end of the twentieth century as it was at the end of the nineteenth. The same is true of such other topical matters as absorbed Conrad in his later novels: colonialism and imperialism, the relations between Europe and Africa, the political turmoil in Latin America, Russia and the West, violence as a revolutionary method. He even wrote, in collaboration with Ford Madox Hueffer, a novel (*The Inheritors*) that concerned itself with figures from outer space intruding into the affairs of earth. Though all these matters occupy us as much as they did Conrad and Conrad's generation—an eloquent tribute to his historical sense—they are nontheless transient.

Conrad is adept at dealing with these timely issues but it is his grasp of timeless matters that cements his enduring reputation. He begins with the traditional questions of good and evil, right and wrong, responsible and irresponsible behavior. But he soon arrives at the conviction that the familiar distinctions among them are no longer verifiable and perhaps not even defensible. Kurtz commits unspeakable crimes and yet there is something great about him. Jim abandons the *Patna*, yet Marlow spends hundreds of pages justifying or at the very least "explaining" the act. In *The Nigger of the "Narcissus"* the mystery of James Wait—is he demon or victim?—remains deliberately unresolved. Conrad throws aside conventional morality and conventional metaphysics in favor of a more sophisticated, less schematic viewpoint best summed up by the statement in *Lord Jim*: "There was not the thickness of a sheet of paper between the right and wrong of the affair."

It is then that Conrad, disburdened of a priori ideas about conduct and morality, grounds his art securely in a passionately disinterested study of human nature itself, with its endless capacity for self-deception and its endless, indeed desperate, need for self-examination. His heroes go forth into the world less in search of dangerous adventure, though that is their invariable lot, as in quest—often subconscious—of self-knowledge. To discover what lies in wait for them within themselves is their obscurely perceived impulse, just as it is Conrad's supreme design to create for them the conditions that will trigger, advance, and at last dramatize their discoveries.

Amid this psychological exploration, there emerges the volatile temperament which absorbed Conrad above all others, which surfaces in his books over and over again, the temperament that is intimately and by now permanently associated with him and his work. If a composite portrait can be drawn of his protagonists, it would mount up to this. His central figures are loners, far more at home in their own company than in society. They are unevenly intelligent, self-indulgent and self-absorbed to the point of solipsism, and given to wide swings, even extremes of mood. They are abnormally susceptible to the virus of boredom and depression—that peculiarly modern disease of the spirit which has found, among the writers of our age, its acknowledged expert in Conrad. But they veer from this to the opposite and equally disorienting state of extreme euphoria.

They bear a startling resemblance to Conrad himself, except that he, unlike them, finally imposed upon his own treacherous and erratic temperament the stern, unrelenting discipline of art. They stand before us as striking instances of a fundamental type of human personality, enough like ourselves to make us uneasily—and fascinatedly—conscious of our kinship. A large part of Conrad's enduring appeal is this creation of a central personality, replete with variations, so rooted in the permanent aspects of human nature that its import, and impact, is universal. In this ultimate way Conrad makes use of and finally masters his timeless subject.

The facts of Conrad's life were first assembled in 1927 by his friend G. Jean-Aubry in the two-volume *Joseph Conrad: Life and Letters*. Mrs. Conrad wrote two memoirs of her husband after his death, *Joseph Conrad As I Knew Him* and *Joseph Conrad and His Circle*. Ford Madox Ford, his early friend and collaborator, wrote a memoir of his own, *Joseph Conrad, A Personal Remembrance*. In 1960 a new biography by Jocelyn Baines appeared, remarkable for its zealous pursuit of original sources, though pedestrian and unilluminating in its extensive comments on the novels.

Over the years a considerable body of criticism has accumulated on Conrad. I will briefly mention the items which seem to me of uncommon interest. John D. Gordan, until his death the curator of the Berg Collection in the New York Public Library where a useful collection of Conrad material is housed, published in 1940 his *Joseph Conrad, The Making of a Novelist*, a valuable analysis of the textual revisions made by Conrad in three of his early works. Gustav Morf's *The Polish Heritage of Joseph Conrad* intriguingly discusses the novels in terms of Conrad's submerged feelings for Poland. A finely shaded, full-length critical study is Albert J. Guerard's *Conrad the Novelist*. Among the more penetrating single essays on Conrad are Morton Dauwen Zabel's "Joseph Conrad: Chance and Recognition" (*Sewanee Review*, Winter, 1945), the section devoted to him in F. R. Leavis's *The Great Tradition* (1948), Robert Penn Warren's introduction to the Modern Library edition of *Nostromo*, and the chapters on *Lord Jim* in Dorothy Van Ghent's *The English Novel: Form and Function* (1953).

The most important volumes of Conrad's letters after Jean-Aubry's are addressed to his cousin Marguerite Poradowska, to his editor Edward Garnett, to his publishers William Blackwood and David Meldrum, and to his friend R. B. Cunningham Grahame. Indispensable to students of Conrad is the bibliography assembled in 1957 by Kenneth A. Lohf and Eugene P. Sheehy, *Joseph Conrad at Mid-Century: Editions and Studies, 1895–1955*.

The George T. Keating collection of Conrad material at Yale University is the richest of its kind in the world. I wish to thank Marjorie Wynne of the Yale Library for her help in making it available to me. Sections of this book appeared in somewhat altered form as articles in *Modern Fiction Studies, The University of Kansas City Review, College English*, and *Nineteenth-Century Fiction* (© 1961). Their publishers—the Purdue Research Foundation, the University of Kansas City Review, the National Council of Teachers of English, and the Regents of the University of California respectively—have kindly given me permission to reprint. I am once again indebted to my wife for her critical reading of the text. This book was completed with the help of a faculty research grant from Hunter College.

I am grateful to J. M. Dent & Sons Ltd. for permission to quote
from Conrad's letters and works, and to Doubleday & Co. for editorial clearance. I also wish to thank the following publishers and
holders of copyright for permission to quote: Roy Publishers for the
selection from *Conrad and His Contemporaries*, by J. H. Retinger;
Janice Biala for the selections from *Joseph Conrad, A Personal
Remembrance*, by Ford Madox Ford; the Bobbs-Merrill Company
for the selections from *Letters from Joseph Conrad, 1895–1924*, ed.
by Edward Garnett, copyright 1955; Charles Scribner's Sons for a
passage from *Castles in Spain*, by John Galsworthy; the Duke University Press for the selection from *Letters of Joseph Conrad to
William Blackwood and David S. Meldrum*, ed. by William Blackburn; the Yale University Press for the quotations from *Letters of
Joseph Conrad to Marguerite Poradowska, 1890–1920*, tr. and ed.
by John A. Gee and Paul J. Sturm.

I have quoted throughout from the Canterbury edition of Conrad's collected works, published by Doubleday, Page & Co. in 1924.
Its pagination is the same as in other editions put out by Doubleday in this country and Dent in England.

I

Conrad as "One of Us"

AFTER CONRAD DIED IN 1924, HIS CRITICAL REPUTATION AND THE POPU-larity of his novels began to decline sharply. Within a relatively few years they had dropped to the low point at which they remained through the 30's, 40's, and early 50's.

The reasons for this slump in fortune go straight to the heart of Conrad. He was acutely distrustful of democracy in an age when the egalitarian spirit continued to flourish. His temper was rooted in the traditions of a landed gentry at a time when this class was being liquidated by political upheavals in the Communist countries and technological ones in the West. He took a dim view of revolu-tions and radical movements—just before they spread through the world and became respectable. He did not believe in the reform of institutions as long as the human heart remained unaltered, a doctrine which ran counter to the theory of the welfare state. And though he was a lifelong critic of imperialism and colonialism—Russian, Dutch, French, Belgian, American, and even British—it was not out of special feeling for the native populations, any more than Jonathan Swift, two centuries before, had any special love for the Irish though he defended them against English exploitation.

Nor did he take established emotions on the usual terms. The devotion of parents to children may be admirable, but in Conrad it can lead to disaster. Patriotism is a noble sentiment, but at times it forces men to assume commitments which prove destructive. The sustaining emotion of love between men and women can wither under the touch of other fine feelings: idealism, refined sensibility, even the instinct of self-sacrifice. The impulse to help others—which in Tom Lingard, central figure of Conrad's three Malayan novels, assumed an extreme form of do-goodism—often leads only to their ruin. Out of good, then, can come evil.

But Conrad's vision embraces its own opposites. At the other end of the moral equation, out of evil comes good, too, and just as inexorably. Marlow's contact with Kurtz in the heart of darkness leads him to light, and the lie that he deliberately and finally utters is a complex kind of truth. The young captain in "The Secret Sharer" protects a murderer and thereby releases the creative energies within himself. Falk eats human flesh; he is, of course, nauseated with himself, but this nausea drives him straight toward love and redemption. The crew of the *Narcissus* are hypnotized by the "nigger" and swayed by Donkin—those twin demons—but it is precisely their initiation into this dark underside of existence that makes possible the release of the ship from its deathlike trance.

Conrad was neither ambiguous nor unclear, but he was elusive. To a postwar generation that required an unequivocal statement about the nature of life, even if it were a statement of despair, meaninglessness, or confusion, this elusiveness seemed unsatisfactory. His moral complications demanded close and attentive involvement; a hard core lay at their center, but one needed to struggle to get at it. Even as he was affirming the necessity of traditional ideals— fidelity, courage, work, duty—he was questioning whether they were enough to stave off corruption and defeat. The exasperated judgment of E. M. Forster summed up the informed reader's sense of baffled vexation: ". . . he is misty in the middle as well as at the edges . . . the secret casket of his genius contains a vapour rather than a jewel; and we need not try to write him down philosophically, because there is . . . nothing to write. No creed, in fact. Only opinions, and the right to throw them overboard when facts make them look absurd." [1] Forster was wrong. There is a jewel in the Conradian casket, the jewel of a created universe. But if it can be asserted that particular treasures reveal themselves at particular times and have an almost instinctively self-protective way of concealing themselves until then, Conrad's moment had, plainly, not yet come.

The nuanced obliqueness of his comments on life extended to his own personality, and was responsible for the diverse and often

[1] *Abinger Harvest* (New York, 1936), p. 138.

contradictory impressions he made upon even those who were close to him. To his wife, he was a genius, to be sure; but also a difficult, unstable, self-centered man-baby who had to be protected from the frictions of everyday life and from the details of practical and domestic responsibilities. What a curious view this was of a seaman who had risen to captaincy in the hard, demanding routine of sailing ships and always prided himself on his sense of meticulous craftsmanship. His maternal uncle and guardian, Tadeusz Bobrowski, regarded the orphaned nephew entrusted to his care at the age of eleven as a fascinating and dangerous battleground where the instinct for order inherited from his mother's family, and the impulse to chaos inherited from his father's, struggled for supremacy.

To Edward Garnett, Conrad was the suffering writer, flogging his imagination to keep it awake at the workbench, constantly denigrating his own efforts, pathetically grateful for encouragement and never quite believing it. Garnett was his first reader, literary confidant, and professional friend. He recommended the publication of *Almayer's Folly,* Conrad's first novel, and when Conrad, blank of mind and at loose ends, was unable to start a second, cleverly nudged him into beginning *An Outcast of the Islands.* The letters with which Conrad bombarded Garnett during the early years of his writing career groan with the agony of enforced creation. Doubts about his own talent, insecurity in the difficult issues of technique and style, the constant psychic irritations attendant upon the plunge into a new life and a new language beset his appeals to Garnett, to whom he clung at times like a drowning man floundering in unfamiliar depths. But in the midst of this turmoil, there is already clearly visible the grown man conscious of his responsibilities, formulating his aesthetic doctrine, stubbornly pursuing the discouragingly remote objectives facing him after the end of his career at sea. No sign of Mrs. Conrad's man-baby here, or of Uncle Tadeusz's split-souled youth.

To Ford Madox Hueffer (subsequently Ford Madox Ford), who collaborated with Conrad in the writing of two early novels, *The Inheritors* and *Romance,* the merchant mariner from Poland now turned novelist was a queer, unclassifiable bird. With a potpourri of languages and background, here he was in England struggling for the *mot juste* in a tongue twice removed from his own. Ford was then a cocky young man who patronized his elders with cheerful insolence, and hinted strongly that he was conferring upon Conrad the inestimable boon of initiating him simultaneously into the mysteries of English and the secrets of art. Mrs. Conrad found him insufferable. But impressed as he was with himself, Ford still found it possible to be impressed with Conrad, whom he regarded as a force, as a phenomenon, though incurably and unavoidably foreign. "When you had really secured his attention," remarked Ford, "he would insert a monocle into his right eye and scrutinise your face from very near as a watchmaker looks into the works of a watch." [2]

To Richard Curle, a young friend of Conrad in his last years, Conrad was simply and altogether a great man. In the admiring eyes of this idealizing and uncritical disciple, he was full of wisdom, replete with an extraordinary knowledge of a wide range of subjects, unfailingly warm, courteous, and friendly. This is quite a different Conrad from the one that Forster saw. The bellwether of the Bloomsbury Group marked him as a severe, rather chilly aristocrat who admitted us with great formality into the anteroom of his confidence, and no farther. Behind the monocle, behind the formidable reserve, lay an utterly concealed and private man.

Since we tend to read others in the light of our own necessities, Conrad's intimates are as clearly illuminated in their portraits of him as Conrad himself. But the qualities they see in him are nonetheless there. He was warm and confessional, yet aristocratic and reserved. He was embarrassingly self-deprecatory, but this was often a mask for his self-belief. The gout that plagued him from his thirty-third year on made him irritable and querulous; most of this emotional destructiveness, however, was directed at himself, and seldom penetrated the armor of old-world etiquette in which he had been schooled. Experience for him was a testing ground of emotions and attitudes. As a seaman he took orders; as mate and captain he gave them. With Mme. Poradowska, a relation of his by marriage and an established literary figure, he was the eager, deferential, almost sycophantic disciple; when he himself became established, it was possible for him to reverse roles and descant, *de haut en bas,* to those who came to him for advice and wisdom. He was son and father, lover and husband, a patriot and refugee from patriotism, an

2 *Joseph Conrad, A Personal Remembrance* (Boston, 1924), p. 3.

almost perfectly amphibious human being who spent half his
grown life at sea and half on land. The protean aspects of his views
on moral conduct have their analogue in the protean aspects of
his personality.

But Conrad was more than a protean figure. He was also a
prophetic one. His novels experimented with time and multiple
narration long before Proust, Gide, and Joyce made these standard
practice in contemporary fiction. As a psychologist Conrad probed
into the split personality, searched for the hidden self, studied the
mechanism of guilt and redemption, and made of inertia, moral
paralysis, and the dreamlike mesmerism of the transfixed will almost
his own special province. The three political novels that Conrad
wrote in succession from 1903 to 1910 were uncanny blueprints of
events to come. Irving Howe has already noted how *Nostromo,* the
first of them, was a preview of recent history in Cuba and Argentina,
down to the very itemization of personalities, motives, and procedures.[3] What happened in Conrad's mythical Costaguana was,
in fact, an imaginative blueprint of revolutions in primitive countries everywhere. The second of the political novels, *The Secret
Agent,* explored nineteenth century anarchism and defined superlatively the motives not of the ideological leaders but of the shabby
hangers-on, the obscure agents, the ambiguous fringe figures who
are standard in every radical movement. The third, *Under Western
Eyes,* was a prescient analysis of Russia and the Russian psyche
almost ten years before the Bolshevik Revolution, twenty years
before the emergence of Stalin, and a half century before the rise
of Khrushchev. In politics, no less than in psychology and art,
Conrad demonstrated how much of the future could be anticipated
and seized by the imaginative mastery of the present.

In an immediate sense Marlow's persistent refrain about Lord
Jim, "He is one of us," applies to Conrad and ourselves. The
phenomena that concern us absorbed him. The spectacle of the
divided man thrust into an ambiguous world is more relevant to the
general psychic frame of the 1970's than when he first proposed
it in the last years of the nineteenth century. The haze that clung
impenetrably to the outer ring of his cosmos is the haze that we see.

3 *Politics and the Novel* (New York, 1957), p. 105.

Our disillusion with doctrinal ideologies was his. The skepticism with which he examined men and their complicated self-deceptions is a cathartic that rouses us to life.

The sophisticated pessimism he embraced as the most durable of attitudes supplied him with a philosophical procedure by which meaning and affirmation could be wrung from resistant experience. The experience remains ours, no less resistant, but blazingly illuminated by Conrad's visionary wrestling with it.

II

The Reluctant Underground

THE TRAGEDY OF POLAND WAS NOT ONLY GEOGRAPHIC, BUT PSYCHOLOGI-
cal. It was bad enough that fate had ringed her with powerful
enemies. Worse still was that the same fate did not equip her to
discharge effectively the role demanded by a malevolent geography.

For nearly two centuries Poland has been forced, against her
own nature and traditions, into a conspiratorial underground, a
role she has played with notable unsuccess. Poland was traditionally
divided between a small nobility and a numerous peasantry. The
nobles were given to stiff-necked patriotism, complicated etiquette,
and grandiloquent gestures. The peasants, largely illiterate, were
equally patriotic, aggressively obstinate, and subject to spasmodic
fits of bigotry. It was a society made for parade-ground wars, headlong cavalry charges, and a relatively simple, straightforward
diplomacy. Instead, it was forced into undercover activities, subtle
Machiavellisms, elaborate pretenses of obedience masking a violent
passion for independence. Partitioned originally among three great
powers, forced to swallow two hated foreign languages, Poland
oscillated throughout the nineteenth century between sudden
bloody outbursts of rebellious ardor and relapses into sullen passivity
bordering on the comatose. There was a touch of disaster and
futility to all her enterprises in bondage, quite in keeping with the
split between her temperament and lot.

"You seem to forget that I am a Pole," Conrad wrote to Garnett
in October, 1907. "You forget that we have been used to go to
battle without illusions. It's you Britishers that 'go in to win' only.
We have been 'going in' these last hundred years repeatedly, to be
knocked on the head only . . ." [1] Conrad's despair about Poland—

[1] *Letters from Joseph Conrad, 1895–1924*, ed. by Edward Garnett (Indianapolis,
1928), p. 209. All future references to this volume will be abbreviated to Garnett.

an emotion endemic to the country—was, in his particular case, heightened by the unhappy experiences of his father, Apollo Korzeniowski, as an unsuccessful conspirator against the Russian occupation.

His father's melancholy private history encapsulates the chronicle of Poland. He was filled with ardor, élan, a capacity to entertain only one political idea at a time, a naïve zeal for the use of short-term methods to achieve long-range objectives, and a rigid inability to live life on any terms but his own. Under normal circumstances, he would have had a career as a scholar or a man of letters. But he lived in an unsettled time, which brought to the surface the restless, unstable sides of his character, and in the end turned even his virtues into faults. The failure of Conrad's father as a rebel personifies the failure of Poland in the same role. Man and country failed for the same reasons. They were both naïve, simple, feudal, brave, filled with chivalrous notions of gallantry and exaggerated heroism when the times called for cunning, concealment, prudence, and sophistication.

Conrad's father was a man of brilliant but unsettled parts. As a student he had pursued oriental languages without finishing. When he lost his own family property through unwise investments, he took to managing the estates of others, also unsuccessfully. But he cut an arresting figure in provincial society, becoming known and feared for a witty, sarcastic tongue. He had literary ambitions, wrote plays and poems of no great distinction, but skillfully translated Hugo, Shakespeare, and Alfred de Vigny into Polish. Highly temperamental and bitterly romantic, he fell in love with Evelina Bobrowska and waited eight long unhappy years for her disapproving father to die and her reluctant mother to give an uneasy consent to their marriage.

The antagonism between the Bobrowskis and Korzeniowskis reflected still another conflict in the history of Poland. Each represented a different aspect of the Polish gentry. The Korzeniowskis were fire-eaters, hotheads, romantic idealists, willing, even eager to die for Poland, impatient of the long view, and allergic to cautious planning. The Bobrowskis were just as patriotic and longed just as much for independence, but they were sober, restrained, willing to get along as best they could with the occupying power while working quietly for a goal they recognized, realistically, to be distant. They disapproved of Evelina's marrying a Korzeniowski, and the later disasters confirmed their opinion.

After their marriage, Conrad's parents lived in the country on a large estate Apollo was managing near the Ukrainian town of Berdichev. There, on December 3, 1857, their son and only child was born. He was named Józef Teodor Konrad Nalecz Korzeniowski.[2] At home the boy was always called by the third of his names, Konrad, which he was later to adopt as his English surname. In his merchant seaman days he was to sign himself in various ship's registers and in letters as Conrad Korzeniowski, Konrad Korzeniowski, K. N. Korzeniowski, and J. Conrad Korzeniowski. He seems to have enjoyed these variants on his name, which in themselves suggest the radical metamorphoses in his life.

In 1861, when Conrad was three, his father repaired to Warsaw in pursuit of a formal literary career. Instead, he became involved with a patriotic group planning a revolt against Russia. Characteristically, he attached himself to the radical wing advocating instant action, was arrested before firing a shot or distributing a proclamation, and was sent into exile. When the next great Polish uprising finally did erupt, in 1863, Apollo Korzeniowski was many hundreds of miles away, in the Vologda region of northern Russia.

His legitimate and justifiable literary ambitions had led him from the relative quiet of the countryside to the great capital, where the temptations of politics operating upon an already aroused patriotic sensibility caught him up in dangerous events for which he was unsuited by nature. Like Poland, he was the tragic victim of a split between his capacities and the pressures imposed upon them. Thirty years later this split was to become one of Conrad's great and recurrent themes.

Apollo's attachment to his wife and son moved him to agree to their company in the harshness of exile. At the camp in Vologda, the inmates were given numbers: Apollo became no. 21, his wife no. 22, Conrad no. 23. Evelina was already in delicate health, and the rigors of their existence hastened her death, which occurred in 1865, when Conrad was seven. After the shock of his wife's passing, Apollo was allowed by the authorities to move to southern Russia where, gazing at the Black Sea, his young son got his first glimpse

---

2 The name Korzeniowski derived from *korzén,* the Polish word for root.

of boundless water. Eventually, broken in health by the ravages of tuberculosis and no longer considered dangerous, Korzeniowski was allowed to return home. His last months were spent in Cracow, a city noted for its churches and mausoleums, memorializing its medieval past, a city of the glorious and epic dead. On his death in 1869 he was given a great public funeral, befitting a man who sacrificed himself, however foolishly, for the national cause, and three years later his son received the freedom of the city as a last tribute to his father, now enshrined in the myth of Poland.

What Russia must have looked like to the small boy is uncertain, though there are powerful descriptions of the endless empty country-side in *Under Western Eyes* and in an unfinished early story, *The Sisters*. What his father seemed like to him is more evident. Conrad had spent his fourth to eleventh year almost exclusively in the company of his father. More than thirty years later Conrad was to recall him in a letter to Garnett:

A man of great sensibilities; of exalted and dreamy temperament; with a terrible gift of irony and of gloomy disposition; withal of strong religious feeling degenerating after the loss of his wife into mysticism touched with despair. His aspect was distinguished; his conversation very fascinating; but his face in repose sombre lighted all over when he smiled. I remember him well.[3]

This restless man, at war with himself, unable to reconcile con-flicting impulses and to come to terms with the world around him, is the one constant figure in his son's novels. The identity and impact of his mother are more shadowy, but she may well have inspired the figure of Mrs. Gould, one of Conrad's most loving and attractive women, who slowly withers in *Nostromo* as her husband sinks in the swamp of his high-minded, unattainable, and finally corrupting ideal. Evelina, the first name of Conrad's mother, is not unlike Mrs. Gould's Emilia, and the similarity in their life situation is striking.

Conrad's early childhood, isolated in an enemy country, cut off from young companions, thrown into the exclusive company of two parents dying visibly before his eyes, exposed him to abnormal

[3] January 20, 1900, Garnett, p. 167.

tension. In the impressionable years before he came to speculate
and philosophize about the nature of things, Conrad intimately
absorbed the attitude of his parents: his father's rebellious lashing
out against oppression, his mother's uncomplaining acceptance and
endurance.

He was eleven when his father died. He was turned over to the
guardianship of his maternal uncle, Tadeusz Bobrowski, and now
came in contact with still a third personality. Uncle Tadeusz was a
believer in order, reason, and balance, and was willing to pay a
price for them by swallowing a little of his nationalistic pride.
Inside the Russian occupation he adjusted himself to political
realities while maintaining his identity as a Pole. Was it possible to
live like a civilized man and still maintain political and patriotic
honor? To this delicate question his answer was Yes, and it served
as a rule of thumb by which he sought to guide his nephew. Since
he felt that an honorable and civilized life was possible in occupied
Poland, he would later oppose Conrad's wish to leave. But once
Conrad had detached himself from the Polish community, he urged
him to embrace another, since civilization involved belonging to a
community and was conceivable only in terms of work, duty, and
professionalism. First, Conrad was to go to France, and then,
England. It was his uncle who would urge British citizenship upon
the hesitating young man. He had opposed his going to sea, but
once Conrad went, encouraged him to perform his tasks as well
as possible and climb in this unexpected profession as high as his
talents would allow. He had distrusted his brother-in-law for
attempting the impossible, and wished to control the impulsiveness
and quixoticism he found in Conrad. Uncle Tadeusz was a great
advocate of the possible. Whatever could be done should be done;
what should be done acquired value only within the framework of
organized society, which alone guaranteed the doctrine of humane
realism he sought to inculcate in the boy turned over to his care.

One of Conrad's childhood companions, Jadwiga Kalucka, remembered him at eleven as a lively, merry boy of extraordinary intelligence. He spent holidays with her family in Lwow. He wrote
comedies, organized amateur theatricals, quoted from Adam
Mickiewicz, the Polish epic poet, demonstrated prodigally the
literary training he had received from his father, and was altogether

the life of the household.[4] Literature and a literary sensibility were quite plainly intimate parts of his earliest experience. During his early years of close companionship with his father, Conrad had enjoyed hearing him read aloud from his translations of French and English writers. The boy himself had occasionally stolen into his father's study and read from the galley proofs.

After his father's death, the five years Conrad spent going to school in Cracow seemed tame indeed. They consisted of a routine of uninspired studies. Like all educated Poles of the nineteenth century, he learned to speak French as a matter of course. But except for geography, everything was academic and cut-and-dried, and aroused in the boy only an irritated and rebellious boredom. And even geography, he remembered many years afterward, was taught by "mere bored professors . . . who were not only middle-aged but looked to me as if they had never been young. And their geography was very much like themselves, a bloodless thing with a dry skin covering a repulsive armature of uninteresting bones." [5] A passion for "the geography of open spaces and wide horizons" had already been aroused by the memoirs of Mungo Park and Captain Cook, which he had come upon in private.

The traditional system of loyalties that most boys accept automatically appeared not to have taken deep hold of Conrad. He did not believe in the superiority or expertise of his teachers; they frankly bored him. Although he always remained on affectionate terms with his relatives, as a family unit they failed to inspire him with awe. He was born a Roman Catholic and brought up in an orthodox way, yet religion never seems to have moved him deeply; he was to grow up a nonbeliever. As to Poland, for all his natural feelings of patriotism and national pride, the last thing in the world he wanted to do was join its underground.

The years in Cracow were punctuated by a romantic attachment to an equally youthful cousin named Tekla that offended the family's sense of propriety, and were climaxed by the crisis over his decision to leave Poland (then completely landlocked) for the sea. His study of geography had roused in him an interest in places far from home. Mungo Park's Africa, the Pacific regions of Captain Cook appeared to him magical. And when he was not reading books of travel and

4 "Conradiana VI," *Poland*, August, 1927.
5 "Geography and Some Explorers," *Last Essays*, p. 12.

exploration, he was losing himself in the sea stories of Hugo, Marryat, and Fenimore Cooper, and the first tenuous thought of becoming a sailor himself took root in his mind.

Once there, this strange ambition flourished vigorously and was not to be dislodged. His uncle did everything in his power to stifle it, without success. Arguments, family conferences, exhortations to nationalism, efforts at passing off the impulse as a passing phase of romantic adolescence were all unavailing. In the summer of 1873, when Conrad was fifteen, a university student was engaged to take him on a walking tour of Switzerland and northern Italy with the express purpose of talking the boy out of his folly.[6] But a glimpse of the Adriatic at Venice seems to have canceled out the tutor's most eloquent arguments. Even his uncle, to whom he was strongly attached, could not deflect Conrad. In the end, with cautious, regretful wisdom, Bobrowski let the boy go. It was typical of his sober realism that he did not allow him to depart unprovided for, but arranged a monthly allowance and gave him letters of introduction to connections in Marseilles.

To the end of his days Conrad remembered the pressure upon him to remain. "Stupid obstinacy" and "fantastic caprice" were among the milder epithets applied. In the struggle to leave he was without allies, and was even unable to summon reasons for his folly. They were not verbalized or analyzed, but deeply and temperamentally felt. He was vehemently assured on all sides that what he wanted to do was wrong. Jarring though this was, it had no effect on his resolve to do it. But his sense of anguish, amounting perhaps to a complex of guilt, remained with him throughout life and created in him a perpetual desire to justify his action. In _A Personal Record_ he recalls the shocked opposition to it in tones whose dryness does not conceal the surviving tension.

I don't mean to say that a whole country had been convulsed by my desire to go to sea. But for a boy between fifteen and sixteen, sensitive enough, in all conscience, the commotion of his little world had seemed a very considerable thing indeed. So considerable that, absurdly enough, the echoes of it linger to this day. I catch myself in hours of solitude and retrospect meeting arguments and charges made thirty-five years ago by voices now forever still; finding things to say that an assailed boy could not have found, simply because of

6 Joseph Conrad, _A Personal Record_, p. 43.

the mysteriousness of his impulses to himself. I understood no more than the people who called upon me to explain myself. There was no precedent. I verily believe mine was the only case of a boy of my nationality and antecedents taking a, so to speak, standing jump out of his racial surroundings and associations. (pp. 120–121)

The pressure exerted to keep him from taking the jump left its mark. He was given to ironic outbursts, reminiscent of his father, followed by moody silences when he was altogether withdrawn.

His passion to go to sea, vague at first, grew steadily more powerful, and was linked in an equally powerful way with a personal need to break out of the dark tunnel of Poland. Since the remote places which made their appeal to him in geography and fiction were invariably reached by water, the sea became the imaginative means of exit from the prison of land. He longed as much as any Pole for his country's independence, but did not believe it would come. He had seen his father and mother swallowed up by Poland's oppressive situation, learned of the melancholy death of his father's two brothers in misadventures that were partly political in character, and was constantly reminded of the heroic sacrifices made by his patriotic ancestors for the Polish cause. These reminders filled him with pride, but also with futility. Polish patriotism was marked by valor and self-sacrifice; yet it seemed always to end in failure and death. He belonged to a country doomed by history to be crushed. The impulse to free himself of these burdensome traditions, to get out from under the weight of this tragic destiny, flared up in him. If his father had rebelled against Russia because he found life in occupied Poland intolerable, Conrad was to rebel against Poland for exactly the same reason. It was the revolt of a youth against iron circumstance which he felt could not be altered, neither by him nor by his compatriots.

His father's tragedy, which Conrad was as resolutely determined to avoid as his nation's, was that of a man cast by circumstance into a role he was unfit to play. Later, Conrad realized that it was not only circumstance but something in his father's own nature that had compelled him to play it. The same tragic fate affected the country; it, too, was thrust into an underground role with a psychic apparatus equipped to function only in the open. This was in due course the tragedy of Lord Jim in the celebrated novel written by Conrad twenty-five years after his exit from the reluctant underground of Poland. Jim, too, was wedded to an ideal of conduct that the resources of his nature were unequipped to realize—the inward division that Conrad projects with an imaginative energy that goes back to his own earliest experience.

The state of the father and the nation was mirrored, also, in the ancient south Polish city where Conrad lived and attended school from 1869 to 1874. Cracow, torn between a glorious past and a drab present, offered still another portrait of a divided self to the impressionable boy. One of his younger contemporaries, J. H. Retinger, grew up in the same town, which he described in a book of reminiscences.

. . . its hundred churches, each of them a reliquary of some past splendor, an unending procession of architectural glory—and the drabness of everyday life. Cracow the most beautiful of ancient towns—and the most uninspiring. . . .
In opposition to the past, the present in Cracow did not supply any spiritual food for youthful, adventurous imagination—there was, indeed, a complete lack of faith in it. . . . The greatest festivities of the town were celebrations in honor of men dead a long time ago, of those who had toiled and suffered for Poland. Festivities of mourning!
In my childish imagination the part of Cracow which was not a temple or museum, was a cemetery! [7]

From this magnificently preserved cemetery Conrad was resolved to escape. As a microcosm of Poland, Cracow reinforced his earliest impressions of his country's fate. His father's feverish, futile, desperate life had come to an end there, and in memorializing him, in placing a stamp of heroic legend upon him, the city fathers were dramatizing his dissociation from the living present. Conrad's experiences during his first sixteen years were remarkably consistent. They built up in his mind an image of existence which was not only to inform his books but to drive him irresistibly into exile.

One of the more fascinating and persistent theories about Conrad postulates a feeling of guilt at deserting Poland in her hour of greatest need, at the time in her history when she was most ground down under the heel of powerful oppressors. Gustav Morf first advanced this idea in *The Polish Heritage of Joseph Conrad*. Morf

[7] *Conrad and His Contemporaries* (New York, 1943), pp. 19–20.

explores all the novels, *Lord Jim* in particular, as subconscious efforts by Conrad to purge himself of the burden of betrayal which he assumed that <u>fateful October day in 1874 when he</u> boarded the <u>train for France.</u> Jim deserts the *Patna* <u>(Poland)</u> with its cargo of sleeping pilgrims (the Poles faithful to their belief in independence), and jumps into the "everlasting black hole" of the lifeboat (exactly like Conrad's "jump out of his racial associations"). He has been urged to abandon ship by the rascally German captain (Germany was one of Poland's traditional enemies). The *Patna,* however, did not go down; by some miracle she stayed afloat. Some time later she was rescued and towed into port by a French gunboat (France was Poland's traditional friend and ally). Jim tries to exorcise his guilt by standing trial and by justifying his actions to Marlow (Conrad addressing himself to his readers, for, according to Morf, his art is an attempt to work out his deeply buried anxieties symbolically, and thus rid himself of them). A subtle variation on this approach to *Lord Jim* is suggested by the émigré Polish writer Czeslaw Milosz: with a <u>slight change of the ship's</u> name *Patna* to *Patria,* the whole drama of national loyalties emerges.[8]

The approach is ingenious, and lends a note of authentic fascination to the reading of the novel. But is it true? It would perhaps be more persuasive if we were sure that the feelings Conrad carried with him on "deserting" Poland required exorcism. There is no real evidence that they did. He was disturbed by the opposition of his family, but though very young and utterly alone he followed his own intent unswervingly and never, in any of his later writings or letters, gave any indication that he regretted his decision. On several later occasions, his uncle, hoping this would win him back, urged him to write travel pieces for Polish magazines; he never showed the slightest interest in doing so. As a young man he returned to Poland to see his uncle, and in 1914, twenty years after his uncle's death, took his English wife and two sons back for a stay that was cut short by the war. These visits were undertaken as perfectly matter-of-fact vacation trips and were scarcely the actions of a man consumed in the deepest part of his self with a sense of treason.

Yet Conrad was visibly upset by Polish attacks upon him after his career as an English writer had begun. Was he indeed a betrayer

8 "Joseph Conrad in Polish Eyes," *The Atlantic Monthly,* November, 1957, p. 226.

who had put even his talent to the service of another country? The accusation may have wounded him because it was true. The reverse is equally plausible. It may have wounded him because it was false. ·Painful falsehoods can rend us as deeply as painful truths; it is sentimental to ascribe to the second a more penetrative power than the first. At any rate, his own private relations with Poland remained friendly. He was gratified when his books were first translated into his native language, the more so because the translator was his cousin. And in many an essay and declaration he espoused the cause of Polish independence, and expressed his pleased surprise when this actually came about after the First World War.

Yet if the theory of guilt is not valid in the personal sense, it has validity in an imaginative sense. The entire syndrome of guilt and treason took sharp hold of Conrad's mind when he was exposed to it as a boy. It became for him a constant of human experience not because he accepted the accusations of treason launched against himself, but because he was intimately involved in them. Against his will he was appointed a central actor in the drama of betrayal, without accepting or giving inner consent to the role of betrayer forced upon him by his accusers. Thus the whole issue penetrated his imagination far more than it did his conscience.

It is therefore conceivable that he called Jim's ship the *Patna* because the name began with the same consonant as Poland and had the same number of syllables. If so, the suggestion of the country behind the ship derived less from Conrad's need to exorcise private ghosts than from an imaginative capacity to derive parallels and find analogies to a situation which he understood very well and regarded as a fixed point of the human condition. To pursue Morf's line is to accept the book as the victim of the man, where it deserves to be accepted as a demonstration of his insight and aesthetic power. We see clearly in Conrad's case how his life experiences fed his imagination and nourished his art, how in the writing of his books, as he observes in the Preface to *The Nigger of the "Narcissus,"* "the artist descends within himself, and in that lonely region of stress and strife, if he be deserving and fortunate, he finds the terms of his appeal" (pp. xi–xii). To the degree that his stories remain victimized by the specific circumstances of his life, to that degree they remain unconquered by the imagination, and serve

mainly as indexes and guides to the biography of one man rather
than as universal statements. To read *Lord Jim* as a compendium of
clues to Conrad's personal feelings is to shrink its range of discourse and turn literature generally into a treasure hunt for disguised personal references, which in any given instance may or may
not be there.[9]

One other aspect of Conrad's life in Poland remains to be men-
tioned, the impact of Shakespeare upon him. When still a boy, he
had read a number of the plays in his father's translations. Centuries
of research have failed to reveal that Shakespeare had a "philosophy," in the sense that Dante or Tolstoy had one. It is hard to say
with certainty that in his work he had opinions or assumed
attitudes, as Dickens did. What Conrad in his extremely impressionable early years derived from Shakespeare was none of these;
even if they existed in articulated form, it is doubtful that they
would have meant anything to him between the ages of seven
and twelve. What he did derive, rather, were examples and situations: bold men hurling themselves into large endeavors, or sensitive figures like Hamlet being trapped into misfortune and disaster.
There was the constant Shakespearian spectacle of the miscast man
forced into circumstances that go athwart his nature: not simply
Hamlet alone, but Othello, driven to endure the devious modes of
jealousy though his character is tuned to straightforwardness and
candor; Brutus forced to assassination and war though essentially
of a quiet, reflective disposition; Hotspur the victim of an age
where his purely medieval pride and honor were out of place;
Romeo and Juliet committed to stealth and subterfuge while their
youthful ardor can flourish only in the open.

Conrad's father was also a miscast man, belonging to a country

---

9 Elsewhere, Morf's comments retain their interest while growing more conjectural and farfetched. He regards Almayer as a composite symbol of Conrad's
paternal grandfather and two paternal uncles who lost their fortunes and lives
speculating, gambling, and drinking. He spots Conrad himself among the crew of
the *Narcissus* in the person of the Finn. This sailor is a foreigner betrayed by
his accent, has a dreaming temperament, and comes from a country under Russian
rule. Finally, Morf regards Conrad's reversion in his last writings to southern
France as a veiled return to Poland, since the two regions have "a strong
temperamental affinity." Though one of the earliest books on Conrad, Morf's opus
remains, for all its wild-eyed speculations and occasional nonsense, one of the
more fascinating.

trapped into a miscast role. To Conrad the plays of Shakespeare were violent, dramatic demonstrations of the same pattern, made all the more eloquent by their richness of action and the phenomenal vitality of their language. These belied the sad ends of the heroes, kept the tragedies from being depressing, and made bearable the idea that life was often too much for the men who lived it. The human lot may be described as a hard and limited one, but if a writer asserts it with enough imagination and gusto, it has a way of shedding its limitations. Shakespeare asserted it with all the imagination and gusto of the Renaissance. To the boy caught within the enclosed world of Russia and Russian Poland in the 1860's the plays supplied whatever élan, whatever impulse to self-fulfillment that he may not have secured from Marryat, Hugo, and Mungo Park.

When Conrad boarded the express on October 26, 1874, for Marseilles,[10] he was still six weeks short of his seventeenth birthday, but he brought with him the emotional baggage of a grown man. The harshness of his experiences had clouded his youthful spirit, but had not crushed it. It deepened the strain of melancholy in him, the melancholy that was later to erupt so frequently into fits of prolonged depression when a sense of his own emptiness, if not of the emptiness of the world, would overwhelm him. He had already learned to protect his inner self by the mask of manners, another of the legacies from Poland. The Polish gentry had wrapped itself for centuries in a thick veneer of etiquette. An elaborate courtliness of gesture and speech had survived virtually unchanged from medieval times and retained a defiantly feudal air into the present. It served as a wall to keep out inquiring eyes, behind which the privacy of emotion could be freely cultivated. Manners coated Conrad like a suit of armor, and would one day harden into a formidable reserve, an impenetrably aristocratic air that would bloom like an exotic continental plant during his years in rural England.

A precocious sense of tragedy, an exultant if vague desire for the

[10] "I got into the train as a man gets into a dream," was the way in which he remembered the incident forty years later (Letter to Harriet Capes, July 22, 1914, Yale).

adventure and excitement of some widening experience outside the claustrophobia of his native country, an encrustation of polished etiquette, and a facility in two languages, Polish and French, were the main items in the assorted paraphernalia Conrad took with him on the train to France.

III

"Where To?"

AN EDUCATED YOUNG POLE LEAVING HIS COUNTRY IN THE 1870's would almost automatically head for France. The ties between the two nations, cultural as well as political, were traditionally close, and French was the language spoken by the Polish gentry.

When Conrad left Poland, it was to Marseilles that he inevitably gravitated, and he remained there during his years in France. Marseilles had distinct attractions for him. It was the greatest seaport in the country and on the Mediterranean, and therefore a natural center for a youth who wanted to become a sailor. Like most seaports it was full of bustle and change, of raw energy and a melting-pot population. It had an established society —the Delestangs, a family of wealthy and well connected shipowners to whom Conrad had a letter of introduction, were representative of it—but there was also the society of the waterfront, sailors, pilots, adventurers, riff-raff, a polyglot of transients from every country in the world, a society of unsettled men with no fixed values, living under the spur of a rough-and-ready pragmatism. Conrad plunged enthusiastically into both worlds. He presented himself to M. Delestang, who brought the young Pole into the circle of royalist sympathizers to which the Delestangs belonged. At the same time Conrad hung about the waterfront, made friends with harbor pilots, was taken along on pilot boats escorting cargo ships through the narrow channels to their piers, and added a strong Provençal accent to the French he had acquired in Poland. The first weeks in France were a time of extreme excitement, an intense embodiment of youthful aspirations.

M. Delestang gave him his first berth as an able-bodied seaman, and soon Conrad was making long voyages to the West Indies. In between sailings, he was caught up in the momentum of his new country. France in the 1870's was enjoying an economic and political boom, a happy circumstance for Conrad coming to it eager for experience from a country closed on all sides and in a state of bleak contraction. The collapse of Louis Napoleon during the Franco-Prussian War of 1870 had ushered in the Third Republic which not even the surge of the Paris Commune impeded for long. By 1874 France had recovered from these shocks and was now in the full tide of the energies released by the newly established government. A republic regime was once again in the saddle, but Bourbons and Bonapartists survived in considerable numbers and actively nursed their hopes of returning to power. At the time, these hopes seemed not in the least quixotic. A Bonaparte had just finished ruling France for nineteen years, and had been overthrown by a losing war, not by an uprising from within. Before him, Bourbons had sat on the throne for thirty consecutive years. The country was alive with royalist centers controlled by restless, able men not yet touched by the pathos of lost causes or affected by the dry rot of movements that history has definitively passed by.

In the south, the royalists, or legitimists, as they often called themselves, supported kings in other countries as well. During the 1870's their favorite foreign venture was the cause of Don Carlos of Spain, who sought to capture the throne in one of the chronic dynastic wars that ravaged Spain through the nineteenth century. Carlos was neither a commanding nor personally attractive figure, but the Carlist war aroused passions that could not have been exceeded in intensity had he himself been Napoleon and Julius Caesar rolled into one. The Delestangs were hot for him though they were not Spaniards, and did not admire him as a man. It was enough for them that he was of royal blood and had royal claims; their energy and money were at his disposal. They drew Conrad, as they did any other likely recruit that came their way, into the feverish partisanship of the Carlist cause, or the Carlist conspiracy as its enemies called it.

Conrad threw himself into the Carlist movement enthusiastically, without really caring about the issues involved. He was not a political partisan or a royalist ideologue, but a youthful adventurer in search of excitement and experience. The Carlists promised both, and Conrad was to derive both from them. There was already visible in him a divided purpose: a strain of skepticism pulling him one way and the impulse to throw himself wholly into life pulling him another. Both were the products of the same experience, the experience in Poland, which made him simultaneously wary of causes and excessive enthusiasms, yet eager to break out of confinement and a sense of hopelessness. His involvement with the Carlists bore the stamp of this division. Conrad, already intensely suspicious of political programs, could not have been more indifferent to the claims of the pretender; he was, of course, equally indifferent to the claims of Don Carlos's rival, now on the throne of Spain. He was never persuaded by the arguments and royalist *mystique* of the Delestangs, though he admired Mme. Delestang, a woman of some breeding and character. Still, he became a gunrunner for the Carlists, spent his own money, risked his neck, suffered physical privations for their cause, all with great enthusiasm and high spirits—but untainted by the slightest trace of conviction. Carlism was the ideal movement for him: it was too absurd politically, run too shoddily, and headed by a man too obviously third-rate to be taken seriously, yet the task of supplying the dangerous and thinly held Basque coast, an enterprise calling for steady nerves and coolness under fire, provided an intoxication made to order for his youthful spirits.

Closely involved in it with him were two persons who aroused in him the most intimate emotions of his years in France. The first was a Corsican sailor named Dominic Cervoni, first mate on the *Saint-Antoine* during Conrad's second voyage to the West Indies.[1] A tough-fibered, physically powerful, immensely self-assured man some twenty years older than the apprentice seaman under his command, he evoked in Conrad a lifelong case of hero worship. He served as a model for Nostromo, the "magnificent capataz de cargadores" in the great novel that bears his name.[2] Cervoni was a competent professional in the career Conrad was now entering.

[1] The dates and external details of all of Conrad's voyages are catalogued in G. Jean-Aubry's *Joseph Conrad: Life and Letters,* the "official" biography published three years after Conrad's death. For all its woodenness of style and the emptiness of the portrait of Conrad, it is a mine of factual information lovingly gathered. Some of the gaps in this information and many small errors in Aubry have been filled in and corrected by Jocelyn Baines in his *Joseph Conrad* (New York, 1960).

[2] Conrad took Cervoni to the well once too often. He stood for the portrait of Peyrol in *The Rover,* one of the half-frozen novels of the writer's old age. It is a last completed version of the Nostromo type, but with all the blood and juice drained out.

He commanded men naturally in a medium where the art of command was decisive. He was intelligent beyond the average, and had a vast fund of experiences that nourished and spiced his conversation. On land, he was equally masterful, with the buxom *patronne* of a waterfront café for a mistress, a large circle of men who looked to him for advice and gazed upon him with admiration, and the perpetual choice of desirable posts at sea that were a tribute to his acknowledged superiority among his fellows.

The two men, the Corsican mariner and his young Polish protégé, had begun their collaboration in a gunrunning venture in the Caribbean. In 1876, while the *Saint-Antoine* was moored in the West Indies negotiating for cargo, they escorted a schooner loaded with arms through the Gulf of Mexico to one of the banana republics engaged in a civil war. Civil wars being endemic to Latin America, they knocked up and down the coast for several weeks, getting at one time as far south as Venezuela, before returning to their ship in Haiti for the homeward voyage to France. This buccaneering interlude [3] was a dress rehearsal for more complicated and perilous maneuvers in the Bay of Biscay on behalf of the Carlists.

Conrad and three of his friends bought the tartan *Tremolino*, and with Cervoni installed as skipper, ferried guns and supplies to the remnants of the Carlist army dug into the Basque littoral of northern Spain (by this time even Don Carlos himself had given up the campaign). Their two hazards were rough seas and the coast-guard cutters of the Spanish navy. They survived the first and, for a time, the second. But one unlucky afternoon in 1877 a fast government vessel drove them ashore. To keep the *Tremolino* from falling into enemy hands, they wrecked it, escaped inland, and after hard overland travel returned to Marseilles bruised in flesh but much exhilarated of spirit. The most serious consequence to Conrad was the <u>loss of his investment</u>. He had been steadily exceeding his allowance anyway; now with the money sunk in the *Tremolino* irretrievably gone, he was <u>deep in debt</u>. It was im-

---

[3] Aubry is reasonably certain that it took place. He describes it first in *Life and Letters,* then repeats it in substantially the same form in *The Sea Dreamer.* Baines regards the episode as a mystery on which no satisfactory light has been shed.

mediately after this that, in an attempt to restore his finances, he engaged in his one venture at the gaming tables. This, too, turned out disastrously. He had borrowed the gambling stake to begin with, and when he lost it all, was more deeply in debt than ever. There was Uncle Tadeusz back in Cracow to fall back on, but Conrad had dunned his guardian several times already for special help; the money had always been forthcoming, accompanied by admonitory notes on the subject of his extravagance and instability. He couldn't turn to the old man again. Aside from the personal embarrassment, there was the nagging matter of his success in this new life. Everyone had predicted failure for him; he could not allow their predictions and sad head-shakings to be so quickly and easily confirmed.

The second person with whom he was closely involved in the Carlist adventure was a woman. For a long time her identity was in doubt; she was referred to in Conrad biographies as Doña Rita, after the heroine of another of his late novels, *The Arrow of Gold*, of whom she was presumably the prototype. Later, Miss Jerry Allen in a biographical study of Conrad, *The Thunder and the Sunshine* (1958), claimed her to be Paula de Somoggy, a young woman of Hungarian extraction who drifted with fascinating mysteriousness from one relationship to another in France and wound up in the Carlist movement as the mistress of Don Carlos himself. When Conrad met her—embracing Miss Allen's theory for the moment—she was not much older than he, though immensely more experienced. They were brought together by their common stake in Carlism, and it was she, in fact, who encouraged him in the gun-smuggling venture. But they had other things in common: they were both East Europeans seeking footholds in a strange country; they were more or less the same age, with the same ardent temperament; like most foreigners searching for new roots, they shared a certain wary mistrust of the world around them while seeking to find a place in it. Toward the end of 1877 they became lovers, a fitting accompaniment to his almost simultaneous initiation into the life of factional politics and guerrilla warfare.

Baines dismisses Miss Allen's tale as poppycock. By a detailed examination of places and dates—his book excels in patient, factual detective work—he proves that while Conrad probably did have a love affair with some woman, it could not have been with Paula.[4] The details of the affair, whether with Paula or someone else, are obscure. It seems not to have lasted very long—like the Carlist movement in which it began, it flared up rapidly and embered out with a suddenness that appears all the sharper because so little is known about the circumstances.

By the beginning of 1878 it had come to an end. At the same time or immediately thereafter, Uncle Tadeusz was informed by one of Conrad's friends in Marseilles that his nephew had suffered a gunshot wound and that his presence was urgently required. By the time he reached Conrad's bedside, the wound was almost healed, but Bobrowski learned to his dismay that it had apparently been self-inflicted.[5] A combination of elements might have driven Conrad to attempt suicide: the loss of his money in the *Tremolino* disaster, his unhappy experience with gambling, his unpaid debts, the abrupt end of his love affair. A final cause may have been the discovery that he could no longer ship out in the French merchant marine because of a French law barring the employment of foreigners twenty-one and over and liable to military conscription by their native countries.

For many years this act was masked as a duel between Conrad and an American named Blunt, who had quarreled with him over the affections of his mistress and then shot him on the field of honor. A similar incident in *The Arrow of Gold* gave rise to this romantic camouflage. When Aubry picked it up for his biography, Conrad made no effort to deny it. He preferred this episode in his youth to pass as an outburst of conventionally romantic spirits instead of the harsher, more complex event which it evidently was,[6] although a man who seeks to commit suicide at twenty is a more

---

4 Baines, pp. 55–57.

5 The circumstances of the presumed suicide attempt were described in a long-lost letter from Uncle Tadeusz to a family friend in Warsaw. The letter, discovered by Baines, was published by him in the *Times Literary Supplement*, December 6, 1957.

6 Did he mislead Aubry deliberately? Or did he simply have an unreliable memory, which seems in any case a faculty designed to present us to ourselves in the most flattering light? That Conrad was not incapable of outright lying Baines demonstrates by an incident in 1881 when Conrad extracted ten pounds from his uncle on the false claim that he had lost all his possessions in the sinking of the *Annie Frost*, a vessel he had never shipped on (Baines, pp. 68–69).

interesting phenomenon than one who fights a duel at the same age.

Suicide and the tissue of motivations leading to it became one of his major themes. No fewer than five of his major characters were to take their own lives. Old Captain Whalley, in "The End of the Tether," allows himself to drown from a sense of lost honor. Martin Decoud, in *Nostromo,* shoots himself because of an overwhelming feeling about "the emptiness of things." Winnie Verloc jumps to her death from a channel steamer at the end of *The Secret Agent* after murdering her husband and being abandoned by her rescuer; it is the earlier death of her half-witted brother, the only person she ever loved, that really drives her to do away with herself. The planter of Malata, in the story of the same name, swims out to his death at sea when he is rejected by the woman with whom he is infatuated. Finally, Axel Heyst acknowledges his failure to grasp the meaning of life by setting fire to his house and perishing in it in the last chapter of *Victory*. At least three of these motives, honor, love, and a conviction of life emptiness, were factors in Conrad's own unsuccessful attempt at suicide, if attempt it was. His fictional versions of the experience may have used his own direct involvement as a jumping-off point. However altered in factual detail, the psychological resemblances would be unavoidable.

Whatever his intentions may have been, Conrad's wound did not prove serious. He mended rapidly and, as often happens after violence, a purgation of temper set in, and the patient recovered his normal spirits. Uncle Tadeusz's alarm was allayed, when he reached Marseilles, by the sight of his swiftly convalescing nephew. But he was more than ever confirmed in his fear of the unstable Korzeniowski blood and delivered his usual admonitions. Then, with his customary practicality he sat down with Conrad to plan the next step. The question of where to,[7] raised when the boy first dreamed of leaving Poland, came up a second time now that his future in France was so abruptly canceled.

On the first occasion the question had almost answered itself. The only European country to which Poland felt something other

[7] "Where to?" are the words addressed by the Russian counterespionage chief to Razumov, the protagonist of *Under Western Eyes*. They supply this climactic novel of Conrad's middle period with its key question, its central directive.

than indifference or hostility was France. Napoleon, at the head of a French army, had been the last man to liberate Poland from the partitionings of the eighteenth century. Waterloo may have been a day of glory for Prussia, Austria, and England; it was a disaster for the Poles. French, moreover, was the second language of the educated classes in the Slavic countries; to speak it was a sign of being wellborn, a mark of grace that set one off from the natives who spoke only the vernacular. Conrad learned it while growing up, which, almost automatically, inclined him to sympathy for the culture that created it. Though physically much closer to Russian and German, Conrad learned scarcely a word of either. When his relatives, finally resigned to his wild maritime ambition, had proposed that he join the Austrian navy as a cadet—Austria was the least oppressive of the occupying powers, and a naval career seemed not unsuited to a gentleman—Conrad refused. He knew no German and was resistant to acquiring it; besides, he wanted to abandon altogether the structure of oppressor and oppressed. The nearest exit from the Polish underground was France.

France also had a seacoast, a merchant marine, an overseas empire, and trading connections everywhere.[8] To Conrad the sea was an escape from land, in its unceasing movement embodying the life of change, possibility, and adventure—or so it had seemed to him before he lived upon it; he was to have other thoughts later. A merchant marine would supply him with the format of his first profession. An overseas empire was a guarantee that the French flag would command respect. Above all, the eminence of France, the French *gloire*, in almost every field in which a nation can be eminent—politics, war, art, language, intellectual influence— exerted a strong pull on Conrad, as it did on Europeans everywhere.

With France's eminence in literature Conrad had already a considerable personal experience, despite his extreme youth. He had read the novels of Hugo and the plays of Musset and Vigny in his father's translations. A systematic study of the French classical writers was a standard part of the school curriculum in Cracow, and continued through the year Conrad spent under the guidance

---

[8] These were, of course, also true of England, as Conrad would one day acknowledge. He claimed in *A Personal Record* that as a boy he vowed that if he ever became a seaman he would be a British seaman. But this seems to have been an *arrière pensée*.

of a private tutor (the same young man who failed in his assignment of disabusing his pupil of his mania about the sea; there is no reason, however, to believe that he failed in his academic assignments). French newspapers and periodicals circulated almost as freely in Poland and Russia as they did in Paris, and events in France were followed with as keen an interest as if they were the history of one's own country. The effect of all this cultural diffusion, backed by the powerful image of France as the savior of Poland, produced in the Poles a Francophilia as deeply rooted as their Russophobia.

In addition to his early intimacy with Hugo and the French romantics, Conrad was soon to acquire a taste for Flaubert that symptomized his passionate preoccupation with craftsmanship long before the start of his own career as a writer. Flaubert's ideas and attitudes, as such, were of little interest to Conrad even when they paralleled his own. He shared Flaubert's distaste for the bourgeoisie, yet it was not the acid portrait of the provincial middle class that impressed him in *Madame Bovary,* but the precision of its language and the immaculate clarity of the frame in which it moved. Similarly with the other novels. Flaubert spent fifteen years in dogged research before he created Carthage in *Salammbô;* Conrad created his South American republic in *Nostromo* in scarcely more than fifteen months, much of it from reading but much out of his own head. Yet he studied Flaubert's historical novel very carefully in an effort to discover the aesthetic mechanism which could control an immense canvas so effortlessly. Flaubert's convictions about the heroic past and the contemptible present, which were to leave their mark on T. S. Eliot and others, aroused little sympathy in Conrad. Conrad was as conservative as Flaubert, but his conservatism was personal rather than ideological; he had an interest in history but developed few theories about it. Though he had an acute distaste for colonial imperialism and distrusted the power of purely material interests, he was never under the illusion that these phenomena were uniquely modern. Their technological development was certainly more advanced; while this added to their pervasiveness, it did not make them more obnoxious morally than in Roman times or Babylonian. The development of technology irritated Conrad personally only in the particular invention of the steam engine. By eliminating the sailing ship, this pernicious phenomenon in his opinion altered for the worse the whole relationship between man and sea.

Flaubert the artist—as contrasted with Flaubert the ideologue, the repudiator of modern scientific civilization, the passionate assumer of attitudes—interested Conrad profoundly. To be sure, a writer had to have something to say; Conrad himself was to suffer acutely from a sense of thematic emptiness. But the act of living churned up its own materials and generated the raw protoplasm of experience. The content of art lay all about in rough fragments. One had only to pick it up and shape it. The shaping was the important thing. But it was also a constant grinding difficulty to perfectionists like Flaubert who not only struggled for the *mot juste* but insisted that there was only one ultimately expressive *mot juste* for any occasion. The trick was to find the suitable form without smothering the idea being shaped and released. Too much form would snuff out its resemblance to life; too little would allow it to run out loosely at the edges. Getting it just right, in equilibrium, required a delicacy of touch that Flaubert carried to the point of mastery. Flaubert's doctrine was legated to his disciple Maupassant, the other French writer whom Conrad examined closely.[9]

How more than *what* became the key word in Conrad's lexicon. He seldom engaged in philosophical discussions, but was always ready to exchange ideas on style and technique. Nor was it only Flaubert and Maupassant who provided him with examples. It was the French altogether, in their mode of pruning trees, laying out gardens, husbanding nature without distorting it, carrying their instinct for order and formality to the edge of the abyss where the artificial threatens to crush the natural, without ever quite falling into it. And while a note of careless impulsiveness ran through the south of France, a note that grew stronger as one approached the Italian border to the east and the Spanish to the west, the dominance of French order—mind imposing itself on the

9 Maupassant, like Flaubert, attracted Conrad solely by the intricacy of his form. A typical tribute appears in a letter to his cousin-in-law, Mme. Poradowska: "I am afraid I am too much under the influence of Maupassant. I have studied *Pierre et Jean*—thought, method, and everything—with the deepest discouragement. It seems to me nothing at all, but the mechanics are so complex that they make me tear my hair" (October 29 or November 5, 1894, from *Letters of Joseph Conrad to Marguerite Poradowska*, New Haven, 1940, p. 84).

chaos of matter—remained. The very structure of the language, assertive rather than suggestive, striving for definiteness and avoiding opacity, the sworn enemy of haze, full of irregular verbs that were somehow regular in their irregularity, encapsulated the national genius for the creation of form. In the end Conrad was to write in English rather than French because there was another side to his temperament that demanded expression. But French left its mark upon him permanently in his preoccupation with the structural side of art.

His principal imaginative statement on the French character came later, in the person of the French lieutenant in *Lord Jim*.[10] This veteran officer, who remains nameless almost as though he were a generic representative of his country, boards the *Patna* when she is rescued by a French gunboat. For thirty dangerous hours, he remains on board while she is towed to port, expecting, as Jim did, that she will sink under him at any moment. What were his impressions of the whole affair? Marlow, the narrative ringmaster of the novel, catches up with him later and poses the question. The two of them go into the whole complicated business of cowardice and bravery, or as far into it as the lieutenant's very lucid yet deliberately limited viewpoint allows.

The lieutenant seizes upon Jim as the interesting man among the absconding officers. All men are cowards, he remarks, and are forced into bravery by a sense of duty, by the eyes of their fellows upon them, or by the examples of others no better than themselves. When these are removed, as in Jim's case, men will relapse to their natural state, and are not to be condemned for it. In any case one does not die of being afraid; the constant presence of fear inside him is man's moral condition. Marlow is struck by the lieutenant's intelligence and his unexpectedly "lenient" view of the situation.

But the Frenchman has set up his own format beyond which he

10 Two of Conrad's late novels, *The Arrow of Gold* and *The Rover*, take place in France. But like almost every other element in them, the setting lacks specific character and might as easily be Italy or Spain as France. Except for a veiled attack on aestheticism as a substitute for life (an attitude embraced by the painter Henry Allègre in *The Arrow of Gold*)—which might represent the French passion for style and art carried to a devitalized extreme—there is not anything recognizably French about these novels. The lieutenant in *Lord Jim* tells us more about France during Marlow's brief encounter with him in Australia than Jean Peyrol, the rover, succeeds in doing through nearly three hundred pages on a farm near Toulon.

will not go. This format is bounded by the fact of universal cowardice at one end and the imperative necessity of maintaining honor at the other. "When the honour is gone . . . I can offer no opinion . . . because—monsieur—I know nothing of it" (p. 148). He refuses to consider Jim's predicament any further. Jim now exists outside the format, and when Marlow asks him whether lost honor can be concealed, he makes his valedictory remark: "This, monsieur, is too fine for me—much above me—I don't think about it" (p. 149). He leaves the café, goes back to his ship, and that's the last we see of him. There is nothing more for him to say. He has looked at Jim through the sharply stenciled frame in which he chooses to accept experience. He has paid for his right to do so by the two scars on his hand and forehead, wounds suffered in his own unmentioned crises. To this he now holds, and will not allow his imagination to venture further. In this he is eminently French, imposing shape and clarity on experience, finding room in it for both the individual and his milieu, disdaining any attempt to break the mold by difficult penetrations into the unexplored, unknown region outside it. An effort to discuss it on any but his own terms is met by the lieutenant's final response to Marlow. He cuts off the conversation stiffly, and leaves. Conrad, fascinated by the French pursuit of design, a pursuit best known to him in the zealous ardors of Flaubert, was nonetheless repelled by the incapacity of the French to get beyond themselves, to acknowledge the existence of the universe which was frameless. It was that universe he was determined to explore, and he was better able to do so outside France. But from the French he armed himself with what they practiced só consummately, the absolute belief in form as a litmus test of art and civilization.

The first stop in the escape from Poland had inevitably been France. But Conrad was now approaching his twenty-first birthday, when he would be denied further berths in the French service. Behind him were an attempt at suicide, a love affair, a lengthy series of improbable adventures, and three sea journeys to the West Indies. He had made friends, gone to sea, dabbled in politics, and fallen in love. Now he faced a future that was suddenly blank. Where to? The question came up a second time, and like the first carried with it its own answer.

After France, there was only one other powerful seafaring country left in Europe outside the Russo-German orbit. If France declared him legally unemployable, England had no such restrictive laws and raised no bars to foreigners. Not, at any rate, in its merchant ships. It was imperative that Conrad leave Marseilles the moment he was physically able. Uncle Tadeusz, at his bedside, assured him that he must. His career had received a severe check; all the more reason to resume it as soon as possible. If not in the French marine, then in the English. Uncle Tadeusz thoroughly approved of England, but he would have approved of Timbuktu had it offered his volatile nephew a chance to recoup his sagging fortunes.

Conrad needed no urging. His four years in France had reached a dead end. With all prospects of employment gone, with his money at the bottom of the sea with the *Tremolino,* and with Paula vanished also, there was nothing to keep him in France. As soon as he could, without taking the risk of thinking about it too long, he signed on with a British freighter named the *Mavis* headed for the eastern Mediterranean. He knew no English.[11] He had met only one Englishman, and that one on his tour of Switzerland back in 1873. He had read Shakespeare and Dickens in Polish. Otherwise, he was as blank and green a foreign young man as ever ventured into a new country.

In due course the *Mavis* returned from Turkey, and landed at its home port of Lowestoft, a brisk but somewhat grubby town on the Norfolk coast, discharging Conrad for the first time on British soil. It was June 18, 1878.

11 Though he had been exposed to three words of spoken English. While helping a Marseilles pilot board a British freighter, he heard a sailor shout at him from above, "Look out there." To those who find hidden import in innocent remarks, the warning might seem prophetic. To Conrad, it only meant the first occasion he had been addressed in English—"the speech of my secret choice, of my future, of long friendships, of the deepest affections . . . of thoughts pursued, of remembered emotions—of my very dreams!" (*A Personal Record,* p. 136).

IV

The Roots of Exile

TO THIS NEW COUNTRY CONRAD CAME AS A COMPLETE STRANGER, without friends or acquaintances, without relations, letters of introduction, or speech. By comparison, his arrival in France had been a kind of homecoming. In England, the fact of total exile became real to him for the first time. Like Yanko Goorall, the refugee from Central Europe in his story "Amy Foster," he found himself alone in a society with which he had no connections. This meant that he had to improvise from day to day and forge a place for himself out of a void.

To find shelter in a strange port, arrange a daily routine, seek another berth was irksome enough. Far more difficult was to be without friends, without ties, and without home. From 1878 until late in 1894 when Conrad met Edward Garnett, he came to know only two people in England well.[1]

During the months that he spent ashore between voyages, he lived in dim lodgings in a state of polite surface relations with landladies, shopkeepers, ships' agents, surrounded by multitudes of Londoners unaware of his existence. At sea, things were better, largely because he had something to do. But he made no lasting friends among the other able-bodied seamen when he himself was one, or among the mates and captains after he rose to their ranks. The close intimacy of shipboard life yielded the imaginative treasures of *The Nigger of the "Narcissus,"* but in Conrad's own case it was a

[1] One was a businessman named Adolf Krieger with whom he had a series of small dealings over the years, winding up with a painful episode over a debt that Conrad had difficulty repaying. The other was G. F. W. Hope, an ex-sailor with whom Conrad went on small-boat excursions, through whom he first met his future wife, and to whom (and Mrs. Hope) he dedicated *Lord Jim.*

generalized group intimacy, and not a closeness of sympathy and understanding between individuals.

A good many people came into his field of vision whom he was able to examine detachedly precisely because he was not personally, not really involved with them. In his Author's Notes and letters, he tells us in great detail of how he met the originals of Almayer, Willems, Lingard, the Arabs in his Malay novels, Lord Jim, and the rest, of how poor he was at inventing characters, and how he had to draw his stories from the materials of his own life. One of his characteristic remarks was: "Imagination, not invention, is the supreme master of art as of life" (*A Personal Record*, p. 25). Yet two of his major novels, *The Secret Agent* and *Under Western Eyes*, were almost entirely invented, with the fragmentary help of newspaper clippings, bits and pieces of memoirs, and a few stray conversations. His most successfully realized figures are often those whom he never knew very well in "life." Paradoxically, those whom he did know well, like Cervoni and Paula, often came out most woodenly in his fiction. Emotional distance was indispensable to him in the process of aesthetic transmutation. He may have suffered long years of loneliness and boredom because he was never drawn into a living circle of companions, but there is no doubt that it was good for his art; or at least, an element that determined its characteristic shape.

He was the outside man looking in, longing to participate in life but obscurely inhibited. Conrad became a great specialist in the paralysis of will, the inability to release oneself into action and hence into life, and the whole contiguous region of moral inertia and sloth. He keenly understood the plight of the foreigner seeking roots in an adopted country and of the exile in the process of finding a new home. Virtually all his characters are foreigners and exiles. Kurtz is a Belgian in Africa. Jim, Marlow, and Lingard are Englishmen in the Malayan Archipelago. Willems, Almayer, and Stein are Dutchmen in the Far East. Adolf Verloc is an Alsatian in London. Razumov is a Russian in Geneva, Nostromo an Italian in South America, Heyst a Swede in the Pacific. The fact of their being outsiders aggravates the difficulties under which they labor. In "Heart of Darkness" Kurtz brings with him to Africa the apparatus of liberal attitudes peculiar to Western Europe; but the Africans have a different set of attitudes, and the conflict between them subjects him to pressures that in the end transform him into a different man, neither the original Belgian nor simply a white man gone native. The foreigners discover, ultimately, that they are foreigners to themselves as well. Conrad projects the shock of this discovery, and uses the external exile as a symbol or as an analogue to the internal one. The social side of isolation and the psychological come together in his fiction to form a complex exploration of one of the abiding and essential themes in the life of man. As his figures struggle for social roots, they struggle also for self-knowledge and self-recognition. The struggles, which begin separately, become one, and give his novels the frame he perpetually labored to find, clarify, and perfect.

Meanwhile, events did occur, and Conrad was caught up in them. After landing in Lowestoft he spent three months on North Sea coastal vessels hauling freight to Newcastle and back, learning his first English and adjusting his sights to England. In September, 1878, he traveled down to London, and wandered through its endless streets in a peculiar state of fear at its vastness, which did not conceal its emptiness for him, mingled with elation at his first plunge into this uncharted sea. He shipped out to Australia a month later, and now began a long series of voyages to the Far East during which he progressed steadily from fo'c'sle to poop deck. He studied assiduously for the three examinations that he took, and passed, at intervals in the 1880's for the right to serve as second mate, first mate, and finally captain. Uncle Tadeusz was deeply gratified. The wild young nephew was settling down, "having a career," establishing himself in that other world that he had embraced after leaving his own. His uncle began urging him to become a British citizen. Conrad had grown up as a Russian national, an utterly uncongenial status. It was not only wrong psychologically, but gave the Russians absolute legal control over him whenever he ventured inside their borders. But Conrad, despite his uncle's promptings, was unready to embrace another citizenship. It meant a final rupture with his origins; it implied a final decision about his future; it involved a definite commitment of loyalty formidable in itself.

For eight years Uncle Tadeusz prodded him in the direction of English nationality. A man had to have ties, he argued in his letters. Since Conrad was building a career in the British merchant marine, it would be good for him professionally to become a British citizen.

Moreover, by creating a new social tie, it would promote stability of character and discipline the wildness in him. Uncle Tadeusz was a firm believer in belonging to a group. To be sure, the human race was a group, but it was too large to mean anything. The family, the community, the nation—these were the groups that gave a man strength. Without them he would zigzag dangerously, like a ship without a rudder. Conrad was alternately amused and irked by his uncle's persistence, but in the end these ideas made a deeper impression than he acknowledged at the time. In his books he was to take the consequences of group belonging and group separation and invest them with a tragic sophistication that made them as different from Uncle Tadeusz's statements on the same theme as "Heart of Darkness" is from *Tarzan of the Apes* as a commentary on Africa. By slow degrees, hesitantly, almost grudgingly, he gave way to his uncle's wishes and finally applied for citizenship in the country to which he had attached himself. It was conferred upon him in 1886. This was something of a special year for Conrad. During it, he also acquired his master's ticket, and wrote his first piece of fiction.

This was a story called "The Black Mate," submitted, unsuccessfully, to a prize contest. It was an elementary but by no means crude or unprofessional account of a subject that Conrad returned to throughout his career: the man who discovers some weakness, wound, or handicap in himself, and the processes by which he seeks to conceal it, deny its existence, pretend it is something else, or learn, on whatever terms, to live with it. The black mate's handicap is a purely arbitrary and external one, the fact that he has turned prematurely gray and cannot find employment because he is taken for an old man. He dyes his hair black and secures a berth, but during a stormy voyage his bottles of dye are smashed and he is confronted with the crisis of the gray showing up at the roots. He wriggles out of his dilemma by acting out an elaborate lie. (Later, no Conrad figure is allowed so easy a way out.) The tale, in general, suffers from an almost total lack of characterization. It is a pure Maupassant story without the stab of pathos that makes Maupassant something more than a clever manipulator of plot. Yet the theme of the handicapped man, which a disciple like Hemingway was to take over from Conrad, appears recognizable and intact in the first tentative writing effort of a man who, though already in his thirtieth

year, was still ten years away from even beginning to think of himself as a writer.

For all the achievements of 1886, the 1880's were troubled years
for Conrad. The sea, once the exotic object of his youthful imagination, began to assume another aspect, the aspect of tedium. The
typhoons, the magnificent swatches of seascape, and the kaleidoscope
of fresh faces not only on board ship but in the islands of the
Malayan Archipelago and the countries bordering upon it supplied
his voyages with their dramatic vitality. But there were also the
long monotonous days, the endless repetition of the same physical
tasks, the lack of intellectual companionship, and the hard work that
began at last to wear him down. "He hated the sea," Ford Madox
Ford recalled in his book on Conrad. "Over and over again he
related how overwhelming, with his small stature, he found negotiations with heavy spars, stubborn cordage and black weather. He
used to say, half raising his arms, 'Look at me. . . . How was I
made for such imbecilities? Besides, my nerves were for ever on the
racket. . . .' " [2] He was knocked to the deck by a swinging spar,
injured his back, and spent several months in a hospital. He began
suffering from unaccountable fits of depression during which he
would throw up comfortable berths and moon about aimlessly on
shore.

There were difficulties about suitable employment. A master's
ticket was no guarantee of a post at that rank, and Conrad was often
forced to sign on as mate because he could find no opening as
captain. The merchant marine was peculiarly sensitive to fluctua-
tions in the economic weather; any slight recession—and downward
turns in the business cycles of the nineteenth century tended to be
sharp rather than moderate—and scores of qualified officers would
be beached for indefinite periods, Conrad among them. The fact
that he was a foreigner in speech, manner, and appearance, though
no longer in nationality, ensured his not being the first to be reen-
gaged when trade improved. Boredom ate into him like acid, and
corroded the reserves of youth and youthful illusion. *Tedium vitae*
settled upon him like a blight, from which his formal professional
successes and his new citizenship failed to rescue him. They were, indeed, ironic commentaries on the hollowness of existence. Profes-

2 Ford, p. 114.

sional advancement had not produced real security. His new citizenship had not brought with it any inner sense of belonging. In 1890 he was almost as much a stranger in England as in 1880. He was still the outsider, wondering whether he could ever summon the energy necessary to grow new roots and even whether new roots were worth establishing.

Periodically, to the alarm of his uncle, he thought of trying his hand at something else. He considered the prospect of becoming secretary to a Canadian politician and going over to the New World. He thought of joining a whaling expedition in arctic waters, a dream that went back to his childhood reading, but it never materialized. There were one or two tentative business offers that involved the investment of his small capital; these, too, faded away. In 1889, despite the rejection of "The Black Mate," Conrad began a novel, _Almayer's Folly_, out of sheer boredom, without the slightest idea that it would ever amount to anything or that it would even be finished. With all these tentative gestures in other directions, he nevertheless remained more or less committed to the sea, and committed to the code of ethics and manners governing life at sea. His later references to fidelity, to duty, to the acts that bind the human community together drew their sustenance from maritime law and tradition. The officer deserting his ship in time of danger—the central incident of _Lord Jim_—is a symbol of the ultimate transgression. Loyalty, responsibility, discipline are all given high marks by Conrad in his private gradebook. And on the everyday level, in the monotonous passage of routine, when nothing exciting is happening, when the dramatic instances of danger are not in view, men are put to their greatest test, the test of meaningful endurance.

It is less what happens _during_ crises than what happens _between_ them that occupies Conrad. The secret weaknesses and salient traits of character are most evident then. Routine can expose psychic texture as much as the moment of peril. Conrad is as concerned with the minds of his characters when things are dull as when they are exciting. Mrs. Verloc, sitting behind the cash register in the dingy shop in Soho, her mind a blank, reveals her single emotion more acutely than when she plunges the kitchen knife into her husband's breast. We become intimate with the crew of the _Narcissus_ during the "ordinary" days at sea and the "ordinary" moments on land when nothing dramatic is happening; the storm, the rescue of the "nigger," the incipient mutiny, aggrandize and intensify an already illuminated landscape. The big scenes make the story; the routine ones expose the men. Since Conrad's years at sea were long interludes of this routine—of which he complained—with only brief interludes of drama, he came to understand in his own mind the psychology of living in the grip of tedium long before it served his purpose in fiction. The passage at the beginning of Chapter II of *Lord Jim* expresses Conrad's view: "He knew the magic monotony of existence between sky and water: he had to bear the criticism of men, the exactions of the sea, and the prosaic severity of the daily task that gives bread . . . there is nothing more enticing, disenchanting, and enslaving than the life at sea" (p. 10). He suffered the sudden, inexplicable nervous crises that it precipitated, the moral inertia that produced the dreadful feeling of life emptiness, and the imperative necessity, a necessity involving his survival as a self-believing man, to come to terms with it.

Coming to terms meant more than mere endurance. It required some specifically human value over and beyond survival. Conrad found it in craft and the pride of craft. If he was to be a seaman, he would be as fine a seaman as possible, which meant performing even the commonplace details of his job as perfectly as he could. It was in this striving for perfection that existence was rescued from the commonplace and invested with a meaning beyond the utilitarian. Duty became to Conrad not simply carrying out the letter of one's task but its spirit as well, and this spirit lay coiled in the potential perfectability with which the task could be done. Fidelity to his ideal state governed his conduct and reflections on the sea.

Since the sea was a dangerous element, its toilers were under additional pressure to master its procedures. Their deadliest enemy was the slacker, and it is no accident that the embodiments of evil in *The Nigger of the "Narcissus,"* Conrad's first novel dealing with life at sea, should be Donkin and the "nigger," the two men who do not work; the one is meanly intelligent and will not, the second is ill and cannot, but whatever their motivation they are a drag on the ship. Inevitably, one of Conrad's admirable characters is Ransome, the cook with the bad heart in *The Shadow-Line,* who, nevertheless, strains himself to the utmost in hard labor when needed. The very quality of his service, quiet, efficient, graceful, emphasizes the human ideal. Conrad devoted himself to this ideal during the long, lonely, tedious years at sea, and praised it warmly in the pages devoted to the craft of his profession in *The Mirror of the Sea*. It was the analogue to his concern with form and style when he took up his career as a writer after leaving the sea, and the link that bound the two careers in "a subtle accord." This concept is implicit in one of Conrad's own statements:

Now, the moral side of an industry, productive or unproductive, the redeeming and ideal aspect of this bread-winning, is the attainment and preservation of the highest possible skill on the part of the craftsmen. Such skill, the skill of technique, is more than honesty; it is something wider, embracing honesty and grace and rule in an elevated and clear sentiment, not altogether utilitarian, which may be called the honour of labour. It is made up of accumulated tradition, kept alive by individual pride, rendered exact by professional opinion, and, like the higher arts, it is spurred on and sustained by discriminating praise.
This is why the attainment of proficiency, the pushing of your skill with attention to the most delicate shades of excellence, is a matter of vital concern. Efficiency of a practically flawless kind may be reached naturally in the struggle for bread. But there is something beyond—a higher point, a subtle and unmistakable touch of love and pride beyond mere skill; almost an inspiration which gives to all work that finish which is almost art—which *is* art. (*The Mirror of the Sea,* p. 24)

But however much the pursuit of well performed duty sustained him from day to day, it did not allay his sense of exile. It was, after all, an abstraction that succeeded in filling the emptiness of time but brought him no closer to the organized community of men. It was true that the ship's company was a kind of organized community, but for too short a period, and the inevitable ending of a voyage, with the dispersal of the seamen never to be reassembled in the same form, only emphasized the transience and ephemerality of maritime life. In port Conrad kept aloof a good deal of the time from contact with other sea captains. He dressed like a dandy, maintained his fastidious manners, and in fact was referred to, by no means affectionately or admiringly, as "the Russian Count." [3]

3 See a letter describing Conrad by a Paul Langlois who knew him during his stay on the island of Mauritius; quoted by Baines, pp. 508–510.

There is a bizarre similarity between this figure cut by Conrad and Axel Heyst twenty-five years later in *Victory*.

During his years in the British merchant marine Conrad never formed any close relationships with others. His letters during the 1880's, written mainly to his uncle in Cracow and his cousin in Brussels, are those of a man absolutely alone in the world. They are sane, clear-eyed, measured in tone, affectionate to his uncle, slightly sycophantic to his female cousin with her small literary reputation —but written out of a void inhabited only by himself. The long voyages to Australia, Malaya, and the Dutch East Indies filled him with experiences instead of relationships, supplied him with materials for observation rather than objects of love,[4] and convinced him of the richness of life without yet giving him a stake in it. At a time of life when most men find the ground under them growing solid, Conrad found it persistently insecure,[5] and this feeling of insecurity became the foundation of his art. His characters, often without knowing it, tread on thin ice, accompanied at every point by the imminent likelihood of their falling through. The lonely years at sea imprinted upon Conrad the acute consciousness that life might be rich but it was also dangerous. The first quality kept his pessimism from morbidity and hollowness; the second invested it with dramatic tension.

Another isolating element was the barrier of language. He spoke English with a heavy foreign accent, which he never overcame. His wife, indeed, recorded the astonishing fact that in his later years it grew more marked, that the longer he lived in England the more

---

[4] In 1888, while on the island of Mauritius, Conrad seems to have proposed to a Eugénie Renouf, and was turned down (Baines, p. 98). This would make her, one supposes, a love object, but too little is known of the episode to identify her clearly. In any case, her rejection of him must have increased his feeling of isolation and insecurity. In a playful questionnaire Conrad filled out on Mauritius, a document now in the Keating Collection at Yale, there was one significant question to which he gave a highly suggestive answer. Question: What trait of character would you have liked to have had bestowed upon you? Conrad's reply: Self-confidence.

[5] Bertrand Russell remarked that Conrad "thought of civilized and morally tolerable human life as a dangerous walk on a thin crust of barely cooled lava which at any moment might break and let the unwary sink into fiery depths" (*Portraits from Memory*, New York, 1959, p. 87). Jim's image, "There was not the thickness of a sheet of paper between the right and wrong of this affair" (*Lord Jim*, p. 130), suggests the subtle, parlous line of separation between solidity and chaos.

like a foreigner he sounded. His sense of otherness was reinforced by his looks, gestures, general appearance. He may have passed for a Frenchman in France, but in England was never taken for an Englishman, not even at the height of his fame as a novelist in English. As a fairly young man in the 80's and early 90's, before his writing career gave him a special foothold in English life, his accent would have been enough by itself to keep him from merging with the people of his adopted country.

The shortcomings of his sea existence were becoming increasingly irksome, but he hung on as best he could. The ideal of practicing his métier with maximum skill kept him going through the darker hours. But performing the same fixed duties over and over, constantly going through essentially the same motions began to weigh heavily upon his spirit and, as he left his first youth behind, upon his body, too. The glamour of the sea, which had lured him for so long, began to fade [6] and was slowly replaced by more complex emotions. The reality of a seaman's life was more exacting than one's youthful imagination realized, and the most exacting thing about it in Conrad's case was the grinding pressure of stark ennui. Storms, typhoons, the risk of accident and death were relatively easy to encompass; they at least gave one something to think about and to do. It was the dull prospect of nothing in particular happening, the prospect that prevailed most of the time, that was hard to endure. In some ways the nothingness of life taxed the spirit far more than its drastic emergencies.

At times the strain of endurance was too much for him and he would break off abruptly. One such *crise de nerfs* took place at the beginning of 1888 in Singapore when he suddenly quit his comfortable berth as chief officer of the *Vidar*. Twenty-eight years later, he described his reasons and state of mind magnificently in the opening pages of *The Shadow-Line,* the last of his great stories dealing with the theme of psychic emptiness.

---

6 Marlow, in one of his asides in *Lord Jim*, describes the process of disillusionment: "There is such magnificent vagueness in the expectations that had driven each of us to sea, such a glorious indefiniteness, such a beautiful greed of adventures that are their own and only reward! What we get—well, we won't talk of that. . . . In no other kind of life is the illusion more wide of reality—in no other is the beginning *all* illusion—the disenchantment more swift—the subjugation more complete" (p. 129).

Another crisis, perhaps the most acute of his career as a sailor, began at the end of 1889. He was without work through the summer and autumn of that year—a particularly long spell of unemployment that forced him to find an escape from idleness. It was then that he started *Almayer's Folly,* not with a view to becoming a writer or ceasing to be a seaman or developing a secondary craft, but solely to kill time. He informs us in *A Personal Record* that he had no clear literary intention: "The conception of a planned book was entirely outside my mental range when I sat down to write; the ambition of being an author had never turned up amongst these gracious imaginary existences one creates fondly for oneself at times in the stillness and immobility of a daydream . . ." (p. 68). But the writing of the opening chapters of *Almayer's Folly,* conceived in a purely amateur spirit, did not save him from the corrosive effects of unemployment. He was also vaguely dissatisfied with his customary sea routes. Now that he had crisscrossed the Indian Ocean and the waters of the Western Pacific, they seemed ordinary to him and had, indefinably, lost their zest. He was in the mood for a fresh turning, not out of maritime life altogether but into some new aspect of it. The old idea of whaling in arctic waters flickered up in his mind again, but died under the impact of a sudden passion for Africa.

The highly publicized explorations of Sir Henry Morton Stanley, who had traced the course of the Congo River, had lent fresh glamour to the Dark Continent. Stanley was lionized in Brussels at receptions arranged by the Belgian government which had extracted a vast fortune in ivory from King Leopold's domain in the Congo. Trade was brisk, opportunities plentiful, the African future a bright mélange of commerce, geographic and scientific discovery, and the fruition of the nineteenth century ideal of bringing civilization to the natives. With the Congo the central artery of trade and penetration, the demand for experienced navigators must surely be great. Or so it seemed.

Conrad, restless, irked at prolonged inactivity, chafing psychically at a career that he had already outgrown without knowing it, leaped at the thought of commanding a boat plying the Congo. Once this desire took hold of him, he pursued it obsessionally. At his request, the men he knew in London shipping circles began making inquiries of their friends in Belgium. He begged Mme.

Poradowska to use her influence in Brussels on his behalf. The fact that he spoke French (an indispensable qualification for the Belgian service) was in his favor. Negotiations began, interviews followed, the captaincy of a river steamship was promised, arrangements were made, and by May, 1890, Conrad was on his way to Africa.

In every way but one the African experience was a disaster. The promise of a steamer, which seemed so firm in Europe, grew nebulous once Conrad reached the Congo. A series of misunderstandings with local agents, coupled with mishaps to the vessels themselves, kept the original agreement from being carried out. He made long overland marches through difficult country to stations along the river, plagued by mosquitoes and enervated by tropical heat. He quarreled with the shipping company's managers who, in his view, deliberately reneged on the contract drawn up in Brussels and refused to assign a river boat to him. He fell ill from malaria, and lay for weeks in the grip of high fever. The African natives, far more primitive and removed from his own civilization than the Malays in the Far East had ever been, haunted him with their atavistic savagery and with the cruelty of their exploitation at the hands of the "civilizing" European traders. Africa was a nightmare that seriously injured his health, exacerbated his already jumpy nerves, and darkened his imagination. But amid these distempers, there was one gain. By putting him under abnormal pressure, Africa taught Conrad a priceless lesson: how to identify the point at which men break under strain and the subtle stages, the concealed gradations, the barely detectible symptoms leading up to it.

He returned to Europe early in 1891 more alone than ever. Where before, he was exiled from Poland and France, and had felt unable to merge with England, he now felt wrenched out of the human frame itself. No sooner had he returned to London than gout succeeded malaria, and he lay in bed for weeks with swollen limbs. His communications to his uncle in Poland struck a new note of black pessimism, which evoked from the aging guardian fresh cries over the Korzeniowski heritage and renewed appeals to take heart and continue. To Conrad's established melancholy, to his sense of dissociation from society and life, to his as yet unacknowledged suspicion that the sea had become a grind and not an adventure, was now added a vision of human nature itself as far frailer in its civilized aspect than even he had thought. All this was aggravated by ill health, which quite by itself darkens the normal coloration of things. In February and March of 1891, though he had just turned thirty-three, Conrad was convinced that his life was behind him.

Nonetheless, he went on living, *faute de mieux*. A stay at a hydropathic sanitarium near Geneva reduced the inflammation in his legs. Still not fit for sea duty, he secured a job as an inspector in a London warehouse, and resumed his sporadic creation of *Almayer's Folly*. His letters to Mme. Poradowska increase markedly at this time. To her he expresses his own fears and insecurities at length, begs for information about her affairs, both personal and literary, is excessively solicitous about her troubles, praises her mediocre books in extravagant terms, and indulges in a good deal of nervous self-deprecation. The flowery verbal courtesies to which he was trained in Polish appear in this correspondence conducted in French, and help create the note of insincerity that runs through Conrad's share of it.

He needed a human being connected with him in some way who was stable enough for him to hold on to; as a relative by marriage, in an established social and intellectual position, she served the purpose. Imagining himself drowning in failure, Conrad clung to her as an image of success. She had been an effective patroness in the matter of the Belgian Congo; she might perhaps help him in some other direction, though at the moment he had no particular direction in mind. He badly needed someone near his own age to talk to. Her advice to him was commonplace, her general ideas were as conventional as her epistolary style was without distinction (so, indeed, was Conrad's during this period; he became a fascinating letter writer only after his literary career began). No matter. She was a life line in a dark time. He clung to her deferentially, tenaciously. Indeed, Uncle Tadeusz was worried lest the friendship between his nephew and the widowed Mme. Poradowska—her Polish husband had died the year before—might develop into something more intimate.[7]

Toward the end of 1891, his health largely recovered, Conrad returned to sea aboard a sailing ship, the *Torrens*, bound for Australia. Once again he signed on not as captain but as first mate,

---

[7] Jean-Aubry, *The Sea Dreamer* (New York, 1957), p. 187.

a condition that he now seemed more or less to have accepted as normal. Conrad's first round-trip voyage on the *Torrens* was uneventful. The second was marked by two small incidents. On the outward journey, a young passenger named Jacques, an ex-Cambridge student en route to Australia in a vain effort to recover his health, became the first reader of *Almayer's Folly*. The lonely first mate struck up an acquaintance with the dying young Englishman and timidly showed him the nine completed chapters of the much-traveled manuscript. He waited anxiously for the verdict. Was the novel worth finishing? Did it interest him? Was the story clear? To these three questions Jacques, surely the most economical critic on record, replied with a total of five words, all favorable. They were: to the first question, "Distinctly"; to the second, "Very much"; to the third, "Yes! Perfectly" (*A Personal Record,* pp. 17–18). This exchange no doubt encouraged Conrad to go on with the book.

On the return journey, another young passenger, John Galsworthy, back from a fruitless attempt to visit Robert Louis Stevenson in Samoa, became friendly with Conrad and spent many hours in his company. He had no way of knowing then that he had met up with a greater man than Stevenson. Galsworthy's description is an acute, first-hand record of how Conrad appeared in March, 1893.

Very dark he looked in the burning sunlight, tanned, with a peaked brown beard, almost black hair, and dark brown eyes, over which the lids were deeply folded. He was thin, not tall, his arms very long, his shoulders broad, his head set rather forward. He spoke to me with a strong foreign accent. He seemed to me strange on an English ship.[8]

He went on to describe the magnetism and power of Conrad's personality, but what chiefly caught Galsworthy's eye was how strange he seemed on an English ship. Conrad was in those years more than a stranger to England; he felt himself disoriented from life itself, outside whatever orbit men were destined for. The long voyages at sea had lost whatever romance they once possessed, and had boiled down to hard, grinding, monotonous labor consuming to flesh and spirit alike.

The second journey on the *Torrens* was at last over. One more chore at sea remained. Conrad signed as first mate aboard a French

8 *Castles in Spain* (New York, 1927), p. 101.

steamer chartered to carry emigrants to French Canada, but the
agents ran into money trouble and the ship, empty of passengers,
never left Rouen. Conrad, salaried but bored, hung about the cafés
of the river front, taking what satisfaction he could out of the fact
that he was spending all these weary weeks in Flaubert's home town.
He occupied himself with writing letters in French to Cousin
Marguerite and in Polish to Uncle Tadeusz, and reflecting about
Almayer who was not far now from seeing his dream of wealth and
racial rehabilitation come apart before his eyes. In January, 1894,
soon after his thirty-sixth birthday, Conrad, released from his static
confinement on the upper Seine, returned to London. The last of his
trips to sea was significantly abortive; it never got under way at all.

Without his knowing it, his maritime career had come to an end,
and a new life, a life on land, was about to begin.

V

The Struggle with Nature

1894 WAS A PIVOTAL YEAR IN CONRAD'S LIFE. HE LEFT THE SEA FOR THE last time early in January. In February Uncle Tadeusz died, leaving him a small legacy. He spent the spring finishing *Almayer's Folly,* which he dedicated to his late guardian.[1] The manuscript was then submitted to the publishing firm of Fisher Unwin. The summer passed in anxious foreboding over the manuscript's fate and in equally anxious correspondence with Mme. Poradowska over the possibility of their collaborating on a French version of the novel.

There is no reason to disbelieve Conrad when he says in *A Personal Record* "that if I had not written in English I would not have written at all" (p. viii), though at this point in his career he appeared to be teetering on the edge of moving over to French. He rejected his first two languages as writing instruments. Once out of Poland, he refused to write Polish professionally. French he found too perfectly "crystallized," to use his own expression, to satisfy a temperament acutely conscious of the haze that hangs over moral issues and obscures the meaning of human destiny. As for English, Ford remembered how Conrad used to rail against its slipperiness:

> Conrad's indictment of the English language was this, that no English word is a word; that all English words are instruments for exciting blurred emotions. "Oaken" in French means "made of oak wood"—nothing more. "Oaken" in English connotes innumerable moral attributes: it will connote stolidity, resolution, honesty, blond features, relative unbreakableness, absolute unbendableness—also,

---

[1] Albert Guerard's subtle hint that Bobrowski's death may have released Conrad's creative energy (*Conrad the Novelist,* Cambridge, Mass., 1958, p. 11) is a tantalizing but improbable suggestion. The bulk of *Almayer's Folly* had, after all, been finished before 1894, at however erratic a pace.

made of oak. . . . The consequence is that no English word has
clean edges: a reader is always, for a fraction of a second, uncertain,
as to which meaning of the word the writer intends. Thus, all
English prose is blurred.[2]

But it was this very blurred quality which attracted Conrad because
it expressed, to begin with, the nature of the universe as he conceived it. French remained incompatible with his metaphysics.
English was by intrinsic character its perfect linguistic medium.

Of course, all the arguments about why Conrad wrote in English,
his third language in order of learning, can be simply resolved by
the statement that he did so because he happened to be living in
England at the time, was a British citizen and a captain in the
British merchant marine, was speaking English and only English
every day, and that it would have been extraordinary under the
circumstances if he had chosen to write in any other language. This
approach, however, based on ordinary common sense, only reinforces externally the affinity that bound Conrad to English from
within. Despite grammatical peculiarities and unidiomatic usages
that persisted to the end of his life, Conrad mastered written
English with phenomenal virtuosity. Ford's image is still the most
apt: ". . . what is miraculous is that he took English, as it were by
the throat and, wrestling till the dawn, made it obedient to him as it
has been obedient to few other men." [3]

But before the year was over, his novel was accepted, and the
question of what language he would write in was settled. He met
Unwin's editor, Edward Garnett, who, with great tact, encouraged
him to start his next novel. This was *An Outcast of the Islands*. In
the interlude between his first two novels, Conrad was gripped by
a characteristic paralysis. Here is his account of it in the Author's
Note to *An Outcast:*

Neither in my mind nor in my heart had I then given up the sea.
In truth I was clinging to it desperately, all the more desperately
because, against my will, I could not help feeling that there was
something changed in my relation to it. *Almayer's Folly* had been
finished and done with. The mood itself was gone. But it had left
the memory of an experience that, both in thought and emotion

2 Ford, p. 229.
3 *Ibid.,* p. 109.

was unconnected with the sea, and I suppose that part of my moral being which is rooted in consistency was badly shaken. I was a victim of contrary stresses which produced a state of immobility. I gave myself up to indolence. Since it was impossible for me to face both ways I had elected to face nothing. The discovery of new values in life is a very chaotic experience; there is a tremendous amount of jostling and confusion and a momentary feeling of darkness. I let my spirit float supine over that chaos. (p. vii)

This inertia is the theme which binds together both novels. They are remarkable studies of men whose vanity and brains have outrun their will power. These men suffer from an acute paralysis of will, which determines their actions, controls their outcries, gives their misfortunes a particular stamp, and brings them at last to their melancholy ends. Almayer and Willems are both the victims of Tom Lingard, a sentimental egotist who derives a self-sustaining gratification from "arranging" and "improving" the lives of others. Both marry native women from greed rather than love. Both stifle in the fecund jungle of Borneo, whose tropicality and profusion sap their vitality and leave them gasping in vain for spiritual air.

Almayer's dream is to accumulate a fortune from a reputed gold mine upriver, return to Holland with his half-caste daughter Nina, the only human being about whom he cares, and rehabilitate himself in Dutch society. Nothing comes of it. Lingard, who set him up in the trading post on the Pantai River, has left him to shift for himself. He is no match in cunning for the native Arab traders, is harassed by his wife as she relapses into native squalor, and is finally "betrayed" by his daughter who runs off with the Malay prince whom Almayer had sought to use as an instrument to secure the gold. Abandoned by everyone, wife, daughter, patron, ally, Almayer collapses altogether, takes to opium, and dies. As a mute symbol of his failure and ruin stands Almayer's Folly, the unfinished mansion he had begun in happier days and then abandoned. Through most of the novel he noisily bemoans his lot but is never able to rouse himself into coherent action. He is so incredibly conscious of himself that he is blind to all else, and even his passion for his daughter comes wrapped in a hard impenetrable coating of self-love. His steady descent into psychic sloth supplies him with the gratification of surrender, his only substitute for the gratification of success. Conrad piercingly exposes the pathology of Almayer's inertia. It emerges as one of the deadlier, more camouflaged disguises of egotism.

This first novel of Conrad's was published in 1895, the year in which Thomas Hardy's last piece of major fiction, *Jude the Obscure*, appeared. It was also the year that saw the end of Henry James's five-year flirtation with the stage, and his retreat, in bitter disappointment, to the growing involutions of his late period. Hardy was the most popular novelist in England when Conrad appeared on the scene, while James, himself an expatriate, was the figure Conrad most admired. A glance at *Jude the Obscure* suggests the texture of English fiction at the time the Polish newcomer entered the field. The novel was full of the advanced social ideas of a generation in revolt against the stuffier sides of Victorianism. It attacked marriage, education, religion, and the cult of progress. It spoke frankly of sex and even nudged the theme of incest, and it did all this so vigorously that the storm of protest that followed from a public still largely Victorian in taste and gentility was violent enough to drive Hardy out of fiction altogether. He had, in any case, looked upon it for twenty-five years as a second-class art, practiced it (though nobly) largely for the money, and longed for the day when he could retire to his first and only real love, the writing of poetry. Yet the structure of *Jude* was as straightforwardly chronological, as filled with coincidences and arrangements as anything in Dickens's time. It was also given to a peculiarly high-flown dialogue which in its most egregious form caused hero and heroine in moments of high passion to break into literary quotations when the direct language of the heart was plainly called for.

All this had its effect on Conrad. He entered literature in a decade when the English were in a "literary" rather than "natural" phase. The artificial formalism of Polish in which he had been nurtured as a boy was reinforced by the high-flown elaborateness of this new language. With Hardy this language tended to be ponderous, with James elliptical and circumlocutory, with the aesthetes of the 90's— Wilde, Beerbohm, the poets of the Rhymers Club, the *Yellow Book* coterie—elegantly mannered. Style drew its sustenance from art rather than life, and entered a mandarin phase. Conrad needed no further encouragement; he was a mandarin by nature. His early prose, despite his feeling for Flaubert, was packed with a good deal of verbal sludge. When enameled with tropical foliage, jungle vegetation, steamy rivers, and the other paraphernalia of the exotic East, it produced what Conrad himself referred to half-jokingly as Conradese.

Not the least cumbersome of his inflations was the habit, pronounced in *Almayer's Folly*, of stating simple things in a complicated way: an eyewitness is described as having gone through an "ocular demonstration"; men do not curse but "hurl objurgations." [4] Even in one of Conrad's most "simply" and "naturally" written tales, "Typhoon," the following unnaturally literary sentence appears: "Unbounded wonder was the intellectual meaning of his eye, while incredulity was seated in his whole countenance." Or, his taste still unsure, he lapsed into dime-store writing, and indulged in phrases like "the glorious beauty of her face" or "the dilated nostrils and the flashing eyes were the only signs of the storm raging within." His dialogue marched stiffly through a variety of gelid phrases; even at the height of his career, his characters, in direct conversation, could still use the expression, "I verily believe." The age marmorealized his prose and made it even more abstract and rhetorical. Conrad struggled against the tendency, broke free of it in his best work, and in the end imposed himself upon the language, but he did so against the resistant element of the times. In this sense, too, his effort to draw sustenance from England proved unlucky. He remained the foreigner, forcing English by an act of temperament to express the artist in him despite all its efforts to release the florid and stylizing man.

A larger issue confronting him in the early novels was nature. Conrad's struggle to master nature instead of being mastered by it was a problem greater than that of language and more serious than the verbal encrustations of English in one of its hothouse periods. The struggle to conquer nature and subdue it to the necessities of his art was fought and decided at the very beginning of his career as a writer. *Almayer's Folly* revealed the danger that confronted

---

4 This suggests James's ponderosities, present even in his beginning work. Herewith three examples from an early novel, *The American* (1877). A cleanshaven man: ". . . save for the abundant droop of his mustache he spoke, as to cheek and chin, of the joy of the matutinal steel." A man swearing: "Newman uttered one of the least attenuated imprecations that had ever passed his lips . . ." A woman weeping: ". . . the eyes were like two rainy autumn moons . . ."

Conrad from within: a passion for the baroque. His experience as a seaman had nurtured this passion by giving it the undulations of immense masses of water, the gorgeous locales of oceans, exotic islands, wild storms, and tropical archipelagoes to feed upon. In addition, he had a natural tendency to sink into passive reverie. Nature provided the perfect material for reverie. It was beautiful and varied; it had texture; it appeared to have "philosophical" meaning. And it was free of the emotional complications and psychological ambiguities marking human life. Our first view of Conrad is as a remarkable painter of the physical scene, but of the physical scene detached from the lives of his characters and inorganic to them.

The central love passage in *Almayer's Folly* comes framed in a magnificent setting. Almayer's half-caste daughter Nina has fallen passionately in love with Dain Maroola, a full-blooded Malay prince. In the thick of night the two drift downriver in a canoe: "They took no heed of thickening mist, or of the breeze dying away before sunrise; they forgot the existence of the great forests surrounding them, of all the tropical nature awaiting the advent of the sun in a solemn and impressive silence" (p. 69). So absorbed are they in each other that the scene around them does not exist, might be threatening instead of calm, ugly instead of enchanting. Here, nature has not very much to do except stand around and be noticed. Conrad himself seems conscious of this for he uses adjectives like *solemn* and *impressive* which represent his own external comment and do not emerge from within the scene.

The passage continues:

Over the low river-mist hiding the boat with its freight of young passionate life and all-forgetful happiness, the stars paled, and a silvery-grey tint crept over the sky from the eastward. There was not a breath of wind, not a rustle of stirring leaf, not a splash of leaping fish to disturb the serene repose of all living things on the banks of the great river. Earth, river, and sky were wrapped up in a deep sleep from which it seemed there would be no waking. All the seething life and movement of tropical nature seemed concentrated in the ardent eyes, in the tumultuously beating hearts of the two beings drifting in the canoe, under the white canopy of mist, over the smooth surface of the river. (pp. 69–70)

The "seething life and movement of tropical nature" is arbitrarily turned off so that we might concentrate on the "ardent eyes" and

"tumultuously beating hearts" of the lovers. The silence is an artificial silence, imposed not by way of heightening the emotion but
of displaying it. The reader is made conscious of nature as a background, as a scenic arrangement entirely outside the characters. No
one excels the early Conrad at scene-painting, but the imminent
peril of allowing this talent to manipulate his art hangs everywhere
over *Almayer's Folly*.

The passage comes to a spectacular end:

> Suddenly a great sheaf of yellow rays shot upwards from behind
> the black curtain of trees lining the banks of the Pantai. The stars
> went out; the little black clouds at the zenith glowed for a moment
> with crimson tints, and the thick mist, stirred by the gentle breeze,
> the sigh of waking nature, whirled round and broke into fantasti-
> cally torn pieces, disclosing the wrinkled surface of the river sparkling
> in the broad light of day. Great flocks of white birds wheeled
> screaming above the swaying tree-tops. The sun had risen on the east
> coast. (p. 70)

The lovers are now forgotten (turned off, as it were, in their turn),
while daylight arrives in a burst of splendor. The description is
superbly dramatic, living up to Conrad's highest expectations of
making the reader *see*, but it stands by itself with the lovers removed from the stage. The emotion and the landscape, though
managed effectively each by itself, have not yet learned to live together.

When Dain and Nina land, they are at once surrounded by the
violence of the tropical jungle:

> . . . all around them in a ring of luxuriant vegetation bathed in
> the warm air charged with strong and harsh perfumes, the intense
> work of tropical nature went on: plants shooting upward, entwined,
> interlaced in inextricable confusion, climbing madly and brutally
> over each other in the terrible silence of a desperate struggle towards
> the life-giving sunshine above—as if struck with sudden horror
> at the seething mass of corruption below, at the death and decay
> from which they sprang. (p. 71)

But though the jungle is violently active, the passion of the young
lovers has reached its first quiescence. They reach shore only to
part, their love fully declared, and so deeply rooted in their hearts
that it is placed forever beyond the reach of the unhappy Almayer.
And the qualities of that love are as far removed as can be from

the confusion, corruption, death, and decay that surround it. Instead of reinforcing each other, nature and man go their separate ways, at times in exactly opposite directions.

For the most part, the landscape in *Almayer's Folly* is an ornamental backdrop, an unrelated montage of which Conrad has an unlimited supply. As the three principal characters go to their final rendezvous, morning breaks upon the Eastern earth:

> The sun, rising above the calm waters of the Straits, marked its own path by a streak of light that glided upon the sea and darted up by the wide reach of the river, a hurried messenger of light and life to the gloomy forests of the coast; and in this radiance of the sun's pathway floated the black canoe headed for the islet which lay bathed in sunshine, the yellow sands of its encircling beach shining like an inlaid golden disc on the polished steel of the unwrinkled sea. To the north and south of it rose other islets, joyous in their brilliant colouring of green and yellow, and on the main coast the sombre line of mangrove bushes ended to the southward in the reddish cliffs of Tanjong Mirrah, advancing into the sea, steep and shadowless under the clear light of the early morning. (p. 186)

The contrasts are certainly effective: the light penetrating the gloomy forests, the black canoe piercing the sunshine, the yellow sand laid side by side with the steel of the wrinkled sea, the green, yellow, and red juxtaposed with the somber, steep, and shadowless. All this has an excitement of its own. Conrad's brushwork is already sure, his chromatic sense full-blown, his instinct for the panoramic and complex as pronounced as it will ever be. Yet if the scene were the edge of a desert in North Africa instead of the jungle in Borneo, the story would be little altered. Two dramas go on side by side in *Almayer's Folly,* the drama of nature and the drama of man. They seldom meet.

The facts of the novel's creation to some extent explain its character. We recall how, in the fall of 1889, beached in England between voyages, Captain Korzeniowski was chafing with inactivity. Out of restlessness, ennui, as an outlet for pent-up energies, he had begun writing *Almayer's Folly,* drawing upon his recent memories of journeys between Singapore and Borneo. He did not even bother to change the names of the principal figures. Almayer, Lingard, Babalatchi, Abdulla were as he knew them in real life.

He kept pecking away at the book during periods of unemploy-

ment or in interludes at sea, and seldom was a novel written in so
sporadic, desultory a fashion. Like a piece of not absolutely necessary baggage it accompanied him everywhere, and must surely have
set some sort of mileage record for a manuscript in transit. Jean-
Aubry, Conrad's first biographer, notes that it journeyed with the
author from London to Poland, from Africa to Switzerland, from
Australia back to England, until finally finished in London in May,
1894. Though not of course his first writing effort, *Almayer's Folly*
bears all the signs of an irrelevant birth, a haphazard composition,
and a reluctant completion. Conrad finished it as he had started it,
for want of something better to do. Little wonder that the novel
should be full of dissociated elements. The wonder is that it hangs
together at all.

In other respects the treatment of nature in *Almayer's Folly* reveals Conrad as he is always to be. Nature is incessantly mobile and
dramatic, constantly in the process of changing from one state to
another. This infusion of energy into the universe seemed instinctive with Conrad, and in any case came to him with his very earliest
impressions. When his Polish friend J. H. Retinger remarked on
how un-English this procedure was, how typically Polish, Conrad
pulled a faded book from his shelf—*Pan Tadeusz,* the great Polish
epic by Adam Mickiewicz—and said: "Here is the reason." No
doubt the perpetual changeability of the sea had something to do
with it, too. The ocean is monotonous—the imaginative sea captain
suffered admittedly from many hours, many days of boredom—but
its monotony is never static. The protean mutability of the sea left
its mark deeply embedded in the fabric of Conrad's first novel, written as it was not simply from memory of the Malayan Archipelago
but while the author was on shipboard pursuing his trade on the
far waters of the globe.

An Outcast of the Islands had a different birth. It was written
more or less consecutively within a single year, late 1894 to late
1895. Again the lack of an appropriate berth at sea was an immense
if unintentional stimulus to Conrad the writer. The leap forward
in aesthetic maturity is staggering. Despite occasional lapses, nature
is as close to the heart of this second novel as it was peripheral to
the first.

The skillful manipulation of external detail is evident from the start. Willems, playing billiards and dispensing gratuitous advice, causes even the billiard balls to stand still "as if listening also." The sea, before the coming of steam, extracts from Conrad a passionate farewell.[5] The contrast of silence and sound is dramatized by the leaping of a fish "which measured the profundity of the overpowering silence that swallowed up the sharp sound suddenly." From the sky Conrad plucks a splendid symbol for Aissa: "Over the courtyard and the house floated a round, sombre, and lingering cloud, dragging behind a tail of tangled and filmy streamers—like the dishevelled hair of a mourning woman" (p. 241). In the wind he finds a movement to embody the hysterical scenes made by Mrs. Willems in Almayer's house: "Those scenes, begun without any warning, ended abruptly in a sobbing flight and a bang of the door; stirred the house with a sudden, a fierce, and an evanescent disturbance; like those inexplicable whirlwinds that rise, run, and vanish without apparent cause upon the sun-scorched dead level of arid and lamentable plains" (p. 303). As Lingard describes the gold mine up the river that will make them all rich, he amuses Almayer's small daughter by building a house of cards; its sudden collapse subtly indicates the hollowness and fragility of their dream of wealth. The unused office, filled with furniture Almayer thought necessary to successful trading, is brilliantly imaged as "a temple of an exploded superstition."

The linkage between Willems and nature springs to life almost from the moment that he arrives in Sambir. Sunk in sloth and moral inertia—a frame of mind Conrad made peculiarly his own province—the disgraced Dutchman is obsessed by what surrounds him:

He heard the reproach of his idleness in the murmurs of the river, in the unceasing whisper of the great forests. Round him everything stirred, moved, swept by in a rush; the earth under his feet and the heavens above his head. The very savages around him strove, struggled, fought, worked—if only to prolong a miserable existence; but they lived, they lived! And it was only himself that seemed to be left outside the scheme of creation in a hopeless immobility filled with tormenting anger and with ever-stinging regret. (p. 65)

[5] The age of steam threatened to eliminate the old dramatic qualities of the sea: beauty, mystery, inscrutability, cruelty, promise. Since these were the qualities Conrad found in the universe, anything that smudged our awareness of them he found tragically regrettable.

The river and the forests are not "arranged" to reflect the emotions of the man, in the traditional romantic fashion. They are themselves, and therefore perfectly convincing. By juxtaposing their intense activity and Willems's intense inactivity, Conrad not only heightens each but uses the one to alter the other. For this "natural" reminder of his withdrawal from life prepares Willems for his extraordinary encounter with Aissa which immediately follows.

He sees her for the first time in the midst of the jungle ablaze with light at high noon, and now ensues one of the magnificent descriptions of sexual impact:

High above, the branches of the trees met in a transparent shimmer of waving green mist, through which the rain of yellow rays descended upon her head, streamed in glints down her black tresses, shone with the changing glow of liquid metal on her face, and lost itself in vanishing sparks in the sombre depths of her eyes that, wide open now, with enlarged pupils, looked steadily at the man in her path. And Willems stared at her, charmed with a charm that carries with it a sense of irreparable loss, tingling with that feeling which begins like a caress and ends in a blow, in that sudden hurt of a new emotion making its way into a human heart, with the brusque stirring of sleeping sensations awakening suddenly to the rush of new hopes, new fears, new desires—and to the flight of one's old self. (p. 69)

The corrupt and corrupting jungle becomes the perfect ecological setting for Willems's fall: "He had been baffled, repelled, almost frightened by the intensity of that tropical life which wants the sunshine but works in gloom; which seems to be all grace and of colour and form, all brilliance, all smiles, but is only the blossoming of the dead; whose mystery holds the promise of joy and beauty, yet contains nothing but poison and decay" (p. 70).

Civilization and barbarism struggle within Willems just as life and death struggle in the jungle. The two conflicts, juxtaposed and analogously linked, immensely reinforce the emotion of the man. Since this emotion is uncontrollably sensual, it comes appropriately enclosed in the bosom of the wildest, most untamed, most thickly tangled nature. For Willems's journey in the novel is from man to animal, from the large city of Macassar and the smaller but no less human settlement of Almayer to the dark enclosure of the Malay jungle. Every stage of this steep psychological descent is accompanied by a similar progression in the physical frame of nature. The way in which these two levels of progression are fused dramatically not only marks off Conrad's second novel from his first but establishes that successful vision of the relationship between man and the sensory universe which was to become one of his supreme achievements.

The deepening struggle in Willems passes through a series of sharply defined stages, each in a suggestive liaison with nature. Conrad makes both him and Aissa superb physical specimens of their races, somehow in keeping with the dramatic grandeur, even the grandioseness of their surroundings. Willems's first sudden sense of his descent into nightmare has a relevant setting:

He looked round wildly. Above the shapeless darkness of the forest undergrowth rose the treetops with their high boughs and leaves standing out black on the pale sky—like fragments of night floating on moonbeams. Under his feet warm steam rose from the heated earth. (p. 80)

The warm steam beclouds his mind, overwhelms his senses, causes him to imagine himself falling to some unpredictable doom:

He struggled with the sense of certain defeat—lost his footing—fell back into the darkness. With a faint cry and an upward throw of his arms he gave up as a tired swimmer gives up: . . . because the night is dark and the shore is far—because death is better than strife. (pp. 80–81)

Other figures in the later novels are to jump or intend jumping to their destruction. In the darkness Jim jumps from the *Patna* to the everlasting dark hole of the lifeboat. Flora de Barral, in *Chance,* is about to leap from a cliff when Marlow's appearance restrains her. Even Almayer has a recurring daydream in which he sees himself falling off a steep precipice, falling "day after day, month after month, year after year." Conrad wraps moral degradation or despair in the physical act of falling. At the end, in a final irony, Willems is drained of all feeling for Aissa while she continues to love him more violently than ever. Their embrace, under these decaying circumstances, culminates in Willems's last vision of his fall into a final corruption.

He stood still and rigid, pressing her mechanically to his breast while he thought that there was nothing for him in the world. He was robbed of everything; robbed of his passion, of his liberty, of forgetfulness, of consolation. She, wild with delight, whispered on rapidly, of love, of light, of peace, of long years. . . . He looked drearily above her head down into the deeper gloom of the court-yard. And, all at once, it seemed to him that he was peering into a sombre hollow, into a deep black hole full of decay and of whitened bones; into an immense and inevitable grave full of corruption where sooner or later he must, unavoidably, fall. (p. 339)

Inside his confused and tormented consciousness Willems falls and rises a dozen times over, his surroundings serving as the ladder on which his descents and ascents are effected, as a barometer record-ing their vibrations.

The emotional struggle between the white man and the Malay woman takes place at one point under the shadow of a gigantic tree. Its size reduces them to a minuscule focus, yet protects their human warmth from the merciless coldness of the cosmos:

The solitary exile of the forests, great, motionless and solemn in his abandonment, left alone by the life of ages that had been pushed away from him by those pigmies that crept at his foot, towered high and straight above their heads. He seemed to look on, dispas-sionate and imposing, in his lonely greatness, spreading his branches wide in a gesture of lofty protection, as if to hide them in the sombre shelter of innumerable leaves; as if moved by the disdainful compassion of the strong, by the scornful pity of an aged giant, to screen this struggle of two human hearts from the cold scrutiny of glittering stars. (p. 154)

Nature, however, is seldom so tender. The novel being a study of deg-radation, and particularly sexual degradation, we see nature chiefly in her fecundity, her teeming regeneration and decomposition. The decay of Willems is accompanied by the awesome decay, the struggle for life and perpetual triumph of death in the proliferating jungle. When at last Lingard repudiates him and condemns him to per-petual exile, Willems is seized by a sudden impulse to kill himself. But the thought of leaving the sensory world with all its intense and ceaseless activity douses the impulse, and the desire to live flares up in him again:

Round him, ceaselessly, there went on without a sound the mad turmoil of tropical life. After he had died all this would remain! He wanted to clasp, to embrace solid things; he had an immense craving for sensations; for touching, pressing, seeing, handling, holding on, to all these things. All this would remain—remain for years, for ages, for ever. After he had miserably died there, all this would remain, would live, would exist in joyous sunlight, would breathe in the coolness of serene nights. What for, then? He would be dead. He would be stretched upon the warm moisture of the ground, feeling nothing, seeing nothing, knowing nothing. . . . (pp. 331–332)

Thus the motivation, the stimulus for one of the last of his conscious acts comes to Willems straight from the heart of nature. By the time he dies at Aissa's hands he has become almost as much the creature of the Malayan forest as she, as much its victim as the victim of the bullet which she fires at him with such unexpected accuracy.

In a letter to Edward Garnett (September 24, 1895) Conrad described his procedure in the final moments of *An Outcast:*

In the treatment of the last scenes I wanted to convey the kind of placidity that is caused by extreme surprise. You must not forget that they are all immensely amazed. That's why they are so quiet. . . . That's why I put in the quiet morning—the immobility of surrounding matter emphasized only by the flutter of small birds.[6]

The craftsmanship throughout the novel reveals the closest, most conscious planning of effects in an effort to fuse together humanity and nature into a single fabric. The effort does not always succeed. There are times when Conrad is still engaged in his early habit of romantic scene-painting, breathing into landscape human characteristics: "At the sun's disappearance . . . the immense cloud . . . hung arrested above the steaming forests; hanging low, silent and menacing over the unstirring tree-tops; withholding the blessing of rain, nursing the wrath of its thunder; undecided—as if brooding over its own power for good or for evil" (*Outcast,* p. 213). Or he will comment portentously and gratuitously on some quite impersonal phenomenon: ". . . the river . . . hurried on unceasing and fast, regardless of joy or sorrow, of suffering and of strife, of failures and triumphs that lived on its banks. The brown water was there,

6 Garnett, p. 43.

ready to carry friends or enemies, to nurse love or hate on its submissive and heartless bosom, to help or to hinder, to save life or give death; the great and rapid river: a deliverance, a prison, a refuge or a grave" (*Outcast*, p. 214).

Nor are his symbols always under control. The tree drifting down the river on the second page of *Almayer's Folly*, lifting its branch "in mute appeal to heaven," embodies perfectly the life of Almayer. But the bluebottle fly which Lingard and Almayer vainly seek to kill, which flies away leaving them "looking very puzzled and idle, their arms hanging uselessly by their sides—like men disheartened by some portentous failure" (*Outcast*, p. 169), symbolizes the futility of their relationship in a way that seems intrusive and commonplace.

Success, however, easily outpaces failure in *An Outcast*. Curiously, Conrad's pursuit of coordination is aided by his detachment from Willems, a detachment that often appears to mask a positive and even contemptuous dislike. In an Author's Note, written twenty-four years after completing the novel, Conrad remembered that "The mere scenery got a great hold on me as I went on, perhaps because . . . the story itself was never very near my heart. It engaged my imagination much more than my affection. As to my feeling for Willems it was but the regard one cannot help having for one's own creation" (p. ix). Not particularly interested in Willems himself, his personal feelings disengaged, Conrad was free to concentrate on the story as an exercise in craftsmanship. For the thirty-six-year-old seaman trying his hand at learning a new trade (though he still thought of writing as only a temporary stopgap), nothing could be more useful. It allowed him to study in a coherent way and at close range not only the problems of his second novel but the directions of his own temperament. The formless drift of *Almayer's Folly* was now sharply arrested, and the movement toward a unifying center set into motion. Henceforth, the separate parts of his fiction were to work together with an intimacy that, more than anything else, bespeaks the decisive role played by *An Outcast* in the formulation of Conrad's art.

One would never suspect from reading Conrad's letters at this time that there was any advance at all in his technical power. Or an advance of any kind. He is anxiously busy making derogatory or self-deprecating remarks about his work:

. . . the last chapter [of *An Outcast*] is simply abominable. . . . As to the XXIV I feel convinced that the right course would be to destroy it. . . . For months I have been afraid of that chapter—and now it is written—and the foreboding is realized in a dismal failure. . . . This letter . . . is a confession of complete failure on my part.[7]

. . . I consider it [*Almayer's Folly*] honestly a miserable failure. Every critic (but two or three) overrated the book. It took me a year to tear the *Outcast* out of myself and upon my word of honour,—I look on it . . . with bitter disappointment.[8]

Nor is it only the first two novels that he disparages. He refers to the stories begun immediately afterward as "dullest trash" and "the most rotten twaddle." Yet he is desperately hungry for approval. Even when the critics approve, he is not satisfied. He must have public popularity as well. Part of his self-deprecation was the ritualistic modesty of the Polish *pan*, part a mask for his own self-belief, part a nervous anxiety over his ambiguous position as half an unemployed merchant mariner, half an untried writer. But underneath the mask and the manners, underneath the protective camouflage of mordant self-judgment, the struggle to master the materials of his new vocation was proceeding relentlessly.

In *Almayer's Folly* Conrad's apprenticeship began. With *An Outcast* it was already over. Perhaps neither novel moves us deeply, any more than it did the author. In them, however, he grasped the elusive linkages that drew his vision of man and his vision of nature together. Thus armed, he was ready for the more intricate and profound linkages of *The Nigger of the "Narcissus," "Heart of Darkness,"* and *Lord Jim,* his first authentic masterpieces that do, unmistakably, move us deeply. The canvas of the first two novels was the battleground on which Conrad won the decisive victory over his centrifugal self. With this victory the master mariner finally gave way to the master writer.

7 Letter of September 24, 1895, Garnett, pp. 41, 43.
8 Letter of October 28, 1895, to Edward Noble, in G. Jean-Aubry, *Joseph Conrad: Life and Letters* (Garden City, N. Y., 1927), I, 183. All future references to this two-volume work will be abbreviated to LL.

VI

The Conradian Centaur

THE TRANSITION FROM CONRAD'S LIFE AT SEA TO A NEW EXISTENCE ON land was appropriately memorialized by his marriage to Miss Jessie George in March, 1896, three weeks after the appearance of *An Outcast of the Islands*.

Jessie George was the daughter of an impecunious London bookseller. She was fifteen years younger than Conrad. Though she lived with him for almost thirty years, bore him two sons, shared a difficult life full of accidents and burdens, not much is known about her. She seems to have had few literary or intellectual interests, though she typed many of the early stories and shrewdly saved the original manuscripts when Conrad threw them in the wastebasket.[1] She wrote two books of reminiscence about him after his death, yet these tell us little about Conrad and even less about herself. One of their astonishing features is her almost total unawareness of how much money problems ate into his spirit; either Conrad was a master at concealing it or she was a miracle of insensitivity. Some of his friends, Hueffer in particular, disliked her intensely; Virginia Woolf is supposed to have referred to her harshly as "that lump of a woman." She suffered a number of leg injuries, endured several operations, had a heart condition, and was for many years a semi-invalid, yet she and Conrad lived together in emotional felicity. He described her once as "a person of simple feelings, guided by the intelligence of the heart. . . ."[2] Although he seldom spoke of her in letters to others, his letters to her are full of sentimental endearment.

[1] Some of these were sold for modest sums to John Quinn, the American lawyer and collector. Over the years they rose considerably in value and became major items in the famous Quinn Library.

[2] Letter to Harriet Capes, March 22, 1902 (Yale).

Theirs was not the first marriage in which the wife failed to share her husband's literary and aesthetic passions. James Joyce's wife was a nonintellectual woman who took little interest in her husband's work and scarcely took him seriously as an artist. Mrs. Conrad took Conrad very seriously indeed. She regarded him as a great writer without, perhaps, being able to explain why, and embraced as one of her wifely functions a duty to "protect" him, if necessary overprotect him, against the vexations of everyday life. He was also something of a strange, even terrifying phenomenon to her. During his courtship he kept assuring her of his morbid conviction that he was soon to die, and urged that they marry quickly so that they might make the most of what little time was left.[3] Then, on their honeymoon in Brittany, Conrad fell victim to one of his fevers. Unconscious, in the grip of nightmares, he raved in Polish, a language of which she did not understand a word. She suddenly found herself alone in a foreign country, on a honeymoon with a strange man who appeared dangerously ill and was now ranting at her in a strange tongue. The whole experience was unsettling; more than thirty years later, she still remembered it acutely.[4]

With two Malayan novels behind him, Conrad began work on a third, *The Rescue* (its original title was *The Rescuer*), dealing with Tom Lingard as a young man long before he met Almayer and Willems. For obscure reasons, he could not get far into it, and after several false starts when even the assistance of Ford Madox Hueffer proved fruitless, he put the story away for the next twenty years; it did not finally appear until 1920. In the meantime, he began writing a series of short stories eventually published as *Tales of Unrest,* and toward the end of 1896 started the first of his celebrated fictional sea voyages, *The Nigger of the "Narcissus."* It was the first of six such tales, each about a voyage dealing with a separate aspect of experience, which in their totality are a remarkably coherent and luminous commentary on vital and inescapable life processes. Each involves a journey on the open sea; each establishes a special relationship between the central figure and his ship; each explores a different area of the psychic landscape. They are not "sea" stories in the sense that they are primarily about life at sea; they are primarily about life,

3 Jessie Conrad, *Joseph Conrad and His Circle* (New York, 1935), pp. 12–13.
4 *Ibid.*, pp. 26–27.

and Conrad was properly irritated when because of them he was regarded as a "sea" writer. He insisted to the end of his life that the central presence of a ship did not make a novel a sea story: "In the *Nigger* I give the psychology of a group of men and render certain aspects of nature. But the problem that faces them is not a problem of the sea, it is merely a problem that has arisen on board a ship where the conditions of complete isolation from all land entanglements make it stand out with a particular force and colouring." [5] But the sea is nevertheless a major element in these tales, as are the ships that carry the men to their several destinies.

The ship serves as a loose symbol of the feminine principle in a variety of incarnations: mother, mistress, home, haven, protectress, the object on which officers and crew can practice their skills and expend their emotions. It is the most protean creature in Conrad—part woman, part craft, part a repository and arena for the energies of those who man her. In one of its manifestations it led to the birth of the Conradian centaur. This fabulous creature, half-man, half-boat, appeared in "Falk" (1903), and is the dramatic instrument by which the sea voyages, fables after a fashion in their own right, are measured. In "Falk" (which actually is not among these six voyages and is, in fact, a tale of a man who through cannibalism ate his way out of the human race and through love is seeking to earn his way back), the narrator, observing Falk for the first time, is reminded of a centaur he had once seen in a childhood book.

Falk's face reminded me of that centaur. Besides, he was a composite creature. Not a man-horse, it is true, but a man-boat. He lived on board his tub. . . . In the last rays of the setting sun, you could pick out far away down the reach his beard borne high up on the white structure. . . . There was the white-clad man's body, and the rich brown patch of the hair, and nothing below the waist but the 'thwartship white lines of the bridge-screens, that led the eye to the sharp white lines of the bows cleaving the muddy water of the river.
Separated from the boat, to me at least he seemed incomplete. The tug herself without his head and torso on the bridge looked mutilated as it were. (*Typhoon and Other Stories*, p. 162)

The boat replaces the horse as the medium for the vitality of nature, and becomes the conduit transmitting the pulsations of the sea to the men aboard. The men, voyaging from one physical

5 Letter to Henry S. Canby, April 7, 1924, LL, II, 342.

place to another, are making analogous journeys from one psychic place to another. The resistant element of the sea, like the universe as a whole which it represents and of which it is an organic part, displays that universe in its violence, beauty, indifference, its constant promise of life, and its recurring threat of death. And the ship is at once the shield and the vessel by which its cargo of humanity survives in and even occasionally triumphs over a hostile and dangerous world.[6]

There are six sea journeys. *The Nigger of the "Narcissus,"* 1897, deals with death; "Youth," 1898, with illusion; "The End of the Tether," 1902, with dissolution; "Typhoon," 1902, with survival; "The Secret Sharer," 1910, with the healed psyche; *The Shadow-Line,* 1917, with the emergent self.

1.

The opening sentence of *The Nigger of the "Narcissus,"* Conrad's third novel, establishes the meaning of the narrative that follows.

Mr. Baker, chief mate of the ship *Narcissus,* stepped in one stride out of his lighted cabin into the darkness of the quarter-deck.

The novel's journey, like Mr. Baker's small step at the start, is from light into darkness. Some sixty thousand words later we come to the final sentences.

Good-by, brothers! You were a good crowd. As good a crowd as ever fisted with wild cries the beating canvas of a heavy foresail; or tossing aloft, invisible in the night, gave back yell for yell to a westerly gale. (p. 173)

The narrator's last view of his shipmates is shrouded in the invisibility of night, his last apostrophe to them a final goodbye. The trappings of death indeed inform the whole last paragraph of *The Nigger:* "dark River," "forlorn stream," "shadowy ship," "a crew of Shades," "shadowy hail." The voyage of the *Narcissus,* from start to

---

[6] One of Conrad's subsequent tales, "The Brute" (1906), deals with a ship which, by some malignant deformation of architecture, has turned into a monster, killing at least one human being on every journey it makes. This mutant among vessels underlines, in reverse, the organic role of the ship in the voyages of the soul embarked upon in his classic stories.

finish, is a penetration into the tensions, powers, and mysteries of death. It is this dimension in the novel that makes it Conrad's first authentic masterpiece, and separates it at once from the limited intensities of *Almayer's Folly* and *An Outcast of the Islands*.

In the celebrated Preface to the novel, Conrad talks eloquently about the appeal of art to the senses, but he speaks also of "the subtle but invisible conviction of solidarity that . . . binds together all humanity—the dead to the living and the living to the unborn" (p. xii). The journey of the *Narcissus* through death is prepared at the outset with the appearance of the crew as "silhouettes of moving men . . . very black, without relief, like figures cut out of sheet tin" (p. 3). The finishing touches to the ship, later referred to as a kind of coffin, are given it by the carpenter. "The carpenter had driven in the last wedge of the main-hatch battens, and, throwing down his maul, had wiped his face with great deliberation, just on the stroke of five" (pp. 3–4). The clarity and precision of his work, and the finality suggested by his finishing exactly on the hour, are preliminaries to the dangerous voyage that lies ahead.

Old Singleton, naked to the waist, resembling "a learned and savage patriarch," is found reading *Pelham*. How account for the spell of Bulwer Lytton's novel, with its "curiously insincere sentences," upon the simple minds of sailors? The answer comes in the form of a question: ". . . are those beings who exist beyond the pale of life stirred by his tales as by an enigmatical disclosure of a resplendent world that . . . comes down on all sides to the water's edge . . . and is the only thing they know of life, the only thing they see of surrounding land—those life-long prisoners of the sea?" (pp. 6–7). Even before the *Narcissus* sails, its men are beyond the pale of life, dissociated from the land which is the center of life, knowledge of which they are doomed to acquire only from books. Stretched out in their berths, their "bodies were lost in the gloom of those places, that resembled narrow niches for coffins in a whitewashed and lighted mortuary" (p. 8). In the harbor at night, the *Narcissus* and the other "ships at anchor floated in perfect stillness under the feeble gleam of their riding-lights, looming up, opaque and bulky, like strange and monumental structures abandoned by men to an everlasting repose" (p. 15).

Mr. Baker is mustering the crew. Seventeen men answer to the roll call. The eighteenth name on his list the mate cannot make out.

"It's all a smudge," he says. Just then the eighteenth man makes his belated appearance. He is James Wait, the "nigger," emerging suddenly from the dark. "I belong to the ship," he cries. Though he speaks in deep rolling tones, towers above the others, and walks with a heavy tread, he is a dying man. If the ship is embarking on a death journey, he belongs to it literally, just as the others belong to it symbolically. The crew return to the forecastle and prepare for sleep: "The double row of berths yawned black, like graves tenanted by uneasy corpses" (p. 22). The last view everyone has that night before the *Narcissus* sails is of Singleton standing silent at the door, appearing—"very old; old as Father Time himself, who should have come there into this place as quiet as a sepulchre. . . . The men who could understand his silence were gone—those men who knew how to exist beyond the pale of life and within sight of eternity" (pp. 24–25). With images of silence and age, sepulchres and eternity, the first chapter of the novel draws to a close—having, in theme, mood, and rhetoric, prepared the way for the somber journey.

As the *Narcissus* leaves the next morning, the tug pulling her to sea resembles "an enormous and aquatic black beetle, surprised by the light, overwhelmed by the sunshine, trying to escape with in-effectual effort into the distant gloom of the land" (p. 27). This night thing leaves behind it in the harbor "a round black patch of soot . . . an unclean mark of the creature's rest." It also suggests the dying Jimmy Wait being carried by the *Narcissus:* ". . . a black mist emanated from him; a subtle and dismal influence; a some-thing cold and gloomy that floated out and settled on all the faces like a mourning veil" (p. 34). He seizes every chance to shake before the crew "the bones of his bothersome and infamous skeleton" so that they begin speaking "in low tones within that fo'c'sle as though it had been a church" (p. 37).

When the great storm begins, the ship "like the last vestige of a shattered creation . . . drifts, bearing an anguished remnant of sinful mankind . . ." (p. 54). As an added touch of the macabre the "hung-up suits of oil-skin swung out and in, lively and disquieting like reckless ghosts of decapitated seamen dancing in a tempest" (p. 54). Mr. Creighton, the second mate, leads a small group up the masts to goose-wing the main-topsail. The violent wind "with a sudden gust, [would] pin all up the shrouds the whole crawling line in attitudes of crucifixion" (p. 56). The high seas pour into the forecastle and wash away the belongings of the men. One of the coats "passed with outspread arms, resembling a drowned seaman floating with his head under water" (p. 58). Wait, trapped in his little cabin, begins to scream and knock "with the hurry of a man prematurely shut up in a coffin" (p. 66). To reach him, his shipmates must pass through the carpenter's shop, wrecked by the sea and bestrewn with tools and nails. These they pass to the boatswain "who, as if performing a mysterious and appeasing rite, cast them wide upon a raging sea" (p. 68).[7] After an immense effort they break into the cabin and rescue the trapped man who by now "was only a cold black skin loosely stuffed with soft cotton wool" (p. 71). They gather round him trying to brace him up "and on the very brink of eternity we tottered all together with concealing and absurd gestures, like a lot of drunken men embarrassed with a stolen corpse" (p. 71). Exhausted, they lie upon the deck where Mr. Baker crawls among them on all fours like "some carnivorous animal prowling amongst corpses" (p. 78). As the gale begins to subside, the ship jerks violently to windward "as though she had torn herself out from a deadly grasp" (p. 88).

The weather turns fair. The *Narcissus* bounds forward and "from that time our life seemed to start afresh as though we had died and had been resuscitated" (pp. 99–100). When the row breaks out between officers and crew, the helmsman lets go the wheel to find out what is going on. The *Narcissus* begins to pitch crazily: "It was as if an invisible hand had given the ship an angry shake . . ." (p. 124). Later, in the forecastle, the men continue to rave at the captain's injustice to Wait, while Singleton, the one figure not taken in by the dying man, stands and listens "like a statue of heroic size in the gloom of a crypt" (p. 129). Under the curse of the "nigger's" presence, the ship is beset by head winds and veers in wayward directions. The sense of unreality, of an illusioned state outside life, grows more intense: ". . . the silent ship, under the cold sheen of the dead moon, took on a false aspect of passionless repose resembling the winter of the earth. . . . And nothing in her was real, nothing was distinct and solid but the heavy shadows that filled her decks with their unceasing and noiseless stir: the shadows darker than the night and more restless than the thoughts of men" (p. 145).

---

[7] Albert Guerard, an astute critic of Conrad, calls attention to a similar passage in the Book of Jonah.

A few moments later the moon "found the ship wrapped up in a breathless silence; a fearless ship that seemed to sleep profoundly, dreamlessly on the bosom of the sleeping and terrible sea" (p. 146).

Wait dies and is buried at sea. Instantly, fresh winds spring up and carry the *Narcissus* swiftly to port. The men are paid off, and gather together on shore for a last drink before dispersing. Conrad sees them "swaying irresolute and noisy on the broad flagstones before the Mint" (p. 171). But his final view explicitly separates them from normal humanity: ". . . swaying about there on the white stones, surrounded by the hurry and clamour of men, they appeared to be creatures of another kind—lost, alone, forgetful, and doomed . . ." (pp. 172–173). They fade from sight, to appear again to the narrator only in his mind's eye: ". . . the spring-flood of memory sets with force up the dark River of the Nine Bends. Then on the waters of the forlorn stream drifts a ship—a shadowy ship manned by a crew of Shades. They pass and make a sign, in a shadowy hail" (p. 173). To their fateful end the *Narcissus* and its crew come swathed in the wrappings of the dark, deathlike journey which they make together.

Wait is the incarnate symbol of death in the novel, just as Donkin is its active agent. The two of them exert upon the crew a terrifying moral blackmail that splits open the cosmic order of the ship and threatens to pull it down into ruins. Conrad may have in mind the drama of the fallen angels. Captain Allistoun and the officers, Baker and Creighton, suggest God and His loyal angelic entourage; their initials, A, B, C, point to the beginning of things. Wait and Donkin are the dark powers, and the crew common humanity contended for by the two sides. Conrad was born a Roman Catholic, became an agnostic, and expressed throughout his life a distaste for Christianity.[8] Unlike James Joyce, who went through a similar progression, Conrad's imagination and art seem not to have been

---

[8] "It's strange how I always, from the age of fourteen, disliked the Christian religion, its doctrines, ceremonies and festivals" (Letter of December 22, 1902, Garnett, p. 185).

". . . the absurd oriental fable from which it [Christianity] starts irritates me . . . it has lent itself with amazing facility to cruel distortion and is the only religion which, with its impossible standards, has brought an infinity of anguish to innumerable souls" (Letter of February 23, 1914, Garnett, p. 245).

haunted by the traumas of Augustinian sin and the formalities of Aquinian theology. But the story of the Fall, given its most celebrated expression in *Paradise Lost,* had long since passed into general mythology. No theological predisposition on Conrad's part was needed for him to use it as a source of reference.

Almost from the start, Wait exercises his spell over the crew. He towers over them in height, moves them with his deep resonant voice, and enchants them with his fantastic egotism, an egotism tainted throughout with self-pity. In a short time these qualities make the members of the crew his willing, even eager victims, the vanity lurking behind their need to pity him leading them on to moral corruption. They remove him from the uncomfortable quarters of the forecastle, install him in a private cabin, rescue him from it during the gale at great peril to themselves, bring him delicacies from the galley, defend him against charges of malingering when he claims to be too ill to work, and then turn about and denounce the captain when that august figure orders Wait confined to his quarters as being morally unfit for duty. They tremble at his changing moods and hasten to gratify his every whim, feeling all the while secretly ashamed of themselves at the thought that they are being "taken in." And in the otherwise bellicose Belfast, the "nigger" attracts his most faithful retainer who guards him with a fierce protective loyalty and is ready to attack anyone who utters the faintest criticism of his new-found master. In the midst of this extraordinary relationship the crew never get a single kind word from Wait, only complaints, recriminations, protestations of virtue.

The only seaman whom Wait does not abuse is Donkin. To Donkin all life is a racket, and he regards the "nigger" as the supreme racketeer. He suggests that Wait has probably malingered on many a previous ship, collecting full wages without doing a stitch of work by pretending to be ill. Since to Donkin this is the ultimate achievement in living—to get something for nothing—he admires Wait and enlists as his executive agent. To make the crew restless and discontented with their lot, to stir them up against the officers (whom he hates because they force men to work for their wages), to sow discord, to foment mutiny—in a word, to raise hell—these are the objects of Donkin's campaign, and to it he devotes the energy that he refuses to devote to the legitimate work for which he is

being paid. What Wait does with great style, Donkin does with calculated cunning. Between them they cast their malignant spells and
turn the voyage into a nightmare.

Wait's toleration of Donkin is significant, for it acknowledges the
alliance between them. He dispenses clothing and food to him for
no visible reason and without expectation of return. He puts up
with Donkin's bad manners though everyone else on board resents
them. In their conversations Donkin does virtually all the talking;
it is he who exerts all the physical and intellectual energy while
Wait embodies all the moral and psychological. Wait is the heart of
evil, Donkin the arm. And when Donkin has done all the damage
he can and has been finally routed by the captain, he turns in his
rage upon Wait and drives the lingeringly dying man over the
edge into death. This climactic scene takes place in the dead of
night, with the crew asleep. The two demons have the field of life
and death to themselves; ironically, the "nigger" lacks even the
protection of Belfast against Donkin's last assault. Yet it is he, and
not Donkin, who remains the dramatic center of the action for it is
in his name, to protect his honor against the captain's order that he
be confined to quarters, that the crew rises in revolt.

The relations between Wait and the crew supply the whole story
with its moral tensions, provide the events of the journey with their
dramatic format, and even make the great gale the physical analogue
of the struggle going on within the collective mind of the ship. Like
the traditional devil he appeals to their best and worst sides at the
same time. Because of his illness they wish to befriend, nurture, and
protect him; because they suspect he is faking, they hate him and
are thoroughly ashamed of their sympathy and hate themselves for
displaying it. They are thrown into a moral disorder which makes
them easy prey for Donkin's propaganda and drives them to the
abyss of revolt against the officers. Their story bears the stamp of the
Conradian progression: what they do stems from what they feel;
what they feel is sophisticated by the element of self-awareness. The
sailors of the *Narcissus* are acutely and miserably conscious of what
is happening to them. But as in a bad case of spiritual measles, the
sufferers are unable to avoid the inevitable stages of the disease.

Among the ordinary seamen only one man, Singleton, is immune
to it. This aged patriarchal figure, so steadfast in his nautical per-

formance, so single in his nature, greets the "nigger's" ailments with calm contempt. ". . . get on with your dying," he remarks; "don't raise a blamed fuss with us over that job. We can't help you" (p. 42). It is Singleton who predicts that Wait will not die until the ship gets within sight of land, and that his death will cause the winds to turn favorable. Throughout the novel he plays the role of a prophet, a special link between humanity and the cosmos. He is always described as existing outside ordinary time, as "Old Singleton," untouched by emotion, undeflected by thought. Even his flesh seems impervious to the ordinary travails: "He had never given a thought to his mortal self. He lived unscathed, as though he had been indestructible . . ." (p. 99). When he does fall, he falls not like a man but like a force in nature, "crashing down, stiff and headlong like an uprooted tree" (p. 97). When he becomes conscious of his own old age, he confronts it not in the faces of his shipmates but in the eye of the timeless sea: "He looked upon the immortal sea with the awakened and groping perception of its heartless might; he saw it unchanged, black and foaming under the eternal scrutiny of the stars; he heard its impatient voice calling for him out of a pitiless vastness full of unrest, of turmoil, and of terror" (p. 99). The outsized Singleton not only is referred to in inflated terms but is seen perpetually in his relationship to the larger world outside the ship. In his strength, in his steadfastness which is only emphasized by his advancing age, in his role as an oracle with the power of accurate prophecy, he strikes in a simple-minded, one-dimensional way an idealistic note that is plainly larger than life.

If Singleton is a taciturn, clear-purposed prophet, the cook is the story's garrulous and demented priest. He is first referred to as "a conceited saint unable to forget his glorious reward" (p. 32). When the men steal food from his galley to appease Wait, the cook knows "that Satan was abroad amongst those men, whom he looked upon as in some way under his spiritual care" (p. 38). Upon seeing three or four seamen in a group, he would leave his stove to run out and preach. In a quiet interlude during the great gale, with the galley virtually wrecked by the sea, he manages to whip up coffee for the wet, bedraggled crew, a feat they look upon as miraculous. He thus discharges what is, after all, a priestly function—the performance of miracles. But he spoils it by assuming an irritating air of superior virtue and holiness. His ferocious evangelicalism comes to its grimly comic climax when he traps Wait alone in the hot little cabin and assaults him with invitations to prayer. From this mordant dilemma the black man is rescued, appropriately, by the one figure on the ship whose authority exceeds that of the priest-cook, the lord captain himself.

Captain Allistoun has iron-gray hair and a hard face the color of pump-leather. He keeps to himself on the poop, speaking little even to his officers. "He, the ruler of that minute world, seldom descended from the Olympian heights of his poop. Below him—at his feet, so to speak—common mortals led their busy and insignificant lives" (p. 31). To emphasize his lordly station in the hierarchy of the ship, Conrad notes that he commanded the *Narcissus* from the day she was built, loved her, "and drove her unmercifully" (p. 30). Baker and Creighton, the first and second mates, are warmer men and are necessarily in closer contact with the crew, but being the captain's officers they share his rightness much as Donkin shares the "nigger's" wrongness. Still, it is the captain, the apex of quasi-divine good, whom Donkin finally assaults with the belaying pin, and it is the captain who personally expels Wait from the ship's company and forces Donkin to take back his murderous weapon and restore it, against his will, to its proper place. The triumph of good over evil is complete, but while the devils are subdued by the gods, the souls of the men remain as before. With the death of Wait, the crew is released from the spell, yet only for the time being. Their susceptibility to temptation remains unchanged. Conrad's metaphysics is too sophisticated and tough-minded to be theologically confined. Captain Allistoun may defeat Donkin and the "nigger" again and again through perpetuity, but his men will remain as errant, as capable of mutiny, as susceptible to nightmare as ever.

The struggle of the larger powers in the universe places the human drama under increased pressure, supplies it with an added dimension, the dimension that pulsates powerfully through *The Nigger of the "Narcissus,"* yet does not create, control, or finally alter it. The ordinary seamen, swaying on the immense ocean between the upper and nether regions, are not the total masters of their own fate. But their fate is not in the hands of any recognizable or identifiable force. This is the mystery that Conrad invokes, the mystery that lies at the heart of his work.

His metaphysics is, indeed, bounded by inscrutability. Over the furthermost horizon of his work there hangs a haze to the edge of which he approaches but does not finally disperse. It is this ultimate element in Conrad which E. M. Forster complained about as synonymous with obscurity, and which F. R. Leavis accused him of seeking to fill by the piling-on of insistent adjectives.

Whatever its philosophical implication, Conrad puts the mist encircling his art to full dramatic use. It makes possible alternative explanations to the baffling questions of *The Nigger*. Does Wait feel himself to be a sick man put upon by others or is he really malingering? Is the storm simply a familiar upheaval of nature or a redemptive occasion for the crew to purge itself of its baser feelings? When the dead "nigger," sewn in his shroud, refuses to slide into the sea during the burial ceremony, is it a sign that death or evil is reluctant to let go its hold on man or only that the cloth is caught on a protruding nail? Conrad dramatizes the answers as coherent possibilities, thereby suffusing his tale with a fascinating suggestiveness that induces the reader to intenser speculation. Twenty years later Conrad made his own conviction about the multiple meaning of art explicit: ". . . a work of art is very seldom limited to one exclusive meaning and not necessarily tending to a definite conclusion. And this for the reason that the nearer it approaches art, the more it acquires a symbolic character. . . . All the great creations in literature have been symbolic, and in that way have gained in complexity, in power, in depth and in beauty." [9]

This ambiguity invites, naturally enough, the multiple interpretations of the new schools of critics. Vernon Young relates the journey of the *Narcissus* in specific details of latitude and longitude to "the subaqueous world of the underconsciousness, the symbol-producing level of the psyche," which he felt to be "the most dependable source" of Conrad's inspiration.[10] Albert Guerard interprets the rescue scene in terms of a difficult childbirth and, invoking Jung, suggests that the wrecked carpenter's shop stands for "the messy pre-conscious with Wait trapped in the deeper-lying un-

9 Letter to Barrett H. Clark, May 4, 1918, LL, II, 205.

10 *Accent*, Spring, 1952. Young, in fact, takes Conrad severely to task for not acknowledging his "cabalistic intent" and for launching into "panicky and often absurd interpretations of his own work": i.e., interpretations that do not agree with Young's. This is not the first instance of a critic chiding an author for his temerity in not agreeing with the critic's view of the author's own writing.

conscious." [11] In a straightforward account, taking no heed of the new depth psychology, James E. Miller, Jr., reads *The Nigger* as a lesson in social community and cohesion learned by the crew.[12] Even the shifts in narrative viewpoint from the third to the first person, which older critics like Edward Crankshaw and J. W. Beach attributed to Conrad's inexperience, now have a conceivable value in terms of bringing us closer to or further from the center of events.

Amid the multiple suggestions and possibilities of the novel, the most persistent remains the death journey. The *Narcissus* comes to life at the beginning of the voyage, is almost destroyed by the gale, revives, only to die again when reaching London. The crew live intensely and magnificently while struggling to save the ship during the storm. Afterward they slip toward death as victims of Wait, and pass through the moral nightmare climaxed by the mutiny. Released by the demise of their incubus, they come alive with the freshening breeze, only to disintegrate again in port.

Seeing his shipmates for the last time on land, the narrator describes them as "creatures of another kind—lost, alone, forgetful, and doomed; they were like castaways . . . upon an insecure ledge of a treacherous rock" (p. 172). After the magnitude of their experience on the *Narcissus,* they now undergo a severe deflation. Singleton, the patriarchal seaman, gropes for his wages in the office of the Board of Trade, cannot sign his name, and is regarded as "a disgusting old brute" by the pay clerk. Charley is taken in hand by his blowsy mother. Belfast goes off muttering sentimentally about the lost "nigger," not one of whose personal possessions he has been allowed to have. A knot of others make their way loudly to the Black Horse tavern "where men, in fur caps with brutal faces and in shirt sleeves, dispense out of varnished barrels the illusions of strength, mirth, happiness . . ." (p. 171). Even the officers are deflated. Mr. Baker resigns himself ruefully to the conviction that he somehow does not have "the cut of a skipper." And Captain Allistoun, no longer a God bestriding the poop, is only a small man with a well dressed wife, who quietly and meekly supervises the paying-off of the crew.

As the crew of the *Narcissus* drift out of sight, they fade into darkness. But Conrad does not leave them shrunken and diminished.

[11] *The Kenyon Review,* Spring, 1957.
[12] *PMLA,* December, 1951.

On the last page they come to life again, this time forever. They are reborn in the narrator's memory, and the journey on the *Narcissus* which bound them together is summed up: "Haven't we, together and upon the immortal sea, wrung out a meaning from our sinful lives?" (p. 173). And in the final sentence, as the recollection of the great gale passes through his mind, the writer hears their voices, pitched to a heroic note, reverberating through the impenetrable night.

The death journey of *The Nigger of the "Narcissus"* is thus rescued from the oblivion of death by the illuminations of a novel destined to rank as Conrad's earliest masterpiece.

2.

The second of the sea voyages unfolds in the story "Youth." The physical journey is made by an ancient freighter, the *Judea,* from London to Bangkok; the psychic one by its second mate, from youth to middle age. The fire that breaks out on the *Judea* lights up the night sky and suggests the exact relationship between the stages of life through which the mate is journeying. The flames of the ship will presently be quenched by the sea, the flames of youth as inexorably by time.

Oh, the glamour of youth! Oh, the fire of it, more dazzling than the flames of the burning ship, throwing a magic light on the wide earth, leaping audaciously to the sky, presently to be quenched by time, more cruel, more pitiless, more bitter than the sea—and like the flames of the burning ship surrounded by an impenetrable night. (*Youth and Two Other Stories,* p. 30)

The mate in question is Marlow, making his debut in Conrad. Now in his forties he narrates this tale of his youth to four middle-aged men who had also spent their youth at sea. The narrative format is not just a device to get the yarn told,[13] but is organic to the

13 Morton Dauwen Zabel, for many years now a fruitful laborer in the Conrad vineyard, observed that the sea yarn told by some tale-spinner ashore was the natural mode of expression to professional mariners. It was as idiomatic, he remarked, for Conrad to unfold so many of his stories in this way as it was for Kipling to be full of "club, mess and smoking-room lingoes" and Hemingway replete with "bar, café, newsroom, and army talk" (Introduction to *Lord Jim,* Boston, 1958, p. xvii).

story. It is not simply an account of youth, with the illusion of an absolute belief in its own powers, but an account of youth as seen through the eyes of men not living through it but looking *back* upon it. Were the story told straight as it was happening to Marlow at the age of twenty, it would necessarily have been filled with the irritations and frustrations that everybody aboard feels during the uncanny mishaps and dogged bad luck that afflict the *Judea*. But twenty-two years later, memory and the sense of loss inevitable with the passing of time have romanticized and glamourized the journey so that we see it as Marlow now does, in terms of its excitement, glory, sense of boundless adventure when all things seem possible, with all the melancholy and defeat purged away. Only in this way can the illusion of youth flare up to the sky boldly and unimpeded like the fire aboard the *Judea*, and at the same time persuade the reader that Conrad, far from arbitrarily editing the theme to make his point, is faithful to the eye, the viewpoint, the tone of idealizing and rueful reminiscence of his middle-aged company. "Youth" acquires not only its frame but its nuance from the harmony established between the angle of narration and the object narrated.[14]

The physical details support the psychic ones. The fire is caused by spontaneous combustion; it is not man-made but in the natural order of things, just as the drawing to a close of youth is in the natural order of things. The explosion which lifts Marlow into the air and hurls him to the deck is appropriate to the exuberant vitality of his high hopes and boundless confidence; when his youth ends, it does so with a bang. Just as the *Judea* never reaches its destination, so the dreams of youth are doomed never to be realized,

[14] The five men, Marlow and his audience of four, are sitting at a table drinking claret. On five occasions Marlow interrupts his reminiscing to say "Pass the bottle." This interjected note, at once humorous and realistic, reinforces the lightness of tone which keeps "Youth" from sinking into metaphysical gloom or becoming overburdened with middle-aged melancholy. Englishmen of an older generation cavil at Conrad's claret appearing in a bottle instead of a decanter, and argue that Marlow would never have had to ask to have his glass refilled; the courtesy would be automatic. They claim that this is further proof of Conrad's foreignness and ignorance of English ways, and belies the opening line of the story, "This could have occurred nowhere but in England. . . ." This is precisely what could never have occurred in England, is the substance of their plaint. So perhaps the "pass the bottle" motif is not so realistic after all, though readers not of that time and place are scarcely likely to balk at it.

and the shrinkage in them is measured by the shrinkage in size from the *Judea* to the small lifeboat which Marlow sails resolutely into a Javanese harbor. And it is a journey he must make himself. The *Somerville* takes the *Judea* in tow, but the fire becomes too dangerous and the towline is cut. Marlow is not towed into port; the journey to the end of youth, to have any meaning, must be made under his own power.

This journey reaches its climax with Marlow's first view of the East, "the mysterious East . . . perfumed like a flower, silent like death, dark like a grave" (*Youth*, p. 38). Insinuative, seductive, aromatic, dangerous—dangerous, especially, to white men—the East epitomizes the approaching period in Marlow's life when, unlike youth, not all things are possible, and a sense of difficulty replaces enthusiasm as the keynote of endeavor. The natives on the jetty who stare silently at the white seamen as they awaken in the morning from an exhausted sleep embody not only the new world in geography but the new world in spirit. Just before this world comes into focus, Marlow says goodbye to his youth.

I remember my youth and the feeling that will never come back any more—the feeling that I could last forever, outlast the sea, the earth, and all men; the deceitful feeling that lures us on to joys, to perils, to love, to vain efforts—to death; the triumphant conviction of strength, the heat of life in the handful of dust, the glow in the heart that with every year grows dim, grows cold, grows small, and expires—and expires, too soon, too soon—before life itself. (pp. 36–37)

In the final paragraph his four interlocutors, their eyes weary, their faces lined with success and failure alike, respond in a last brief resurgence of the emotion Marlow has evoked and now laid to rest.

Nowhere do the beneficent aspects of nature blaze more splendidly than in "Youth," an appropriate accompaniment to the narrator's recollected state of mind. Sky, stars, and sea outdo themselves in luring Marlow's youth, in affirming it and encouraging its luster. Nature and youth are in league, as it were, against the conditions of life; the alliance does not endure, but nature as seen through the eye of youth burns forever in the incandescence of memory: "The sky was a miracle of purity, a miracle of azure. The sea was polished, was blue, was pellucid, was sparkling like a precious stone, extending on all sides, all round to the horizon—as if the whole terrestrial globe had been one jewel, one colossal sapphire, a single gem fashioned into a planet" (p. 20).

The journey of the *Judea* is in space, but it carries Marlow in a deeper sense on a journey through time. The beginning of life is represented by the young Marlow; the middle by the East which is his destination; and the end by the ship which, groaning from the infirmities of old age, commanded by a captain and first mate who are both very old men, carries him there. These three stages are the theme (as Conrad himself tells us) of this entire collection of tales, *Youth and Two Other Stories* (1902), of which the second, "Heart of Darkness," deals with two men in their maturity, and the third, "The End of the Tether," is an account of old age. Conrad always insisted that his short-story volumes had some inner unity of spirit or mood. The thread binding together what is certainly his finest single collection is that sequence of time stretching across the life of man whose stages are already defined at the beginning of the sequence in "Youth."

3.

Captain Whalley, in "The End of the Tether," is a superior man trapped in an inferior universe. There are two aspects to his situation, the outer and inner, but his entrapment is the same in each. The outer is the change in the world from sail to steam, which Conrad regards as degenerative; this change is symbolized in the contrast between Captain Whalley's old clipper ship *Condor,* in which he had made voyages of discovery, and the steamer *Sofala,* a decaying vessel with bad boilers which he, at the age of sixty-seven, is forced to use as an instrument of shabby, dingily competitive trade. This change, a part of "modern progress," is of course inevitable. The inward dimension is equally inevitable, the relentless decline in Whalley from the prime of life to old age, a decline symbolized by his growing blindness. The physical decay of the man and the physical decay of the world combine to give the story its large dimension and lend it a note of heroic pathos.

The theme of decline binds the other figures with equal force.

Whalley's daughter, whom he loves deeply [15] and for whose sake he compromises his honor, is married to a weak invalid whose incapacity compels her to run a dreary boardinghouse in Australia. Sterne, the instinctively disloyal and impudent first mate, is so poisoned with the ambition to become a captain that he connives against every captain he serves under and is consumed by frustration when he does not succeed. Massy, who owns the *Sofala* and is her chief engineer, hates captains too, not only because he has to pay their salaries but because he regards them as functionless parasites whom the law forces him to accept as masters on his own ship. Massy is one of those Conradian villains "with an amazing sensitiveness to the claims of his own personality" (p. 269)—Schomberg, Donkin, Brown, Sotillo, de Barral, Scevola are others—caught up in a perpetual anger and hatred of everything, of the men around them, of themselves, of life, who look upon the world as a deliberate conspiracy to do them in. Massy lives only for the Manila lottery, whose numbers he manipulates in feverish combinations; only with this is he at home, outraged as he is with humanity. Like the decayed boilers which he tends as engineer, like the *Sofala* which he owns, Massy embodies the destructive principle at work in the whole story. He and Sterne represent the seamen of the new age, misanthropic, viciously self-centered, whose pursuit of money and mean ambition corrode the human in them. The *Sofala* is a poor thing, and Massy had come to hate her "for the repairs she required, for the coal-bills he had to pay, for the poor beggarly freights she earned. He would clench his hand . . . and hit the rail a sudden blow, viciously, as though she could be made to feel pain" (p. 268). The new men and the new era are no longer unities, but are split apart by the corruptions of money and vanity, and the absence of love.

The theme of dissolution is further highlighted by the shift of landscape. The open sea is the arena of Whalley's early achieve-

[15] Thomas Moser suggests that this love is incestuous, as is Almayer's for his daughter (*Joseph Conrad, Achievement and Decline,* Cambridge, Mass., 1957, pp. 52–53, 218), but the textual evidence he summons is meagre and unconvincing. Conrad may well have been interested in incest as a theme. Ford claimed in an introduction to Conrad's unfinished *The Sisters* (New York, 1928, pp. 6–7) that, in fact, the subject fascinated him. But the possibility of incest neither explains nor adds anything to "The End of the Tether." A "normal" paternal devotion is quite enough to render Whalley's actions credible.

ments. He "had steered across the unsurveyed tracts of the South Seas, and had seen the sun rise on uncharted islands" (p. 167). On the open sea he had discovered Whalley Island and Condor Reef, and found the Whalley Passage. In it he had buried his wife, his boon companion aboard the *Condor* and the sharer of his fortunate time. The open sea is the center of creativity, where able men can rise to greatness. The *Sofala*, by contrast, is a river creature, and the river along which she plies her "monotonous huckster's round" is a thing of mud and mangroves, of rocky inhospitable reefs against which Massy treacherously dashes her to her death at the end, of squalid little clots of native habitation, and occasional somber masses of jungle vegetation suggesting the fecund and inhuman darkness of primeval times. The passage of the *Sofala* along its river course is masterfully described:

> The thump of the engines reverberated regularly like the strokes of a metronome . . . and the smoke pouring backwards from the funnel eddied down behind the ship, spread a thin dusky veil over the somber water, which . . . seemed to lie stagnant in the whole straight length of the reaches. (p. 257)

Stagnation and confinement, a meanness of outlook and the monotony of routine are the features of the river in which the *Sofala,* appropriately, in her ugliness and meanness of shape, and the ugliness and meanness of the man who owns her, finally sinks. And with her Captain Whalley, trapped in the new age which the *Sofala* apotheosizes.

The story is a passage between two points, and the dual note is struck throughout. There are the two ages of sail and steam, the two ships, the two bodies of water, the two types of human beings, the two Whalleys, the two marriages (Captain Whalley's and his daughter's), and the two races, white and Malay, whose abyss of incommunicability amid the closest physical contact is suggested by the old Malay serang serving as Whalley's eyes without the slightest inkling that his master is going blind. In each instance the gap between the two widens irresistibly.

In "Youth" the curve of life is on the rise; in "The End of the Tether" on the fall. In the final dissolution, everyone is torn away from his life center. Whalley embraces his own death. To be sure

that he does not rise to the surface and be tempted to swim, Whalley
stuffs his pockets with the pieces of iron used by Massy to deflect
the compass and steer the ship on the rocks. By this gesture he means
literally to be weighted down by the instruments of corruption
emanating from the man with whom he is in partnership. He thus
assumes the burden not only of his death but of his guilt. Massy,
clutching the insurance money, leaves the sea altogether and rushes
off to his maniacal gambling in Manila. Sterne, frustrated in his desire to become the captain of the *Sofala,* comments ruefully on his
bad luck, now once again reaffirmed. Van Wyk, the fastidious young
Dutch planter (a faint prefiguration of Axel Heyst), had become
friendly with Whalley, and is so disturbed by the old man's end
that he leaves his prosperous river plantation altogether and returns
to Holland.

The story reaches a superb coda when Whalley's daughter reads
his last letter. "She slipped his folded letter between the two buttons
of her plain black bodice, and leaning her forehead against a window-
pane remained there till dusk . . . giving him all the time she
could spare" (p. 339). The irony of this last phrase braces the scene
against excessive pathos, just as her remaining there till dusk subtly
recapitulates the remorseless movement of time. The final sentences
break into the emotional life of the daughter and through the mixture of her feelings supply a frame into which the whole tale fits.

Gone! Was it possible? My God, was it possible? The blow had come
softened by the spaces of the earth, by the years of absence. There
had been whole days when she had not thought of him at all—
had no time. But she had loved him, she felt she had loved him
after all. (p. 339)

The plot of "The End of the Tether" is not quite as deftly
handled as its theme. Captain Whalley's involved financial arrangements with the *Sofala* thicken the narrative flow. Nevertheless,
like the boat, "the thump of its engines reverberating regularly like
the strokes of a metronome," the story beats on in a surge of power.
Whalley lends it his own qualities, a commanding physical presence,
a largeness of purpose, and an immense dignity. Like Conrad's art
in general, the story does not arouse our love. It does something
more difficult; it arouses our wonder and admiration.

4.

Though "Typhoon" was written before "The End of the Tether," it was published later. Afterward Conrad thought it had been composed later, too. André Gide, who once remarked that one ought to learn English just to read Conrad in the original, translated it into French—a rare action for a writer of considerable reputation.

"Typhoon" is a drama of survival. The great storm flogs and punishes the *Nan-Shan* as brutally as it did the *Narcissus*. Conrad organizes the violent upheavals of nature with the finesse and energy of a professional impresario, but it is not nature that concerns him but man. And the man at the center of the story, Captain MacWhirr, is one of Conrad's remarkable creations. He deliberately appears to us stupid, unimaginative, pedantic, lacking in a sense of humor, unloved by his drearily snobbish wife whose only secret "was her abject terror of the time when her husband would come home to stay for good," regarded as a freak by his chief mate and as an object of patronizing amusement by his chief engineer. Conrad can say of him bluntly: "Captain MacWhirr had sailed over the surface of the oceans as some men go skimming over the years of existence to sink gently into a placid grave, ignorant of life to the last . . ." (*Typhoon and Other Stories*, p. 19).

Yet MacWhirr is the hero of the story, and not only a hero in a verbal or structural sense, but a hero in truth, a real, a genuine, and finally even an admirable hero. For he displays two qualities essential to survive the crisis in the China Sea, and is the only man aboard to do so. Jukes, the first mate, is more intelligent. Rout, the chief engineer, more interesting, sensitive, and aware, but in the end it is MacWhirr who comes up with the right answers to the questions of life and death. One quality is courage, the other a passion for order and justice; the two enable the ship and the ship's company to limp into port as a battered but civilized entity instead of a disorganized, self-destroying mob. Furthermore, these qualities are concealed in MacWhirr so deeply beneath his visible surface that their emergence under pressure comes as a great dramatic surprise, indeed as a revelation, and provides "Typhoon" with a psychological equivalent to its geographic journey down the China coast.

During the preliminaries, while the *Nan-Shan* is getting under way with its live cargo of Chinese coolies returning home, Mac-Whirr is the relentless butt of ridicule. Even his physical appearance on the first page of the story is grotesquely comic, in the style of Dickens.

Captain MacWhirr . . . had a physiognomy that . . . was the exact counterpart of his mind . . . it had no pronounced characteristics whatever; it was simply ordinary, irresponsive, and unruffled. . . .

He was . . . so sturdy of limb that his clothes always looked a shade too tight for his arms and legs. As if unable to grasp what is due to the difference of latitudes, he wore a brown bowler hat, a complete suit of a brownish hue, and clumsy black boots. These harbour togs gave to his thick figure an air of stiff and uncouth smartness. A thin silver watch-chain looped his waistcoat, and he never left his ship for the shore without clutching in his powerful, hairy fist an elegant umbrella of the very best quality. . . . (pp. 3–4)

He has "just enough imagination to carry him through each successive day and no more" (p. 4). It is "as impossible for him to take a flight of fancy as it would be for a watchmaker to put together a chronometer with nothing except a two-pound hammer and a whipsaw in the way of tools" (p. 4). He speaks very little, and cannot understand how others can speak so much; what he does say is highly uninteresting; his letters home, which bore his wife and arouse no response in his two children, consist largely of place names and details of weather. When the ship is transferred to Siamese registry, he has a comic argument with Jukes who objects to sailing under a Siamese flag. It is the foreignness of it that bothers this honest English sailor. He is gruff to the Chinese coolies, "as became his racial superiority" (p. 13), Conrad cannot refrain from adding with a touch of irony directed at the English.[16] MacWhirr cannot under-

---

16 In Conrad's general distaste for colonialism and European hegemony over native peoples, the English are specifically included, though he does attack them less severely than he does the Belgians, Dutch, French, and others. Yet Charles Gould, the Englishman in *Nostromo*, is one of his supreme symbols of imperialist exploitation, no less destructive because it is carried out on personally idealistic grounds. And Conrad had sharp things to say about the English during the Boer War (Letter to Cunninghame Graham, October 14, 1899, LL, I, 284–285).

He nevertheless developed a *mystique* about Britain, which he regarded as

stand Jukes's irritation; as long as the flag, a white elephant in a
red field, is hung straight and not upside down, there can be nothing
queer about it in the captain's eyes. Jukes gives up the argument:
"I don't believe you can make a man like that understand anything. He simply knocks me over" (p. 12).

When the barometer falls precipitously, MacWhirr is prepared
for dirty weather, but he scorns the idea of going off course to
avoid the typhoon. He reads a book on storms, but throws it away,
"contemptuously angry with such a lot of words and with so much
advice, all head-work and supposition, without a glimmer of certi-
tude" (p. 33). The idea of skirting the storm, using up extra fuel,
arriving behind schedule for the sake of avoiding trouble or making
his Chinese passengers more comfortable seems to him absurd. Exhausted by all the palaver and by the suddenly oppressive heat, he
gives orders to plow straight ahead on course, and falls asleep. When
he wakes, the typhoon is at hand. It is plain that the great trial into
which everyone, ship and men alike, is now plunged, was brought
about by a deliberate act of will on the captain's part. He could
have avoided it, but chose not to. The central action of the story
is thereby evoked by the character of its central figure.

The raging storm pounds the *Nan-Shan,* batters the crew, demoral-
izes the coolies. Jukes is convinced that all is lost. While he wrings
his hands, shouting "My God! My God! My God! My God!" (p. 42)
and thinking despairingly, "She's done for," he hears MacWhirr's
voice from a great distance saying, "All right" (p. 44). A sudden
blow of the wind drives him into the captain's arms and he clings
to him "in the manner of two hulks lashed stem to stern together"
(p. 46), asking, "Will she live through this?" (p. 47). And "after
a while he heard with amazement the frail and resisting voice in his
ear, the dwarf sound unconquered in the great tumult. 'She may!' "
(pp. 47–48). Virtually everyone aboard falters in spirit. The crew

---

the bulwark of civilization. This led him at times into small chauvinisms that
support Jukes's feeling of superiority to other races and even extend it to
other Europeans. Here is Marlow in "Youth" commenting on the admirable
behavior of the English crew of the *Judea:* ". . . it was something in them,
something inborn and subtle and everlasting. I don't say positively that the
crew of a French or German merchantman wouldn't have done it, but I doubt
whether it would have been done in the same way. There was a . . . hidden
something, that gift of good or evil that makes racial difference, that shapes the
fate of nations" (*Youth,* pp. 28–29).

huddle under the bridge, groaning together in the dark at each heave of the ship. Rout and his assistants at the engines struggle in acute despair. The second mate, a direct descendant of Donkin, "was lying low, like a malignant little animal under a hedge" (p. 59). And Jukes, at the crest of the typhoon, falls into the psychic apathy which is the signature of a Conrad novel. He was "as if rendered irresponsible by the force of the hurricane, which made the very thought of action utterly vain" (p. 51). He sinks into "a trance of confounded stoicism" (p. 51), feels "a searching and insidious fatigue" (p. 52), and is "corrupted by the storm" that breeds in his heart "a craving for peace" (p. 53). As the ship, physically and emotionally, threatens to collapse, it is shored up by the countervailing spirit of MacWhirr whose fiber, perhaps because it is uncomplicated and unveined by an excess of intelligence [17] and imagination, stands the strain. By a deliberate act of will, he has caused the crisis, and by a deliberate act of courage survives it. It is true that during the second part of the hurricane, which takes place offstage, MacWhirr does endure a moment when he feels the end has come, but it does not disable him.

The storm, however, is not the only emergency faced by the *Nan-Shan*. Rioting breaks out among the Chinese as their possessions, chiefly silver dollars, scatter through the hold, with their owners in half-crazed pursuit. Jukes's advice is to leave them strictly alone, but MacWhirr cannot tolerate the thought of fighting aboard his ship; it violates his sense of order. "If the ship had to go after all, then, at least, she wouldn't be going to the bottom with a lot of people in her fighting teeth and claw. That would have been odious. And in that feeling there was a humane intention and a vague sense of

---

17 Like Bergson, Lawrence, and Hemingway, Conrad has his violent anti-intellectual moments when he is convinced that the capacity to think is man's gravest handicap. ". . . if we could only get rid of consciousness," he wrote to Cunninghame Graham on January 31, 1898. "What makes mankind tragic is not that they are the victims of nature, it is that they are conscious of it" (LL, I, 226). And to Garnett on March 29, 1898: "I would like to make a bargeman of him [Borys, his older son]: strong, knowing his business and thinking of nothing. That is *the* life my dear fellow. Thinking of nothing! O! bliss" (Garnett, p. 136). In *Lord Jim*: "Imagination, the enemy of men, the father of terrors . . ." (p. 11). And Marlow in the same novel: "Hang ideas! They are tramps, vagabonds, knocking at the back-door of your mind, each taking a little of your substance, each carrying away some crumb of that belief in a few simple notions you must cling to if you want to live decently . . ." (p. 43).

the fitness of things" (p. 85). But if order is one of the elements of civilization, justice is another, and the captain is responsive to this as well. He wants to recover the dollars and return them to their rightful owners in order to be fair to all. They may all go down, but they will go down in good shape. In the end he painstakingly divides the money evenly among the Chinese, and the three dollars left over "went to the three most damaged coolies, one to each" (p. 102). All this he does by force of character; when his officers and crew arm themselves with rifles in case the coolies should break out again, he gives them a tongue-lashing. "For God's sakes, Mr. Jukes," says he, "do take these rifles away from the men. Somebody's sure to get hurt before long if you don't" (p. 100).

MacWhirr is right on every count, and "Typhoon" turns out to be a paean in his honor. The man without brains emerges, unexpectedly, as the voice of reason. The man who distrusts speech and cannot understand what people have to talk about utters singularly right words when more articulate men are mute. The man without imagination or foresight becomes the upholder and defender of civilization in its manifest ideals. What a mystery is here! Rout's last letter home expresses his wonder: the captain is a simple man but he has done something clever; what it is the chief engineer doesn't say, remarking to his wife that she couldn't understand how much there was in it; he is so moved by the event, so shaken by the whole experience that he suddenly longs for her to come out and live with him in the Far East. Jukes, meanwhile, concludes the story with a letter to a friend in a comfortable Atlantic billet, detailing the experience at great length and remarking about the exploits of the captain, "I think that he got out of it very well for such a stupid man" (p. 102). Jukes, for all his intelligence, cannot get beyond the surface of MacWhirr, and attributes his success to luck.

Conrad, however, sees below the surface and records, not without some amazement on his part too, the remarkable facts within. It is possible for salvation to come wrapped in dullness, for a human being to be both stupid and responsive, for mindlessness and apathy to conceal purposive energy and will. Retracing our steps in "Typhoon" we observe that the mystery of MacWhirr was sounded at the beginning, amid the pejorative preliminaries. What, after all, caused him at fifteen, the son of a Belfast grocer, to run off to sea against his family's wishes? The lives of men do have their mysterious sides, observes Conrad, and proceeds to one of his central statements:

It was enough, when you thought it over, to give you the idea of an immense, potent, and invisible hand thrust into the ant-heap of the earth, laying hold of shoulders, knocking heads together, and setting the unconscious faces of the multitude towards inconceivable goals and in undreamt-of directions. (pp. 4–5)

The affinity between MacWhirr and Conrad, who also ran off to sea as a boy against his family's wishes, is too obvious to be missed.

"Typhoon" chronicles, of course, a struggle for physical survival, for human order against the disorder of nature. It is also a psychic penetration into one of Conrad's most deceptive figures,[18] a relentlessly common man who, under pressure, reveals himself remarkably and astonishingly uncommon.

5.

The fifth of Conrad's classic sea journeys, "The Secret Sharer," has drawn the attention of critics, anthologists, and psychologists perhaps more persistently than any of his stories with the exception of "Heart of Darkness." Its meaning has also aroused more dispute. Is Leggatt, the fugitive who killed a man and is now boldly fleeing the law, the young captain's alter ego? His *doppelganger?* His lower self? His higher or ideal self? The man the captain secretly longs to be? His secret unconscious self? These possibilities attach themselves to the theory that the story is rampant with psychological symbolism. At the other end are those who prefer the tale on straight literal terms. Leggatt is simply Leggatt, and "The Secret Sharer" an account of an adventure in which the captain is strangely and dramatically involved, during which he acquires self-confidence and the mastery of his ship. To find anything more arcane than this in the story, according to the literalist school, is to create symbols where none exist.

18 Robert Penn Warren's brilliant gibe at Galsworthy as a MacWhirr of literature (in his introduction to the Modern Library edition of *Nostromo*), however relevant to Galsworthy, is untrue of MacWhirr and reveals how insistently his portrait is swallowed on surface terms.

Nor do the devotees of the buried meaning viewpoint agree on the merits of the story. One of them[19] takes Conrad severely to task for being so obvious in pointing out his intentions, sprinkling nearly every paragraph with references to depth psychology and with giveaway words like my double, secret, depths, inside, dark, sleeping suit, which reduce everything to a clinical level and cause us to lose interest in the narrative itself. For the most part, however, the story is read as a masterpiece of penetration into the divided self.

Two versions of Leggatt appear at once: the man as he is and as the captain thinks him to be. To Conrad, to us, he is a distinct person with his own identity; to the captain, he is plainly more than that; he feels for Leggatt a mysterious and compelling affinity. The story has its physical side where everyone exists distinctly and objectively; the psychological side is determined, indeed created, by the necessities of the captain's mind. At the center of this mind is the lesion from which Conrad himself confessedly suffered so mordantly, an afflictive lack of self-confidence. The lesion is compounded of several elements: the captain's extreme youth, the fact that he is embarking on his first command, and a strain of nervous anxiety in him which is beyond explanation, which is perhaps rooted in his temperament. The strangeness of the night scene in the Gulf of Siam at the start of the story is a projection of the captain's own acute sense of disorientation. He is a stranger to the ship, a stranger to the crew, a stranger to himself even; no wonder that the slightly eerie aspect of the river, pocked with "fishing-stakes resembling a mysterious system of half-submerged bamboo fences" ('*Twixt Land and Sea,* p. 91), dominated by the miter-shaped hill of the Paknam pagoda, should seem strange to him, and to us. No wonder that in his state of uncertain nerves he should break precedent by assuming the anchor watch himself, forget to pull up the side ladder, and be half-mesmerized altogether in the clutch of a growing anxiety as to "how far I should turn out faithful to that ideal conception of one's own personality every man sets up for himself secretly" (p. 94).

When Leggatt appears naked and exhausted, clinging to the bottom of the ladder, his "broad livid back immersed right up to the neck in a greenish cadaverous glow" (p. 97), the captain feels a

[19] Marvin Mudrick, "Conrad and the Terms of Modern Criticism," *The Hudson Review,* Autumn, 1954.

"horrid, frost-bound sensation" gripping him about the chest. He leans over the rail to make him out more clearly: ". . . the sea-lightning played about his limbs at every stir; and he appeared in it ghastly, silvery, fish-like" (p. 98). These sensory details are entirely faithful to the visual facts; the "unnatural" or "abnormal" note proceeds from the captain's unsettled state, the very state which, upon his hearing Leggatt's calm, resolute voice and his astonishing self-possession under desperate circumstances, moves the captain to state: "A mysterious communication was established already between us two—in the face of that silent, darkened tropical sea" (p. 99). On Leggatt's part, this communication marks the appearance of a miraculous rescue; on the captain's, the appearance of a man who has all the qualities of decisiveness, ability, and courage he himself seems to lack. In protecting him, in rescuing him, he may somehow draw these qualities from Leggatt and by absorbing them into himself proceed to meet the crisis of his first command successfully. Meanwhile the physical identity of Leggatt, the fact that he is not simply a projection of the captain's subconscious, is reaffirmed throughout by the captain's own remark, "He was not a bit like me, really" (p. 105), and by the nerve-racking scene in which the captain of the *Sephora,* the ship on which Leggatt as first mate had killed a mutinous seaman, comes looking for the fugitive, desperately eager to see him punished for his "crime."

The ordeal of concealing Leggatt from the prying eyes of his pursuer and later from the unsuspecting eyes of the steward and the rest of the ship's company taxes the young captain to the utmost and makes the competent handling of a new ship seem relatively simple by comparison. He lies to the party from the *Sephora* and incurs the growing hostility of his own officers who look with alarm upon his unstable nerves, his queer flare-ups of temper, and his dubious sailing procedures. At last the captain carries the ship itself into grave danger by bringing it in close to a rocky shore at night in order to allow Leggatt to escape unnoticed. By saving the fugitive and releasing him into freedom, he is somehow achieving his own maturation, and for it he is willing to pay a heavy price. The price proves almost fatal to himself and to the men under him for the ship comes within a hairbreadth of crashing on the rocks. Only the fortuitous appearance of the captain's white hat marks the drift of the current and gives him the saving mark necessary to turn the ship in time. He had voluntarily thrust his hat on Leggatt's head to protect it from the sun; and the hat had slipped off while the fleeing man was swimming to shore, slipped off in time to save the situation. The captain, having successfully survived the ordeal, feels a surge of confidence in himself, leading him to "the perfect communion of a seaman with his first command" (p. 143).

As in "Typhoon," the crisis of the story is both created and overcome by the will and energy of the captain. His weaknesses and uncertainties cause it; his will to overcome them finally masters it. Leggatt, for all his resolution, is a relatively passive figure throughout. The things that happen, the things that are done, happen and are done because of the captain, from the mistake with the ladder at the beginning, so suggestive of his confusion, to the protective gesture with the hat at the end, so indicative of his healed psyche. The image of the white hat on the black water appears again in the final paragraph where this time it is seen against the towering black mass of land looking "like the very gateway of Erebus." Erebus is the spirit of primeval darkness but is also the father of day. The white hat is a prefiguration of day, as indeed is Leggatt, "a free man, a proud swimmer striking out for a new destiny" (p. 143). The new destiny is, of course, not only his but the captain's.

Once again the ship is the seismograph on which psychic vibrations are recorded. At the outset the captain rests his hand on the ship's rail "as if on the shoulder of a trusted friend" (p. 92), but it is then at anchor before the voyage of self-discovery begins and the communion between them has yet to be earned. It can be earned only in action; not the routine action of ordinary seagoing, but action of some extraordinary kind. The redemption of Leggatt who appears from the depths of the sea—the creative medium of all the sea journeys in Conrad's fiction—and returns to it at the end provides the captain with his opportunity. His seizure of it supplies "The Secret Sharer" with its essential frame.

6.

The Shadow-Line was originally called First Command, but Conrad discarded this title once the composition of the story was under way. Although it deals, to be sure, with a young sea captain who acquires command of his first ship, this is only the scaffolding for another—it was to prove the last—of Conrad's rich psychic studies of the emergent self. In due course *First Command* was abandoned, and *The Shadow-Line,* far closer to the story's meaning and inward discourse, arrived at. The work, written and published in the middle years of the First World War, was dedicated to the author's elder son, then in combat in France. Conrad, as he had done before, was using the actual historical crisis, subjecting its participants to severest pressure, as an external analogue to the crisis experienced by his narrator.[20] This crisis had nothing to do with war or history, but it was no less severe and involved the crossing of the same shadow line.

Adorning page one is an epigraph from Baudelaire: ". . . — D'autres fois, calme plat, grand miroir/De mon désespoir." [21] And it is the doldrums with which the story begins. It is not the sea of nature that has fallen into a period of stagnant quietude, but the narrator, and it is not his body or the air around him that has been seized by an ominous emptiness, but his mind. As so often happens with the doldrums of nature, the young captain has drifted into his mysteriously, for no apparent reason, and without visible change of circumstance. He had been contentedly occupied for two years as first mate aboard a steamship trading in the islands of the Malay Sea. Then suddenly, from one moment to the next, he quit his post. "One day I was perfectly right and the next everything was gone— glamour, flavor, interest, contentment—everything" (p. 5).

His captain wondered what ailed him. The second engineer thought it was woman trouble. The chief engineer blamed it on a deranged liver. The narrator himself had no theory, only the overwhelming sensation that everything he had been doing was dreary, prosaic, and without truth. "What truth? I should have been hard put to it to explain" (p. 7). His ignorance only adds to the acuteness of his abrupt dissatisfaction with his job, with himself, with his life, with everything in general uncaused by anything in particular.

Waiting for passage back to Europe, he checks in at the Officers' Home, and finds it a striking externalization of his mood. The first

[20] In an Author's Note, composed in 1920, Conrad links the two: ". . . there was a feeling of identity, though with an enormous difference of scale—as of one single drop measured against the bitter and stormy immensity of an ocean" (*The Shadow-Line,* pp. viii–ix). But the one drop contained the same elements as the ocean.

[21] "At other times, the doldrums, mirroring my despair."

man he sees, a stranger dozing on the verandah, opens "one horribly fish-like eye" as he approaches. The other guests are scarcely more prepossessing. A man named Hamilton, an impecunious snob behind on his bills, cuts him dead. A Captain Giles, full of benevolent platitudes, is spoiled by "a curious air of complacency." The establishment is run by an "unhappy, wizened little man" whose chief intention is to keep the place as untenanted as possible. It is hot, empty, tomblike, cumbered with cardboard boxes, dreary furniture, "grimy antimacassars" scattered over "horrid upholstery," and a smell of decaying coral. The manager greets him with a whine of dismay on learning that he is to be a guest, and later tries to cheat him. Even the newspapers, the only reading matter offered, "were old and uninteresting, filled up mostly with dreary stereotyped descriptions of Queen Victoria's first jubilee celebrations" (p. 16). After a day or two the conversation, consisting of complaints from the manager, unintelligible exclamations from the fish-eyed man, banalities from Captain Giles, and an offensive silence from Hamilton, wears our narrator down to a state of almost total life paralysis. After a particularly labored and inane discourse by Captain Giles, he reaches bottom.

The whole thing strengthened in me that obscure feeling of life being but a waste of days, which, half-unconsciously, had driven me out of a comfortable berth, away from men I liked, to flee from the menace of emptiness . . . and to find inanity at the first turn. Here was a man of recognized character and achievement disclosed as an absurd and dreary chatterer. And it was probably like this everywhere—from east to west, from the bottom to the top of the social scale.

A great discouragement fell on me. A spiritual drowsiness. Giles's voice was going on complacently; the very voice of the universal hollow conceit. And I was no longer angry with it. There was nothing original, nothing new, startling, informing to expect from the world: no opportunities to find out something about oneself, no wisdom to acquire, no fun to enjoy. Everything was stupid and overrated, even as Captain Giles was. So be it. (pp. 22–23)

The account of his descent into this abyss of emptiness is one of the flawless sequences in Conrad. His arrangement of an outer situation to encase and intensify the inner state of nervous desolation is replete with inventive detail, finally reinforced by the suggestion that men like the narrator have come to the Officers' Home before to stay for a few days and have remained a lifetime. The East is filled with white men who lost their spirit, grew soft, and declined into vague misfits.[22] The twilight and stuffiness reigning in the Home give it, from one angle, the aspect of a mausoleum. In entering it, the narrator has taken a last step away from life.

His psychic identity has all but disappeared. Torn away from his lost self, devitalized, on the edge of an annihilation of personality, he is abruptly confronted with his main chance, the chance he has been waiting for without hope, the opportunity to command his own ship. It is like a breath of wind foretelling the end of the doldrums into which he has sunk almost without trace. The opportunity, fortuitous, accidental, unexpected, is delayed by the devious maneuvering of the manager. It is Captain Giles, that dull man, who alerts the narrator to what is going on. The sudden call to action, exacerbated by the flagrant attempt of the manager to rob him of his chance, rouses him from his lethargy and supplies him with the handhold in the external world which can often wrench men from the grasp of their enervated selves.

This brings the first part of the story, dealing with the inner life, to a close. In part two the young captain emerges from sterility by responding to the challenges and responsibilities of the outer life, incarnate once again in a ship and its crew. She is anchored in Bangkok, and to reach her the newly appointed captain must be ferried as a passenger aboard another vessel. Her master is unaccountably hostile, but nothing can dampen the narrator's rising optimism. And when he catches a first glimpse of his new command, looking like "an Arab steed in a string of cart-horses" among the moored ships, the "feeling of life-emptiness which had made me so restless for the last few months lost its bitter plausibility, its evil influence" (p. 49).

But ill luck hangs over the ship like a miasma, and the captain, sucked into it, must call upon all his newly found vigor to survive. Three misfortunes occur: an outbreak of cholera among the crew, aggravated by the discovery that the quinine bottles had been emptied; a dead calm in the Gulf, which keeps the ship drifting aimlessly and undermines the morale of the company; and the obsessive,

22 Or fell into the pit of miscegenation. The white men in Conrad like Almayer and Willems who marry Malay women usually come to a bad end, and their degradation is specifically symbolized by their crossing of racial barriers.

spectral aura of the previous captain who had gone mad and died
at sea (the superstitious first mate thinks it is he who is responsible
for all the calamities). Since these difficulties are outside his consciousness, the narrator-captain endures them, somehow, more easily than
he did his earlier melancholy. The crew is prostrated with disease,
but with the aid of the cook, a man named Ransome with a bad
heart but an excellent, quietly courageous disposition, he manages
to pull them through. The lurid story of his predecessor eats a little
into his spirit; he manages to shake it off and even to rid the impressionable mate of his obsession. The doldrums in the Gulf last
longer, yet dogged patience is in the end rewarded by rain and
wind, energizing the ship and sending it finally on its way. These
scenes are managed with skill, though they do not take hold of our
imaginations as did the descent of the captain into his well of psychic
sterility.

Characteristically, when, en route to his final destination, he returns as captain to the port where the story had begun, everything
is changed. "It is strange how on coming ashore I was struck by the
springy step, the lively eyes, the strong vitality of everyone I met"
(p. 130). The torpor has vanished. The appearance of things has
become infused by the narrator's newly charged spirit.[23] Even
Captain Giles, whom he meets again, talks sensibly and "began to
interest me for the first time" (p. 132). The vigor of mind, the affirmation of temper, the rush of life energy have transformed the
world in the eye of the beholder, and even the abrupt reminder of
Ransome's weak heart in the last line of the story cannot chill his
élan. The descent and ascent of mood, which is the substance of *The
Shadow-Line,* proceeds through stages that are psychologically unequivocal, with a ship and a sea journey as the agents guiding the
shift in direction. Conrad's rhetoric falters in places; after twenty
years of professional writing, he still clings to his misguided passion
for vaguely grandiose adjectives like impenetrable, inconceivable,
and inexpressible. But these do no more than briefly jar the narrative current.

[23] Though he remarked earlier that his depression had been rooted in a failure
of confidence ("I always suspected that I might be no good" [p. 107]), his plight
is different from the captain's in "The Secret Sharer." His is a crisis of nerves,
not a crisis of self-esteem; his newly charged spirit draws its sustenance from the
current of action into which he is thrust, not from a personal demonstration of
power or ability.

The story remains a penetrating representation of the human soul enervated and then replenished. Written in 1915, published two years later, it was the last of Conrad's sea journeys, in which the dimensions of mind are explored in harmony with the dimensions of space. It was also to prove the last of his great works.

VII

"The Eye of Others"

UPON HIS RETURN IN 1896 FROM AN EXTENDED HONEYMOON IN BRIT-
tany, Conrad's literary life began in earnest. The first two Malayan
novels had already appeared and a third, *The Rescue,* was under
way, though its troubles were beginning to mount. A number of
stories soon to be part of *Tales of Unrest* had been written in
France, and *The Nigger of the "Narcissus"* begun. Yet Conrad still
did not regard his new vocation as permanent; as late as 1898 he
was still looking for posts at sea. On October 16, 1898, he wrote to
Cunninghame Graham's mother: "I will without scruple use and
abuse everybody's goodwill, influence, friendship to get back on
the water. I am by no means happy on shore." [1]

His day-to-day living was now being done on land, and his land
commitments were drawing him into a tangle of experience so increasingly involved that the sea, ironically, became the element to which
he longed to escape. He was subjecting himself to still another radical change of environment, but he was no longer a boy of seventeen
eager for adventure; he was a grown man, in his late thirties, striving for success in a new career. And the career he had chosen, the
difficult, hazardous, insecure career of letters, was as ambiguous and
amorphous as any that lay within reach. To this radical shift in
fortune he was bringing a wife and, very soon, a son; a set of highly
uncertain nerves, aggravated by equally uncertain health; an abnormal capacity to look on the dark side of things, profess discouragement, and descant on the ultimate futility of all human effort.
But these burdens, amounting almost to a certain bill of disqualifi-
cation, could not wholly conceal what lay underneath: a hard de-

[1] LL, I, 251.

termination not merely to survive but to succeed. Conrad's capacity for unhappiness and self-deprecation was unbounded, but more powerful still was his passion for life. Actually, in self-estimation he ranked very high; his effusive modesty and mannered courtesies were devices to keep his sense of superiority from being offensive. However much his philosophy may have convinced him of the folly of human hopes, his instincts and vanity spurred him to hopes and efforts of a most tenacious kind.

These opposing tendencies were a constant anguish but they did not disable him; they became, in fact, a characteristic and even necessary part of his procedures as a writer and as a man with a precarious living to earn. They were evident, with an effect equally paradoxical, in his relationship to money. It was a point of personal pride for him to support his family, but he did not hesitate to borrow heavily during the many years when his books did not sell. He complained bitterly about the failure of the public to buy his novels, yet did not hesitate to heap scorn upon the man who "forks out the half crown" as a stupid fellow quite incapable of appreciating the aesthetic riches being offered him. He was forever schooling himself to be content with a *succès d'estime* and always irrepressibly longing for popularity.[2] His father and mother belonged to the landed gentry, and even after all their troubles there was still an inheritance for him when they died. And for all his complaints and grumblings, Uncle Tadeusz had always paid his debts and come through in emergencies. When he was short of funds, it never occurred to Conrad to reduce expenses. Money would be somehow forthcoming.

After the death of his uncle he made investments on his own; these invariably failed, leaving him little to go on in his marriage. When his early novels proved financial failures, he swallowed his pride and borrowed from his agent, J. B. Pinker. The anguish of not being able to support himself and his family never left him, but again it did not undermine him. He suffered, borrowed, endured humiliations, but struggled on. His life situation may have been in desperate conflict with his tastes and standards; he did not allow himself, least of all his creative self, to be ground down between them. The outcries in his letters on how hard it was to earn a living,

---

[2] Henry James suffered from the same longing. But while James's hunger for a great public success went unrealized, Conrad in his last years did win a large audience and earn considerable sums of money.

punctuated with savage, deprecatory attacks on literature as a way of doing so, may give the impression of a man who hated what he was doing and misanthropically lamented its futility. Nothing could be more misleading. His railings and outbursts expressed not the conviction of failure but the passion for success. They touched off his disappointment, his injured self-esteem, his wounded pride, without ultimately concealing his determination to persevere, his finally unshakable will to achieve. The strain of remonstrative, self-pitying pessimism in Conrad was an overlay to the iron in him. His life, his art acquired their tone from the first, their substance from the second.

The grinding, chronic shortage of money aside, Conrad faced the problem not only of establishing himself in a new profession but making a place for himself in a new society. He was now no longer a bachelor free to come and go as he pleased, withdrawing from the world when the mood seized him or being gregarious when he chose, but a married man anchored necessarily in a fixed position. Responsibilities at sea had been demanding and derived from a rigid code of conduct; yet they were transient and came to an end when a voyage was over. His land responsibilities were less clearly defined—fidelity, courage, skill were easily applicable to the life of a mariner; on land they seemed abstract and amorphous, had no time limit, and could not be instantly measured.

The pressure upon Conrad now increased immeasurably. The changeover from an itinerant and unattached sailor to a domesticated novelist living in the English countryside brought with it a maze of fresh difficulties. He had to get his books written, market them, negotiate with agents and publishers, struggle with the complexities of a demanding art, wrestle with a language which he spoke as a foreigner, find suitable houses to settle down in, pay bills, make friends, work his way somehow into an English milieu, and learn to be a husband and father (not easy for a man who remained unmarried until he was thirty-eight and embarked on fatherhood at forty). In addition to all this he had to bear the constant burden of gout which in his case was both organic and psychosomatic, struggle with the later burdens of his wife's serious accidents and ailments and the more ephemeral but no less worrisome ailments of his two growing sons. And all the while he staggered on under the weight of an ardent, highly strung temperament, which was at the same time the source of his productive genius. When the old voyages had come to an end, he could rest between them, or change posts and try another part of the world. In this new life there was no letup, no protracted pauses for stocktaking, no possibility of even temporary withdrawal without the imminent danger of general collapse, of everything falling in upon him irreparably.

The story of the eighteen years between the appearance of *Almayer's Folly* in 1895 and the publication of *Chance* in 1913 deals essentially with how he bore up under these pressures. To the act of writing, made all the more difficult by the slow, erratic movements of his imagination, he addressed himself from the start with unremitting effort. He would spend whole days at his desk, and nothing would appear. The blank pages became nightmares to him; he despaired of ever getting on. But somehow he did get on; by grimly sticking to his task, he goaded his treacherous muse into renewed activity, groaning all the while. The transformation of nervous energy into phrases, Conrad's definition of creative writing, was a process which racked him with its fits and starts. He grasped for help wherever he could. In matters of critical judgment he submitted to the advice of Garnett; submitted is perhaps not quite the right word since he solicited his advice eagerly and always seemed painfully grateful for it. His eagerness for assistance led him to the collaboration with Ford Madox Hueffer shortly after the two men met in 1898.

Collaboration was more common in those days than now. Conrad's motive was apparently linguistic and technical. Despite three published novels English was still difficult for him, and the act of organizing a piece of fiction still a formidable task. Working on a novel with someone to whom the language was native and who was at the same time aesthetically knowledgeable might prove the very thing. Hueffer came into his orbit then, and Conrad seized his chance. Hueffer appeared to fill the bill perfectly. Though his father was German, his mother was English; he had been brought up in England and English was his native tongue. Some sixteen years younger than Conrad, he had already published one novel and was thought of as a coming man. Moreover, he carried himself with an air of overwhelming assurance as though there were no doubt of his genius in his own mind and ought not to be any doubt of it in the minds of others, a conceit he managed to carry off not with insolence and abrasiveness but with easy charm. As a final fillip, he spoke French fluently. Hueffer himself was more than willing to enter a literary partnership with a man who was not only equally bilingual but had an unusual personality and a considerable reputation among the more perceptive critics.

The relationship that followed had its ups and downs, its periods of achievement, its difficult moments, its quarrels and reconciliations, its obscure sides. It is an altogether fascinating interlude in the history of Conrad. Two novels were published under their joint names; though neither is a great work, each is a respectable piece of craftsmanship, and Conrad's willingness to include them in the collected edition of his own works can be understood. *The Inheritors* (1901) is one of those blends of supernaturalism and political satire popular at the time, and its mixture of fourth dimensionists (creatures from another sphere assuming human form and bent on conquering the earth from within) and characters drawn from the political and literary circles of the hour may be psychologically superficial, but it is smoothly and professionally concocted. Conrad's contribution to it was minor. *Romance* (1903) was an out-and-out Caribbean adventure story with pirates, gold, beautiful girls, and island politics skillfully scrambled; Conrad claimed to have written the whole of Part Four. Both novels wisely concentrated on events rather than character, plot being a more maneuverable substance in the hands of collaborating authors than the complexities of human nature.

That Conrad profited from the relationship may not be precisely demonstrable, yet it helped him over a difficult time. The days and nights spent with Hueffer—they often stayed up all night talking and arguing about literary problems—supplied him with the intimate professional discussion of his craft that he so plainly lacked and badly needed. He had had a "literary" childhood of sorts under the distracted wing of his father, a man of letters in the traditional European sense when he was not leaping hotly into the political bonfire. As a boy he himself had written plays, and as a young man had indicated in his letters an easy facility with words and enough individuality of eye to nudge his uncle—himself the author of an extended memoir—into suggesting that he contribute articles to the Polish press. But all this "background" was vague, diffuse, and uncoordinated. It made the transformation of the seaman into the novelist something less than miraculous, yet does not dilute the accuracy of Conrad's reference to himself as an amateur when he began dabbling at *Almayer's Folly*. He was an amateur. He had written nothing imaginative (with the single exception of "The Black Mate") since his heroic drama "The Eyes of King John Sobieski" at the age of eleven. He had had no contact whatever with the literary world or literary men since his father's death, and despite his wide reading among the French novelists of the nineteenth century, there is no evidence that until his thirty-eighth year the thought of such contact had ever crossed his mind.

When, by imperceptible degrees, he slipped into the writer's life after another kind of life altogether, he felt a strong and in this case perfectly natural urge for communication with other men in the same field. Hence the eagerness of his reliance on Garnett, and the intense, almost boyish enthusiasm with which he discussed writing problems with Noble, Sanderson, Galsworthy, Stephen Crane, H. G. Wells, and Cunninghame Graham, whom he met before the end of the century. To work at close range with an experienced native professional like Hueffer would supply a last orientation and provide him with a final assurance. So at any rate was his hope, and it seems, in fact, to have been realized. The long conversations between them on questions of style and aesthetic theory, the selection of words and phrases, the planning of scenes, the exchange of ideas and the pursuit of the *mot juste*—carried on with the concurrent intimacy of their wives and children—probably levered Conrad into an easier working arrangement with his new language and an increased fluency in his new trade. The distempers and misunderstandings that accompanied all this were a small price to pay for the value received by each from the other, and were, in retrospect, trivial.

Hueffer has been much abused by zealous defenders of Conrad, but unjustly so. He may have patronized Mrs. Conrad, exaggerated his own importance in Conrad's maturation as a writer, and struck a note of excessive vanity in his book of reminiscences on their collaboration. But he never lost sight of Conrad's genius and regarded him as the noblest man he knew. And his services did not end with *Romance*. On and off for years afterward he took Conrad's dictation when the older man was stricken with gout, helped with correspondence and editorial details, made valuable suggestions with regard to *Nostromo* and *The Secret Agent,* and supplied the intellectual companionship to which Conrad had responded from the beginning. There was bickering between them, too, and occasional bitterness, and long periods when they were completely estranged. Yet when Hueffer started *The English Review* in 1907 Conrad contributed the pieces that were later published in book form as a *A Personal Record,* and when Hueffer started *The Transatlantic Review* in 1923, during the last year of Conrad's life, he had little difficulty in persuading Conrad to contribute to it as well. Whatever others may have said about his feelings, Conrad appears to have retained an essential harmony with Hueffer that survived their occasional frictions. At the start, at any rate, if not later, Hueffer was one of the life lines that Conrad clutched in his early struggle for literary security.

No less arduous than his struggle to master the act of writing was his struggle for approval, not simply in his own eyes but in the eyes of others. Almayer and Willems had fallen from their ideal images of themselves; the only shock left to them was the discovery of how they looked to those around them. Conrad's hunger for the esteem of others was at first in direct ratio to his uncertainty about his creative energies, but it continued unabated and as an autonomous craving long after this uncertainty was reduced by the completion of one substantial work after another. He anxiously solicited the good opinion of his friends, was gratified by good reviews, stung by bad ones, and dreamed of conquering the great reading public. This external image of success was the obverse of his secretly nurtured ideal of imaginative art. Success with himself was not enough; he craved success with others. The pursuit of these twin demons, concealed inside the sheath of a seductively high-minded ideal analogous to Conrad's own, became the theme of *Lord Jim,* a novel remarkable for its many voices and interlocking tonalities that appeared in the first year of the new century.

It is the first of his books to introduce the full Conradian orchestra, replete with motifs and variations: cowardice and bravery, society and its outlaws, the whites and Malays, a smorgasbord of English, Dutch, Germans, and French, noble savages and ignoble Europeans, the process of joyless sin cathartized by joyful expiation, the assaying of false idealism and true, the manipulation of the time dimension, like so much taffy, to suit the splicing of narrative comment, and an astonishing projection of the sensory universe, land

as well as sea, in a blaze of light and darkness. The reader can dive
into this babel of riches at any one of a dozen points, and is indeed
invited to do so. He can cling to the story of Jim himself or to the
many figures who comment on Jim or to the deliberated theme of
moral redemption or to the persistent refrain of "one of us," which
Marlow sounds and others tacitly take up. One can search for
buried symbols—the wreck over which the *Patna* passes may be the
hidden weakness in Jim, just as the split hill in Patusan may represent his split self.[3] Or approach the story in the footsteps of Gustav
Morf as an exorcism in art of Conrad's private guilt feelings about
Poland. The novel is so rich in character and inventive situation
that a half-dozen of the figures who appear relatively briefly, Brierly
and his breathtaking suicide, Chester and the adventure of the
guano island, Brown with his festering hatred of the world he feels
has betrayed him, could each in his turn serve as the subject of a
full-length tale. Their presences enrich the affair of Jim and supply
it with an all-star cast.

In the prodigal multiplicity of the book, there is a unifying center,
a thread that leads us through the mazes of the labyrinth to an
ultimate clarity. This center is embodied in certain remarks of the
French lieutenant: "Man is born a coward. . . . But habit—habit
—necessity—do you see?—the eye of others—*voilà*. One puts up
with it" (p. 147). The novel is a demonstration of one phrase in
this statement, "the eye of others." Until he becomes concerned
with that eye, Jim behaves badly; once he becomes responsive to it,
he behaves well. It determines his actions as fixedly as the lunar
cycle controls the movements of the tides.

The human community appears in two forms in the book. There
is the community referred to by Marlow as "us" in his recurring
comment, "He was one of us." This is the community of white
Europeans struggling to maintain their favored position among the
Asiatic Malays. Disgraceful conduct on the part of one weakens
them all, and Jim's cowardice hits them very hard. Equally disturbing is his insistence on giving himself up for trial; this public spectacle will dramatize before the natives the downfall of a white man.
Brierly, one of his white judges, wants to get rid of him—hustle
him out of town or bury him twenty feet underground. The demands of the white community, however, make little appeal to Jim.

3 Dorothy Van Ghent, in her book *The English Novel: Form and Function*
(New York, 1953), discovers these and other ingenious arrangements.

Its members are scattered all over the Pacific; its ideals are too impersonal. Jim does not at any time feel a sense of belonging. In his experiences on the training ship and later as a young mate he always kept to himself, nourished his high-flying dreams of heroism, thought of himself as above everybody else, was responsive only to the claims of his own nature. Marlow, to be sure, regards him as "one of us." Jim is white, English, youthful, handsome, rugged-looking; he looks like "one of us." But Jim never feels it or claims it. The claim that is overwhelmingly real to Marlow is only an abstraction to him, and Marlow's persistent vexation with Jim lies rooted in this sharp division of loyalties. Before, during, and after the trial Jim remains a "loner," as detached from the white men and their private codes in the Pacific, as he is from his father the vicar who mouths his untested platitudes back home in the safety of rural England. The eye of others in this instance had no effect upon Jim because he is blind to its existence.

The second community in the novel is the Malay tribe headed by the old native chieftain Doramin, and it is the only one to which Jim ever becomes attached. After rescuing the tribe from a series of brutal oppressors, Jim becomes Doramin's adopted son and blood brother to Dain Waris, the crown prince, as noble a young savage as appears anywhere in Conrad's fiction. Jim assumes the responsibility of leadership, becomes the arbiter of everyday disputes, acquires a Malay bodyguard who swears to defend him with his life, and grows into an incarnation of wisdom and power, into *Tuan* or Lord Jim.

As Lord Jim his life acquires a social texture it had hitherto lacked. He has friends, enemies, responsibilities, a woman who loves him and whom he loves, a fixed place in the world, and the sense of achievement that comes only when the gap between the real self and the ideal disappears. The earlier trauma of cowardice and bravery no longer obtains. On Patusan he behaves bravely a dozen times over. When the final trouble comes, the great trouble, it attacks him not through the desire to save himself—which caused him to desert the *Patna* despite his vows as an officer—but through the desire to save others, to avoid bloodshed, to behave in a humane and statesmanlike way. He gives Brown and his ruffians leave to depart in peace. This turns out to be a mistake in judgment, a fatal mistake that leads to the murder of the crown prince and others, but it is a mistake implicit in Jim's youth, his inexperience, his new-found humanity, and not in the old paralysis of mind and self-worshipping imagination. And he pays for it without wavering, going to his death with a clarity and decisiveness in remarkable contrast with his sullenness, egotism, and persistently self-pitying tone in the days when he was simply Jim. By redeeming Dain Waris's death with his own, Jim shores up the faith of the tribe in the cosmic order and acknowledges with this supreme gesture his newly established function as an agent of society. Being now a *tuan,* considered such by organized society, he behaves like one. We are what we seem to be in the eyes of others.

On the *Patna* Jim was entirely alone. The eight hundred passengers making a religious pilgrimage to Mecca were an anonymous blur to him. His fellow officers, from the coarse, flabby German captain down, were a distasteful lot for whom he felt only contempt. The only eyes upon him during the crisis when the ship seems about to go down at any moment are those of the two silent Malay steersmen gazing at him impassively. Their blankness suggests the emptiness of the social universe Jim inhabits, a universe that provides him with no countervailing pressure against the sickening paralysis of will into which he sinks. Left to himself, stripped of the support normally to be expected from his fellow officers, surrounded by crowds of strangers from another race and who are, moreover, asleep in the hush of night,[4] he is forced to decide between dying heroically or living ignobly on the sudden spur of the moment and in complete loneliness and isolation. As in a dream, no longer conscious of his own actions, he hears the voices of the deserting officers urging him to jump, and as though he were someone else he does jump, "into the everlasting dark hole" of the lifeboat. Shame, and an obscure desire to be both vindicated and punished, drives him to give himself up for trial. There he meets Marlow, the courtroom spectator on whom he makes so singular an impression, and Captain Brierly, one of his judges, who takes his own life soon after delivering the verdict. He turns the judgment he has rendered on Jim inward, and collapses under the sudden, shocking discovery of the possible Jim lurking within himself.

Drummed out of the merchant marine, Jim wanders from one

---

[4] One of them awakens, seizes Jim as he rushes past to release the lifeboats, and begs him for water. In a panic, Jim strikes him with a lantern, then out of fear that he will arouse the ship, thrusts a canteen in to his hand, and gets rid of him at last (pp. 89–90). This small incident inside the larger scene of the desertion suggests at once the utter dependence of the passengers upon Jim and the gulf between them as human beings.

obscure job to another, still nursing his dream of heroism, still yearning for a chance at redemption, and fleeing at every mention of his debacle. All this time, while Marlow seeks persistently to get him another start somewhere, anywhere, Jim remains an outsider, unconnected with anyone. Even his connection with Marlow, this older man who listens to and befriends him, is purely egoistic; he uses Marlow as a confessional and unloads all his grievances upon him. At last, through the intervention of Stein, a kind of older, wiser, more successful Jim, Jim is given his chance on Patusan, a remote and isolated peninsula cut off from the larger sea world by a narrow, winding, jungle river. In Patusan comes his great chance, probably his final one, to wipe out the memory of the *Patna*.[5]

As in his other novels Conrad is committed to the principle of un-love. He keeps the reader at a maximum emotional distance from his hero, and prevents any warmly sympathetic identification between them. In this he is in revolt against the practice of nineteenth century English fiction, and all those Pips, Pendennises, David Copperfields, Adam Bedes, and Richard Feverels who arouse in us a close personal response. This attachment, which begins in sentiment and often rushes unrestrainedly into sentimentality, Conrad distrusts at every stage. He does not wish us to love his protagonists but to understand them, and love can be as blinding in fiction as in life. Jim is a notable example of the hero to whom the reader is not permitted to get emotionally close. He is himself a cold, self-centered egotist, and scarcely a passage in the novel allows us to forget it. His early dream of heroism is tainted by the constant image of himself as being "above" others, "higher" than the rest. His favorite perch on a ship is atop the mainmast, and the quality of his ideal vision has the unpleasant egotism of an assumed superiority. During the trial he seeks from Marlow a personal vindication not justified by his cowardly desertion, simply on the self-pitying grounds that he was not really to blame. Afterward, he nurses his wound for all it is worth though belligerently ready to drive his fist into the face of anyone who so much as mentions the *Patna* humiliation to him. He is a classic case of psychic masturbation.

[5] The names Patusan and Patna are obviously related to each other, the first being Patna with the letters *u* and *s* added. Is there any significance to this? Patusan becomes an anagram of Patna with the addition of *us*, the very element that transforms the pilgrim ship with its total incommunication into a living society of responsible and interacting men. The theme of "us" has, of course, already been struck by Marlow.

Even on Patusan his new-found ties are not quite natural. He is more the rescuer than the compatriot, more a *tuan* or lord than an equal. He remains a white man among the Malays, their leader, counselor, benefactor to be sure, yet somehow an outsider. He is in love with Jewel, but when the last crisis comes and he must decide between her feelings for him and the spur of his outraged honor, he brushes her aside and goes to his death unflinchingly. Moreover, he does so without hesitation. As she begs him to run off with her to that outside world of which she has hitherto been in dread, as she clings to him frantically, there is never a doubt in his mind as to what he must do. "He goes away from a living woman to celebrate his pitiless wedding with a shadowy ideal of conduct" (p. 416), Marlow writes at the end. Jim's capacity to sacrifice the concrete for the abstract, the real for the ideal, the living tissue of emotion for the veiled and inscrutable dream, removes him from the dimension of love and identification altogether and thrusts him, instead, into the harsh, bracing light of ironic definition. He is a fascinating figure, but a deliberately cold one.

His effect on others is abrasive. He reduces Jewel to a hollow shell "leading a sort of soundless, inert life in Stein's house" (pp. 416–417), drives Brierly to suicide, is responsible for the death of his best friend, the crown prince, and rouses even the experienced, life-tempered Marlow to a state of agitated moral confusion. He suffers acutely himself and is the cause of suffering in others. The French lieutenant is sympathetic to him up to a point, but when the question of lost honor comes up, he shies nervously away and abruptly takes his leave. Even Stein, the one ideal figure in the novel, the man who combines physical and spiritual success, who defeats his enemies and finds the rare butterfly he has pursued for years, who triumphantly demonstrates his own advice to men that they should "in the destructive element immerse" [6]—Stein who understands Jim, gives him his glorious opportunity on Patusan, looks upon

[6] This utterance by Stein, one of the famous statements in Conrad, has intrigued a whole generation of critics, most of whom are baffled by its meaning or find it cryptic and deep. The destructive element would appear to be life, and the call to immersion would be a call to live it not only actively but actually. The man who tries to rise above it, as Jim does, and gets too far removed from its actuality, is sure to drown, for a removal from life is death. Yet to survive involves not passive submission but exertion. "The way is to the destructive element submit yourself," says Stein in his Teutonized English, "and with the exertions of your hands and feet in the water make the deep, deep sea keep you up" (p. 214).

him as his surrogate self, reliving in this youth his own earlier life—
even Stein crumples visibly after Jim's death. The final sentences
of the novel record this deflation, the analogue of Jim's: "Stein has
aged greatly of late. He feels it himself, and says often that he is
'preparing to leave all this, preparing to leave . . .' while he waves
his hand sadly at his butterflies" (p. 417).

Moreover, as part of the ruthless examination to which Jim is
subjected, he is as much and as often one of "them" as he is one of
"us." Though detesting the captain of the *Patna*, decidedly one of
them, Jim nevertheless jumps into the same boat with him and commits the same crime. After the trial, Chester, another one of them,
offers him a job on a guano island; the bird excrement suggests how
far Jim has sunk in the common estimation, almost as far as Captain
Robinson, the corpselike wraith accompanying Chester, the man
who ate human flesh and became a pariah. The bellwether of
"them," the most ferociously intelligent and able of the lot, Gentleman Brown, invades Jim's secret heart and makes his fatal appeal
there.

And there ran through the rough talk a vein of subtle reference to
their common blood, an assumption of common experience; a
sickening suggestion of common guilt, of secret knowledge that was
like a bond of their minds and of their hearts. (p. 387)

The sharing of a common guilt in the desertion of mankind—momentary in Jim's case, permanent in Brown's—links the two of them
indissolubly together. They are blood brothers quite as much as
Jim and Dain Waris, presently to be slain by Brown, are blood
brothers. By way of a final definition, Marlow balances his claim
of Jim as one of us by references to him as a "flawed sovereign,"
whom he would not trust aboard his own ship even after Jim's
triumphs and seeming vindication on Patusan. Marlow himself is
painfully and persistently aware of the "them" element in Jim. "He
appealed to all sides at once—to the side turned perpetually to the
light of day, and to that side of us which, like the other hemisphere
of the moon, exists stealthily in perpetual darkness, with only a
fearful ashy light falling at times on the edge" (p. 93). The tension
between the "us" and "them" sides of Jim keeps the story in perpetual counterpoint.

Jim himself is too egotistical for us to like and treated too ironically for us to love. The pleasant, sentimental glow aroused by the heroes and heroines of nineteenth century English novels evaporates under the heat of Conrad's uncompromising moral curiosity. Jim, projected impersonally, becomes the protoplasm of human nature itself, and his story is universalized into a series of demonstrations in which Jim becomes the catalytic agent by which a multitude of other characters are brought to light as well as life. The novel resolves itself into a series of psychological episodes rather than a series of chronological events, rids itself of the strait jacket of time-narration. Events are introduced not in order of time but in order of consciousness, not because they happen one after another but because of the psychological vibrations they arouse. But Conrad does not get away from the event to concentrate wholly on the psychological vibration, as does James. He incorporates them into a fusion that is his special mark as a writer and creates the particular Conradian illusion of living simultaneously in the act and in the consciousness of the character experiencing it. This reminds us that Conrad is a rousing storyteller, a fact occasionally forgotten in the pursuit of his elusive meanings or demeaned in an age of criticism perversely disposed to look down upon the magic of storytelling as an inferior aspect of fiction.

Moreover, Conrad's brand of storytelling transcends plot and is not limited to discovering what happens. The arrangements, circumstances, and avenues of entry into an incident compel the eye as much as the formal existence of the incident itself. The details of Brierly's suicide are beautifully rendered, but it is the crafty blend of hints as to why he did it with just enough left unsaid that sets the event reverberating through the rest of the novel like a warning bell. The drowning of little Bob Stanton while trying to save a lady's maid much larger than himself occupies scarcely more than a page in the narrative (pp. 149–150), yet it exposes the ridiculous side of heroism and by so doing reveals the juvenile element in Jim's dream; in the desire to be a hero, there is always the danger of being a fool.

The final chapters dealing with events that take place after Marlow's last view of Jim are assembled in a letter from Marlow to one of the men who had listened to Marlow's tale during the long evening on the verandah of an Eastern hotel. This man is selected as the privileged listener because he is skeptical of Jim's redemption

and scornful of racial intermingling; he doubts that any good can
come from a lone white man acting outside the frame of his own
community. The last chapters are sharpened by the intimate presence of this doubting observer whose disbelief keeps the final melodrama from being taken on its own terms. Jim's death has a stagy
quality—as Doramin shoots him, he casts an unflinching glance to
the right and left, he falls with his hand on his lips—heightened by
the consciousness of a man who does not believe in the meaningful-
ness of the death at all and therefore is a counterweight to our accepting it as such too easily. A dozen other arrangements serve as
sounding boards for the critical action, lending it a resonance that
creates a constant moral and psychological accompaniment to the
physical unfolding of plot. Conrad's curious double and triple
platooning of his narrators, added to his ruthless subordination of
time to theme, lends *Lord Jim* and the novels following it a vibrant
tonality, a suppleness of comment that prefigure the art of the new
century.

The switchboard through which the comment passes is Marlow,
the same man at about the same age in life who related "Youth,"
only this time dealing not with his own youth but Jim's. Whatever
his usefulness to the author in the four tales in which he appears as
narrator, Marlow is of particular value to Conrad as a bridge to
England, or, more exactly, to the quality of being English, to Eng-
lishness. The five years from 1895 to 1900, from *Almayer's Folly* to
Lord Jim, are the period of Conrad's first and most serious attempt
to establish himself in England, not simply as a welcome foreigner
but as a man who could, however expatriated to begin with, take
root from within. Marlow is Conrad's most sustained effort at
getting inside an English skin. He is not Conrad *in toto;* he is Conrad in his English manifestation, the Pole striving to be a Briton;
he is the British Conrad not alone as he wishes to be but as he imag-
ines himself in the ideal sense. "There but for the grace of God
goes God," Winston Churchill once observed of Sir Stafford Cripps.
Marlow, but for the grace of God, is Conrad if, in another incarnation, he had been born English.

Aside from the fact that he is English and an officer in the British
merchant marine, that he bears an English name and speaks the
language idiomatically, Marlow embodies the ideas and functions
which Conrad associates with the genius of his adopted country.

Marlow assumes a middle-of-the-road position on everything and seeks to mediate between the extremes; in this, he embodies the British spirit of compromise, which manages somehow to cling to pragmatic reality without wholly losing sight of principle. In "Youth" he mediates between the attractive illusions of youth, which he plucks from memory, and the gritty deflations of middle age, the frame circling the story. In "Heart of Darkness" he mediates between the illusioned, sentimental innocence of Kurtz's Intended and the complex satanism of Kurtz himself, between the light of civilization and the darkness of primitivism, between colonializing Europe and exploited Africa. In *Lord Jim* he seeks to restore Jim to a balance between his warring selves, and serves throughout not simply as the agent of his salvation but as a buffer muting the impact of the social disapproval that threatens to vitiate Jim (with his rich capacity for sullen unhappiness) altogether. In *Chance,* a much later novel filled with ramified polyphonies, Marlow demonstrates for the last time his capacity to keep contending sides in orbit and to prevent the complicated conjecturing that informs the story from tearing it apart. He is, throughout, the supreme compromiser, the moderator of the show who yet does not renounce his own views; his role as a technician is constantly reinforced and humanized by his private apparatus of moral opinion and amateur philosophizing.

He is also a preserver, not a destroyer. Conrad saw the British Empire as the preserver of civilized values, a great stable force in a sea of anarchy. Marlow seeks to save. He saves Jim, saves himself by telling the necessary lie to Kurtz's fiancée, saves Flora de Barral from committing suicide, saves the crew in the lifeboat after the sinking of the *Judea.* When he is not saving, he is recording, totting up moral accounts, building a system of communications strong enough to withstand the malignant and hostile disorders that afflict men. He strains at every point to hold things together, not out of a naïve faith in the virtues of keeping a stiff upper lip but from a sophisticated awareness of the treacheries of human nature and the deformities of society. More than Jim, more even than Stein himself, he embodies the dictum of "in the destructive element immerse," and by his exertions strives to preserve not only himself but those around him, those within reach. His exertions remain unceasing, a supreme display of virtuoso energy, in itself a mark of an informing, life-producing vitality.

He is British in his insularity, too, managing to maintain his national identity despite years in foreign parts. The code of behavior implied in "one of us" is the code of the colonizer, conscious of his power position among the native peoples and anxious to maintain it not by force but by moral example. The white man's leadership is justified by his constant display of unflagging courage, by the steadiness of his character—to be sure. But it is exerted more subtly by the bond of mutuality, the strength of which the whites acknowledge. Not only are their eyes upon one another, but the eyes of the Asiatics are upon them as well, and each man's action expresses the power of the group. Jim's conduct, despite his acknowledged indifference, undermines the position of the group not simply by its individual example but by the doubts aroused about each of themselves in the minds of the others. This is the irritant that forces its way into Marlow, causes him to question himself, moves him to seek exculpation or justification for Jim, and leads him to tell the long tale to his listeners with the commitment not just of a chronicler but of a special pleader. More than anything else, Marlow is the conscience of the community, with whom all its members are involved as communicants; it is to Marlow that Jim confesses himself, that Brierly expresses his first doubts and discontents, that Brown (even the outlaws from the community are accountable to it) unfolds his deathbed outpourings, and that the anonymous listeners on the verandah give their protracted attention. "You are so subtle, Marlow," exclaims the host in the middle of the tale (p. 94), after a particularly involuted comment by Marlow about his own powers of understanding. But for the most part they sit in absorbed silence, the story being not only Jim's and Marlow's but theirs. It is to them that Marlow delivers his moral report, plays the role of honest broker, and invokes the white man's burden—discharging, in short, the historical functions of the Englishman.

Marlow is also the agent of civilization as against primitivism. Civilized men have to plunge into contact with the primitive— their own primitive selves as well as primitive societies—before they can get to the bottom of their own natures, but they must not linger there too long. If they do, they may be hopelessly split away from their civilized selves as was Almayer after his marriage to a Malay woman, or drowned in a swamp of suppurating, enervating, mindless sensuality like Willems in Aissa's arms, or become prey to satanic temptations like Kurtz in the heart of his African darkness. Marlow follows Kurtz to his final station, hears his last words, serves as his spiritual executor by bringing back his body and delivering a last message to his grieving sweetheart, but returns to Europe before he himself sinks irretrievably into the Kurtzian quagmire. In *Lord Jim* he makes the long journey to Patusan to see Jim on his new terrain with his own eyes, but Patusan—static, airless, primitive—begins to suffocate him, and he can hardly wait to get back to the civilized world "where events move, men change, light flickers, life flows in a clear stream, no matter whether over mud or over stones" (p. 330). The trip down-river toward the open sea defines in geographic terms Marlow's psychic claustrophobia.

> . . . we sweltered side by side in the stagnant superheated air; the smell of mud, of marsh, the primeval smell of fecund earth, seemed to sting our faces; till suddenly at a bend it was as if a great hand far away had lifted a heavy curtain, had flung open an immense portal. The light itself seemed to stir, the sky above our heads widened . . . a freshness enveloped us, filled our lungs, quickened our thoughts, our blood. . . . (p. 331)

When, accompanied by Jim, he reaches the sea, he is like a man released from some underground chamber the moment before asphyxiation.

> I breathed deeply, I revelled in the vastness of the opened horizon, in the different atmosphere that seemed to vibrate with a toil of life, with the energy of an impeccable world. This sky and this sea were open to me. . . . I responded with every fibre of my being. I let my eyes roam through space, like a man released from bonds who stretches his cramped limbs, runs, leaps, responds to the inspiring elation of freedom. "This is glorious!" I cried. (pp. 331–332)

Jim leaves him at this point, at the precise line of separation between the two worlds (and the two selves). "This is my limit," he says, for only within the tight, closed area of the primitive enclave can he thrust his amorphous dream of glory into a manageable format. But the fact that as a *tuan* he is apart from the Malays keeps him from "going native."

This does not mean that Conrad believes the civilized is "good" and the primitive "bad." (He is neither a naïve Victorian like Tennyson on this subject nor a sophisticated one like Kipling.) As life frames they are different and, in the end, incompatible, though native society produces just as many admirable figures as does civilization and civilization just as many rascals. Primitive men like Dain Maroola, Dain Waris, Hakim, Babalatchi, and Doramin can stand comparison with the best Europeans, and are infinitely superior on any scale of values to white men like Cornelius, Donkin, Schomberg, and Massy. But it still remains true that the races may intermingle only up to a point; when that point is exceeded, disintegration sets in. Willems and Kurtz are the most prominent examples of this, but Conrad's work abounds in other instances. In this sphere of experience Marlow is the instrument by which pressure is measured. He himself approaches the point of collapse on several occasions but in each case, by some instinct of preservation that Conrad associates with the British spirit, pulls back in time. He remains here, as elsewhere, the embodiment of civilization and, even more pertinently from his creator's peculiarly personal view of him, the embodiment of his country.

Conrad had acquired his formal British citizenship in 1886 largely at the urging of his uncle. He did not pay his inner allegiance until the birth of Marlow in 1898, and Marlow was his own idea, needing no urging from his uncle or anyone else. As a narrator in the stream of fiction, Marlow can be traced to his predecessors in *Bleak House, Wuthering Heights,* and the novels of Henry James, and to that most garrulous of all narrators, the schoolteacher turned sailor who calls himself Ishmael in *Moby Dick.* As the spokesman for Western society and Western ethics wherever challenged—in Africa, in the waters of the Far East—Marlow derives from Conrad's abandonment of his own role as a "loner" during his sea years and his drive to find a place for himself within the English enclave of Western society. If, as Conrad, Conrad did not wholly succeed in the personal sense, Marlow was a resounding success as his imaginative surrogate.

In this way art—that harsh taskmistress—softened her forbidding face and came to the aid of life.

VIII

Life and Death in Costaguana

SOON AFTER FINISHING "LORD JIM" CONRAD BEGAN DEPRECATING IT. Caught up in this typical mood, afflicted by the sense of failure that accompanied his greatest creations, he turned his bitterness upon himself. "The *Outcast* is a heap of sand," he wrote to Garnett on November 12, 1900, "the *Nigger* a splash of water, *Jim* a lump of clay. A stone, I suppose, will be my next gift to impatient mankind —" [1] The stone turned out to be *Nostromo*, a huge iceberg of a novel, which Robert Penn Warren accurately described as "one of the few mastering visions of our historical moment and our human lot."

The road to it was as difficult as any traversed by Conrad, but it was not marked by any spectacular new departures. His land life had begun to settle into a well defined routine, and the period from 1900, when *Lord Jim* was finished, to the end of 1904 and the completion of *Nostromo,* more or less followed the tracks grooved out by the experiences of Conrad's initial period as a writer during the last five years of the old century. It was a nervous, anxious, arduous time, striated with periods of brooding inactivity plagued by gout and a general sense of the wretchedness of existence. Conrad's talent for suffering was as great as his talent for fiction. The two capacities were more subtly intertwined than appeared on the surface. For in the midst of the blackest, most sterile despair his imagination would rouse itself to its most productive efforts, and the blank page at

[1] Garnett, p. 172. Garnett, however, was convinced that Conrad was most pleased with himself when most self-depreciatory (see his comment in the Introduction to *Letters from Joseph Conrad,* p. 27). But since Conrad deprecated his work, whether good or bad, virtually all the time, there is no basis for judging Garnett's skepticism.

which he had been staring for hours on end with deadening discouragement would begin to fill.

In this spasmodic fashion he struggled along, drawing what satisfaction he could from the occasional conviction that he was writing well and from the continuing admiration of his friends. There was little to be found in the continuing indifference of the public, in his mounting debts, and in the gloomy certainty that life, his life at any rate, was bound to be difficult, and that in the distribution of the pleasure-pain principle, pain was sure to predominate over pleasure. Halfway through *Nostromo*, he wrote to Galsworthy: "No work done. No spring left to grapple with it. Everything looks black, but I suppose that will wear off, and anyhow, I am trying to keep despair under. Nevertheless I feel myself losing my footing in deep waters. They are lapping about my hips." [2] And when the novel was done, he made a formal announcement of it to Garnett in his accustomed manner: "I drop you these lines just to say that Nostromo is finished; a fact upon which my friends may congratulate me as upon a recovery from a dangerous illness." [3]

Side by side with his imaginative writing during this period, Conrad was constantly reflecting upon the nature of art and upon the secrets of the writing process. His old instincts as a "loner" persuaded him to avoid schools, eschew *isms*, and escape theories and systems. "Theory is a cold and lying tombstone of departed truth," he had written to Garnett.[4] In the Preface to *The Nigger* he had dismissed Realism, Romanticism, Naturalism, Sentimentalism, calling them "temporary formulas" which the artist would have to abandon when, alone with his conscience and consciousness, he got down to serious work. "You stop just short of being absolutely real," he wrote to Arnold Bennett on March 10, 1902, "because you are faithful to your dogmas of realism. Now realism in art will never approach reality. And your art, your gift, should be put to the service of a larger and freer faith." [5] This larger faith was a frame that stretched beyond the tenets of a particular aesthetic viewpoint, and encompassed the ideal values that bound together all men, writer and reader included, in a feeling of unavoidable solidarity. The

[2] Letter of November 30, 1903, LL, I, 322.
[3] Garnett, p. 190.
[4] Letter of March 15, 1895, Garnett, p. 34.
[5] LL, I, 303.

ultimate aim of art, like that of life, may be obscured in mist, but its immediate aim is to communicate, and the artist must be free of dogmatisms if he is to proceed unhampered. His years of unattachment had bred in Conrad a highly developed sense of dissociation, an aversion to being tied down, a conviction that ideologies and fixed viewpoints were nets to contain art, not release it. "One does one's work first and theorizes about it afterwards," he was to state in 1920 in the Author's Note to *Tales of Unrest* (p. v).

He studied the prevailing doctrines, only to reject them in the end. ". . . where is the thing, institution or principle which I do not doubt?!" [6] He could not be a social reformer like Shaw and Wells,[7] or like his friends Galsworthy and Cunninghame Graham; he did not believe in social reform and doubted that literature should be used as a vehicle for it. Nor could he be the kind of writer that he thought Jane Austen was—a mere painter of social manners; this was altogether too restrictive and, besides, to paint society one had to be inside it, which is precisely where he had never really been; his characters were not representations of social types, classes or attitudes, but representations of human nature. Conrad was familiar with the work of the mid-nineteenth century decadents, Gautier, Baudelaire, Huysmans, and their English imitators like Oscar Wilde, but he had no sympathy for the morbidly subtilized pursuit of their attenuations of consciousness that threatened to drown them in the same immense pesthole of pathology into which Dostoevsky, whom Conrad looked upon as the destructive demon of modern literature, had plunged. Conrad wound up as he began, a free lance, and turned out what he himself soon labeled, *sui generis,* Conradese.

He allied himself more closely than before to the principle of doubt. "The fact is," he advised Galsworthy, "you want more scepticism at the very foundation of your work. Scepticism, the tonic of minds, the tonic of life, the agent of truth,—the way of art and salvation." [8] If *Lord Jim* supported the claims of society as a ground-

---

[6] Letter of March 8, 1895, Garnett, p. 33.

[7] On February 16, 1905, he wrote to Cunninghame Graham: "The stodgy sun of the future—our early Victorian future—lingers on the horizon, but all the same it will rise—it will indeed—to throw its sanitary light upon a dull world of perfected municipalities and W.C.s *sans peur et sans reproche.* The grave of individual temperaments is being dug by G.B.S. and H.G.W. with hopeful industry" (LL, II, 12).

[8] Letter of November 11, 1901, LL, I, 301.

work of human action, *Nostromo* would show all the ways in which society betrayed and undermined it. Conrad refused to take anything for granted and was forever on the alert against being taken in by his material. His characters were often victimized or sustained by illusions, but it was essential that he not be. Unless he could see through their illusions, and indeed see through the characters themselves, his art would lose its vigor and become sentimental.

At the center of Galsworthy's work was his belief in the liberal conscience, in the improvability of institutions by men of good will —the typical nineteenth century belief. But it was a belief Galsworthy assumed rather than examined, though it became the touchstone by which all social and individual conduct was judged in his work. Conrad did not believe in the liberal conscience or in the improvability of institutions as such; to him these were the reflections not of some maneuverable machine but of human nature. As long as human nature was unchanged, it was fruitless to change institutions; change alone would not bring improvement, though it was part of the modern temper to think so. Yet Conrad's complaint about Galsworthy lay not in his doctrinal disagreement over liberalism, but in his friend's failure to subject this central conviction to the same ruthless examination to which, say, he subjected such a figure as Soames Forsyte. Because he did not, his novels, in the last analysis, rested on sandy ground. Here and there, individual achievements—Soames being the most notable—survived; the work, as a whole, suffered from Galsworthy's lack of tough-mindedness. Conrad's letters to him are filled with enthusiastic compliments and warm encouragement, yet do not conceal his awareness of Galsworthy's compromised vision.

Whatever the price he would pay in popularity, Conrad did not intend to compromise his, and in *Nostromo* put this vision, and the skepticism that produced and refined it, to an ultimate test. Among the multitude of questions posed by the novel, one commanded the author's particular attention. Suppose every conceivable motive, ideal, and illusion animating human conduct were stripped away, shown to be false or untenable, what then? On what basis could humanity survive? On the basis of a belief in reality. Reality defined as a distinct source of experience apart from one's self, not indeed as a purposive process or a meliorative one or leading to some meaningful end—there is in Conrad no faith in abstract ethics, no religious conviction, no attachment to reform, and no teleology—but as a thing in itself, carrying its own solidity simply by virtue of its existence. This instinctive belief links his characters to themselves and to one another. They are alive, and the act of being alive carries with it its own momentum and, in some mysterious way, its own conviction. It is when this conviction of one's own existence dims or snaps, as with Martin Decoud, that life loses its identity and sinks back into the anonymous flux. Decoud's suicide shows Conrad in the characteristic act of examining his own conception of reality. Even it has its limits and, under certain conditions, can be metamorphosed into its own antithesis and become nonreality. In this way he remained ruthlessly faithful to the principle of skepticism, exposing to its harsh gaze even his own ultimate acceptance of life on no terms but its own, which meant embracing the possibility that there were times when even life might lose its preservative power.

For the most part, however, this power is maintained, and keeps the figures in *Nostromo* going even after they have lost their illusions. It was the same power that kept Conrad going during the public failure of his great achievements and served as a hard floor beneath which his pessimistic railings at the world and at himself could not sink. Amid his many difficulties—gout, recurrences of malaria, acute sense of displacement, his unsuccess in a new profession after his old one had petered away to its barren close, amid the stresses and strains of language, of art, of family life to which he was never by nature quite attuned and which he never wholly accepted [9]—the will to continue remained unflagging. He never ceased to believe in his own identity which, indeed, as his pessimism grew more pronounced, appeared more and more sharply defined in his own mind; in his later years, it became possible for him to refer to himself, at first ironically and then soberly, in the third person. His hold on life was continually tested and confirmed by his persistent awareness of the element of dissolution embedded within it. He had attempted suicide at twenty and later projected

[9] As a father, he was occasionally enthusiastic and often irritable. Being at home all the time greatly increased the jarring upon him of the domestic round. He never seems to have gotten over his astonishment at being a father at all, and used to complain ruefully that his two sons (born eight years apart) each entered the world on Tuesday, his best working day, thus playing havoc with his weekly schedule.

the syndrome of dissolution in his novels, of which the most celebrated and complex example was Decoud's. The death of Decoud
throws into sharper relief the continuing life of the Goulds, Dr.
Monyghan, Captain Mitchell, the Garibaldino, even for a time Nostromo, just as Conrad's philosophical gloom throws his essential
passion for life into a light made all the more bold by the pressure
to which his pessimism perpetually subjects it.

At the very end of the novel Linda Viola, deserted by Nostromo,
addresses the dead man with a cry that rings over the whole darkened gulf, "I cannot understand. But I shall never forget thee.
Never!" (p. 566). This cry, coming from her perch atop the light-
house where she turns the beacon on nightly, brings the story to a
final affirmation. Life is perhaps no more to be understood than
Nostromo by Linda, is no more perhaps than the narrow beam
of light cast by the beacon on the immense darkness of sea and
heaven, but it, like him, is unforgettable. Dr. Monyghan, who hears
the cry, feels it to be proof of Nostromo's ultimate success, proof that
he still "dominated the dark gulf containing his conquests of treasure and love" (p. 566). The magnetism of the life process survives
and on occasion transcends its defeats.

Nostromo deals with the cycle of life and death in the mythical
republic of Costaguana, but it also summons almost every other theme
encompassable in fiction. It is a full-scale account of politics, society,
the historical process, geography, economics, morality, love, revenge,
primitivism, civilization, and imperialism (not the crude early kind
of physical conquest described in "Heart of Darkness" but the
sophisticated, advanced form of capital investment, referred to in
the book as Material Interests). There is even the theme of race
relations, in the struggle between the Blanco aristocrats and the
Negro masses.

To transform the story into a microcosm of earth and man, Conrad equips his scene with multiple ramifications. The landscape
includes the ocean, a gulf, islands, an extended seacoast, a plain,
foothills, the snowcapped peak Higuerota, a rampart of mountains
virtually cutting off the province of Sulaco from the rest of Costaguana, a city, villages, hamlets, and every kind of weather including a peculiarly windless, cloudbanked darkness that settles
over the coast at night. In this totalism of nature there appears a

wide gallery of human beings. ". . . Aristocracy and People, men and women, Latin and Anglo-Saxon, bandit and politician," remarks Conrad in his Author's Note, set down "with as cool a hand as it was possible in the heat and clash of my own conflicting emotions" (p. xi). A maze of nationalities, races, and religions appears: Englishmen, Americans, Latin Americans, Italians, Frenchmen, Spaniards, Indians, Caucasians, Negroes, Catholics, Protestants, and Jews. Five languages are heard, not alone in their formal but in their dialect versions as well. Extensive reading had supplied Conrad with a mass of authentic information about South America,[10] supplementing his brief view of it in the 1870's. He proceeded to transfuse it into the intensely visualized and extraordinarily mapped state of Costaguana, which becomes not simply his "broadest canvas" as a writer but his most nearly universal frame of reference as a psychologist, moralist, and philosopher.

On its external side *Nostromo* dramatizes Conrad's disagreement with Galsworthy and Cunninghame Graham, the first a liberal, the second a socialist reformer. It demonstrates the bankruptcy of society, the folly of equating revolutionary change, whether economic or political, with betterment, and the illusory hollowness of trust in abstract ideals. It not only refutes the reformers; it also refutes *Lord Jim,* and nothing is more typical of Conrad's suspicious mind than his insistence upon reexamining his own premises. Jim had failed because he was alone, and succeeded when he entered the human community. Nostromo is drawn into the human community to begin with, and it is this which fails him. In the form of Guzman Bento the tyrant, society puts Dr. Monyghan to the torture and abuses Don José. It betrays the republican ideals of the Garibaldino and leaves him beached on a private atoll of disillusionment. Society resists the attempts of Charles Gould to stabilize it, and the efforts of Mrs. Gould to humanize it. And on the political side, it is a failure both as primitive nationalism and as finance imperialism. In the first instance it is simply the plaything of irresponsible men-children armed with guns, in the second the plaything of material interests that are totally inhuman because they are not primarily concerned with the advancement of human welfare. Dr.

[10] For a detailed account of the documentary sources of *Nostromo,* see Baines, pp. 293–297.

Monyghan's observations late in the novel sum up the point decisively:

There is no peace and no rest in the development of material interests. They have their law, and their justice. But it is founded on expediency, and is inhuman; it is without rectitude, without the continuity and the force that can be found only in a moral principle. Mrs. Gould, the time approaches when all that the Gould Concession stands for shall weigh as heavily upon the people as the barbarism, cruelty, and misrule of a few years back. (p. 511)

The "one of us" theme that permeated *Lord Jim* is turned inside out: the one is constantly betrayed by the us. Having demonstrated in the earlier novel the successful possibilities of society, Conrad now examines the multiple ways in which it fails. At the root of the failure is its mutability. Society is forever at the mercy of forces more powerful than itself; whatever equilibrium it achieves is only an uneasy stalemate among contending pressures, a stalemate inevitably of short duration. The principle of mutability is established at the very start by the flight of President-Dictator Ribiera, routed by an uprising against him (Part I, Ch. II). Eighteen months earlier (Part I, Ch. V), the same man had been guest of honor and center of attraction at a luxurious reception in the harbor attended by railroad magnates from England, the leaders of his own Blanco party at home, and General Montero, his markedly nonwhite, crudely plebeian War Minister soon to head the revolt against him. The contrast between these two events illustrates the protean nature of society and political institutions. It is characteristic of Conrad that he should introduce Ribiera's two appearances in the novel in reverse order of time, with his downfall (in which he barely escapes with his life and only because of the timely intervention of Nostromo and his cargadores) coming first.

Nostromo himself is soon to go through the same experience, upended by social transmutations for which he is in no way responsible. He is a kind of reverse Jim, instinctively brave, resourceful, reliable in emergencies, faithful to his word, willing to risk his life for the good of the community. However, he does so out of vanity, the vanity of being thought well of by others. The vanity of an excellent reputation is the most social of all qualities, approved and sanctioned by society, owing, in fact, its very existence to society.

Nostromo is the social artifact through and through, and serves in the novel which significantly bears his name as the barometer that records the health, the fortunes, and the vicissitudes of the state.

After he has been betrayed by the state and no longer believes in it, he continues for a time to defend it almost by reflex action. The last of his great deeds, the six-day ride through dangerous country to Cayta to summon the army of Barrios which, upon its return by sea, overthrows the Monteristas and restores the moderate rule of the material interests, is done simply out of habit. But, though continuing to serve them, Nostromo believes himself abandoned by the "hombres finos," as he now calls Captain Mitchell, Gould, and the others, whose unrewarded servant he feels he has been. Accordingly, he does not sail with Barrios into the harbor, but jumps overboard in the Gulf when he sights the empty rowboat in which Decoud had committed suicide. He clambers into it, paddles to the Great Isabel, and resolves to steal the buried silver. This is his revenge on the betraying state.

By stealing the silver, he feels that he is depriving the state of the thing it holds most dear. In the end, however, he succeeds only in undermining himself. Theft, and the necessity "to grow rich slowly" as he puts it, imposes upon his candid nature a stealth and secretiveness not natural to it. In the dark of night, coming to remove more ingots from the treasure, he is killed by the Garibaldino who mistakes him for an unwelcome suitor coming to rob him of his younger daughter. Ironically, Nostromo, in truth, does intend to run off with the girl, and his death, though accidental and technically a case of mistaken identity, is not at bottom a case of mistaken identity at all. In avenging himself upon society, Nostromo betrays the Garibaldino, betrays the older daughter Linda to whom he is betrothed, betrays his own self, and so effects his own defeat. But it is a defeat stemming in the first place from his abandonment by society. Nostromo—*nostre uomo,* our man, the our representing the act of social possession—finally becomes his own man, but becomes it too late. Jim succeeded when he at last became "one of us." Nostromo was overthrown because he was altogether "our man" and not sufficiently his own.

The problem of equilibrium between the individual and society is delicately poised in *Nostromo* and affects everyone. Dr. Monyghan, tortured by the old tyrant Guzman Bento and his clerical agent Father Beron,[11] confessed to crimes he did not commit and accused innocent friends of fictitious conspiracies. Dr. Monyghan was a stubborn prisoner, but in the end "his subjugation had been very crushing and very complete. That is why the limp in his walk, the twist of his shoulders, the scars on his cheeks were so pronounced. His confessions when they came at last were very complete, too. Sometimes on the nights when he walked the floor, he wondered, grinding his teeth with shame and rage, at the fertility of his imagination when stimulated by a sort of pain which makes truth, honour, self-respect, and life itself matters of little moment" (p. 373).

Thus outraged by the state and humiliated by his own weakness, he turned into a sour, misanthropic man gloomily living out his days and suspecting others of the same corruption he had found in himself. He disliked Nostromo because of the cargador's reputation for incorruptibility, which he found an unbearable reproach. Only Mrs. Gould, to whom he attached himself with single-minded zeal, saved him from utter morbid solitude. It is she who deliberately withholds from him the news of Nostromo's thievery, and thus prevents Dr. Monyghan from sinking into the morass of his vengeful self. His equilibrium, such as it is, is maintained by a single slender life line to a woman whose fragility emphasizes the tenuousness of his connection with the world.

Mrs. Gould—the most attractive and appealing of Conrad's women—also suffers from a steady corrosion of her ties to the world. A natural idealist, a creature to whom the necessity to love is the equivalent of life, she falls under the spell of her husband's dream to bring civilization and order to Costaguana through the development of the silver mine. Their marriage begins under the spur of this imperative.[12] While Charles Gould develops the mine, she devotes herself to the miners and their families, seeking through personal acts of charity and kindness to improve their lot. Before

[11] After the torture, Father Beron would return "with that dull, surfeited look which can be seen in the eyes of gluttonous persons after a heavy meal" (p. 372). After this startling image Conrad goes on to remark: "At no time of the world's history have men been at a loss how to inflict mental and bodily anguish upon their fellow-creatures" (p. 373). There is nothing unique about Father Beron. His inquisitorial instincts, we are told, have a long ancestry.

[12] Yet in the room where Gould proposes to her, there stands a cracked marble vase (p. 61), ominously foreshadowing the canker that is to devour the ensuing marriage.

long the whole community comes to love her, to depend upon her, to be grateful for her existence, from Blanco aristocrats like Don José, to Nostromo, Dr. Monyghan, the Garibaldino (for whom she gets spectacles, a gesture symbolizing her humane function), and the humblest natives in the town created by the mine on the sprawling side of the mountain. Yet amid these favorable auspices, surrounded by auguries of good fortune, the blight that attacks everyone in the novel attacks her as well. Her husband, absorbed by the silver mine, is at last obsessed with it, gives it more and more of himself, and allows his wife to wither emotionally. More demanding than a mistress, the mine cozens Gould out of his marriage and replaces Mrs. Gould as the object not so much of his affections as of his vital energies.

Still, something might have been saved if the ideal of civilization represented by the mine had been advanced, at whatever cost to their personal lives. But the blight that falls upon them personally settles first upon the ideal, and poisons it, too. Far from producing order and stability, the silver arouses the greed of politicians hungry for office. It creates a state within a state, subject not to the laws of the community but to the demands of the moneyed powers symbolized by Holroyd, the American millionaire whose capital makes the San Tomé mine possible, and by Gould himself, who is soon referred to as the King of Sulaco. It corrupts Nostromo, drives Sotillo to murder Hirsch, encourages native uprisings by the stimulation of antiforeign sentiment, and unhinges the ties between men by substituting material demands for human imperatives. When Gould discovers all this, it is already too late. His marriage has atrophied. Instead of attending his wife, he has attended the mine; instead of loving her, he has loved it. Dr. Monyghan, in love with Mrs. Gould himself, watches it all and suffers mutely. The mine, operated by Gould's father and uncle, had not prevented the tyranny of Guzman Bento. Revived by Charles, it had not prevented the Monterista uprising. At the end of the novel the Monteristas are overthrown, the San Tomé is in full operation again, foreign capital is once more pouring in freely, the province of Sulaco has seceded from Costaguana and, following Decoud's blueprint, set itself up as an independent state. Yet in the cycle of history, in the mutability of institutions, the present "moderate" phase is surely temporary, and the seeds of another revolutionary uprising based on the old slogans of death to the foreigners are already visible. Society, in the eye of history, is a quicksand in which the characters struggle for footing, and always in vain.

The Goulds are possessed by the illusion of historical progress in its typical nineteenth century form: that the world can be made better by good will, energy, and unselfish idealism. Moreover, they cannot rest unless they are making it better. They fail despite their most zealous, well-intentioned efforts; and because the success of their marriage depends on the success of the silver mine, when the mine fails to fulfill its ideal purpose their marriage decays. They, too, like Nostromo, pay a heavy price for their faith in society, and reveal the folly of giving up their selves for its sake. Central to Conrad's ideology is the failure of ideology—whether sentimental liberalism, anarchism, imperialism, nihilism, capitalism, or even nationalism. Costaguana is strewn with the wreckage of formal programs for social betterment—Gould's, Don José's, Decoud's (whose blueprint, ironically, materializes after he himself has ceased to believe in it), Holroyd's, Father Corbelàn's, and others.

But life in *Nostromo* does not cease with the bankruptcy of social ideas and idealism. Mrs. Gould's personality survives the end of her social commitment in a way that Nostromo's does not. There is a sweetness of temper in her, a natural kindliness and courtesy, a moral energy that affects those around her, a power of communication that carries with it the power to evoke communication, that place her in sharp contrast to her husband. Charles Gould is an aloof, silent man, impressive in his self-possession, but cold, withdrawn, and forbidding. When her dream fades, she falls back on the resources of her personality and maintains her human place in life even though she has been badly wounded. Her relations with others remain intact, as does her fastidious sense of values. The final demonstration of her intactness comes on Nostromo's deathbed when he wishes to tell her the location of the buried silver. She refuses to listen; she does not want to hear; the silver she now recognizes to be a curse crushing not only her husband but all men who give themselves to it. By her refusal she acknowledges the end of her illusion, passes moral judgment upon it, and manifests her capacity to survive in her personal self now that it is over. As she leaves the dying man, Dr. Monyghan, eager to confirm his suspicion that the incorruptible Nostromo has been corrupted, begs her to tell him the capataz's last words. " 'He told me nothing,' said Mrs. Gould, steadily" (p. 560). With this comment, not strictly the truth, she repudiates the false dream represented by the silver, preserves Dr. Monyghan from a last outburst of destructive cynicism, and re-asserts her own capacity for purposive action in the personal if no longer in the social sphere. As we see the first lady of Sulaco at the end of the book, she remains "considered, loved, respected, hon-oured, and as solitary as any human being had ever been, perhaps, on this earth" (p. 555). Her solitude is the price she must pay for the treachery of the social idealism which had stultified her mar-riage.

Society as an illusory or disintegrative force leaves its mark on everyone and forces everyone to submit to the test which Mrs. Gould, though deeply injured, manages to pass—the test of person-ality. Each of the characters, thrown back upon himself, endures it in his own particular way. Mrs. Gould and Dr. Monyghan, blessed with intelligence as well as sensibility, manage to maintain a pre-carious balance. Charles Gould has so abandoned his private self and made so irrevocable a commitment to the mine that after its failure as a social agent he continues to cling to it as the only thing left for him to do; the draining of his lifework of its value leaves him no less aloof than before, but pitiable instead of impressive. Like his wife, he continues externally to function as before, but joylessly now and without zeal. Decoud, a man of powerful intelli-gence, suffers from a lack of feeling, or rather from a lack of faith in the validity of his feelings. He is in love with Antonia de Avel-lanos, a beautiful and patriotic Blanco, puts aside his own skepti-cism about Costaguana politics, and throws himself into the cause of political reform in order to win her favor. But when isolated with the treasure on an island in the Gulf, his passion begins to blur; his intelligence comes to the fore and convinces him of his own insig-nificance in the vast scheme of nature. When his sense of his own identity vanishes altogether, Decoud kills himself. His personality is exaggeratedly rational; this creates the disharmony that under-mines him. The indistinctness of his love—his one genuine emotion —is dramatized and indeed made convincing by the vagueness of Antonia as a person. She is an assemblage of glossy adjectives, a handsome exterior with nothing inside. In Decaud's fevered mind, she appears for the last time not as a woman but "gigantic and lovely like an allegorical statue" (p. 498). Her inchoate dimness in the novel makes it possible for us to believe that in his crucial hour, and alone, Decoud forgets her with remarkable speed and forthwith plunges himself through death into "the immense indifference of things" (p. 501).

If Decoud's tragedy lies in the subordination of his heart to his rational powers, Nostromo's is the reverse. He suffers from an excess of feeling uncontrolled by any trace of the disinterestedness or perspective that usually accompanies ideas. When the fixed world dissolves before him, Nostromo abandons himself utterly to his feelings of betrayal, as Decoud abandons himself to his intellectual skepticism. All the sensible advice Nostromo had received in advance from people like Mrs. Viola, warning him that he was being used by the gentry to serve their interests and not his, he brushed aside, so that when his disillusionment comes he believes the warnings in retrospect with far more conviction than they deserve. In this way he swings from one kind of mindlessness to another, and succeeds only in subverting his magnificent natural attributes. That Conrad admires these attributes is plain from the famous passage describing Nostromo as he awakens from the long sleep after the coup with the silver:

Nostromo . . . arose full length from his lair in the long grass. He stood knee deep amongst the whispering undulations of the green blades with the lost air of a man just born into the world. Handsome, robust, and supple, he threw back his head, flung his arms open, and stretched himself with a slow twist of the waist and a leisurely growling yawn of white teeth, as natural and free from evil in the moment of waking as a magnificent and unconscious wild beast. Then, in the suddenly steadied glance fixed upon nothing from under a forced frown, appeared the man. (pp. 411–412)

His "suddenly steadied glance fixed upon nothing" reveals Nostromo's particular self. At home in the world of the sensory and concrete, he is helpless in the flux of emotion and idea, with its treacherous and unpredictable shifts of direction. These shifts are indicated by his change of name. He is Nostromo until emotionally upended by the Montero uprising. The approaching change is indicated when he runs into Dr. Monyghan in the dark and feels "an inexplicable repugnance to pronounce the name by which he was known" (p. 425). He gives no name at all but announces himself simply as a cargador. Afterward he is called by his real name, Captain Fidanza, restored to him, as it were, when he is thrown back unhappily upon himself. As Captain Fidanza, he is a thief of both money and love, and cut off from ties with society. Self-interest is his single motive. It is a motive uncomplicated by ideological considerations, for though he considers himself exploited by the English capitalists, one of the lower classes destined to be oppressed by the upper, he refuses to contribute financially to the proletarian cause. In this he is faithful to his new role and new self. He refuses to pay any heed to others, all others, whether of his own class or not. Nostromo has all but disappeared in the tidal wave of events and another man cast up in his stead. He is the supreme victim of the mutability which in Conrad's eyes embodies and undermines the social and historical process.

Another of its victims is Hirsch, the Jewish hide merchant, whose career, like Nostromo's, depends on the stability of the social order. When it breaks up, when trade is no longer possible and the ordinary protections enjoyed by individuals in normal times are removed, he dissolves into a quivering mass of palpitating and hysterical fear. Since in Conrad events have a way of thrusting men into situations where their hidden weaknesses will be brought to the surface, Hirsch finds himself in exactly those emergencies where personal initiative and steady nerves—the qualities he most painfully lacks—are demanded. He takes refuge on the lighter just before Decoud and Nostromo take off on their perilous journey. In the collision with Sotillo's troopship, he is swept off freakishly and falls into the hands of the invading army. Interrogated on shore as to the whereabouts of the missing silver, he gives forth such a burble of incoherent answers that Sotillo hangs him up by the wrists, and then, while Hirsch is in this crucifixion posture, shoots him dead in a sudden spasm of frustrated rage. Throughout these peculiarly painful and embarrassing scenes, the Jew apotheosizes the man who draws all his sustenance from society, who depends utterly upon society as a fixed, formulated, and permanent entity—the very attributes it does not possess.

The heart of the social theme in *Nostromo* is polarized by the positions of Captain Mitchell, who believes in society through thick and thin despite all evidence to the contrary, and Martin Decoud, who does not believe in it at all. Captain Mitchell is one of those men in Conrad—Captain MacWhirr is another—announced to us as insensitive, unimaginative, and unaware. But whereas with MacWhirr this is an outer shell beneath which another man lurks, Captain Mitchell is, throughout, stubbornly inflexible in his vision of life. This vision rests on a single imperative: the world is essentially a decent, orderly place, successfully resisting the forces seeking to make it otherwise. When bad times come and the harbor falls into Sotillo's hands, when Mitchell himself is made prisoner in his own warehouse, his chronometer stolen,[13] his personal dignity affronted, when law and order to all intents have given way to disordered outlawry, he never for a moment doubts that this is only a brief, unpleasant interregnum and that in due course things will come back to normal. He has no grounds for this conviction except his own faith that it is so. But this faith, instinctive, unreasoning, sustains him in the moment of danger, moves him to confront Sotillo courageously, maintains his dignity in his demand that his purloined watch be returned, and altogether enables him to live through the crisis with a genuine if crotchety heroism. He is wrong about everything, wrong in his belief that Sotillo is only an irritating nuisance and not a dangerous man, wrong about the world being a stable place governed by traditional decencies, wrong about his own importance in the scheme of things.[14] Yet these errors, by their very nature, tilt him toward life and enable him to survive more or less intact. Courage and dignity in his case are at once externally right and internally wrong; they are the husks of virtue rather than virtue itself since they are the products of stupidity and insensibility.

By contrast, Decoud is intelligent and acutely sensitive, but these qualities lead him to death. His conviction that society is amorphous and unreliable is supported by far more evidence in the novel than Mitchell's belief to the contrary. His belief that nothing in the universe can stand the test of analysis except his own sensations is borne out by the whole history of his native Costaguana, whether

[13] The chronometer is a symbol of his attachment to orderliness. Its theft is a sign of disorder, and as such affects him painfully.

[14] In Mrs. Gould's salon, he appears "slightly pompous . . . a little disregarded and unconscious of it; utterly in the dark, and imagining himself to be in the thick of things" (p. 112). Threatened by Sotillo, he feels no physical fear: "It was not so much firmness of soul as the lack of a certain kind of imagination" (p. 338). His pompous manner and garrulous style of speech express his sense that all is well with the world and himself in it.

seen at home in Sulaco or from his earlier vantage point as a boulevardier in Paris. By a remarkable paradox his capacity to be objective leads him to believe only in his own subjectivity, while Captain Mitchell's total incapacity to be objective leads him to embrace the permanence of objective principle. Decoud is betrayed by a passion for Antonia, which compels him to actions he cannot rationally justify. He thus commits himself to the very social process he does not believe in, and sets into being the chain of events that end in his suicide. His enforced solitude on the Great Isabel is the final test of his own subjective reality. It is a test which Decoud does not pass. In the eye of the immensely indifferent universe, confronted with the undifferentiated emptiness of things, his self-belief and at last his self crumble under the pressure of an insupportable nothingness. Captain Mitchell could have remained on the island till doomsday without turning a hair, absolutely certain that sooner or later he would be rescued. Devoid of any belief in the efficacy of outside human agencies, Decoud is thrust against the naked cosmos. The confrontation is too much for him. He dissolves into the formlessness of matter. Just as Captain Mitchell is saved by his credence (however unsound) in society, so Decoud is lost by a leap (inspired by Antonia) into the very social and political involvement to whose value he never for a moment subscribed.

Nostromo deals not alone with society in general but the society of a particular period, place, and epoch. Costaguana is not only a country, but a South American country. It represents social and political institutions with certain universal and unchanging characteristics, but also those of a primitive, semifeudal community coming in the late nineteenth century in convulsive contact with the energies of the advancing industrial age pouring into it from the outside. The results of this contact are morally dubious and physically unsettling. The railroad puts an end to popular feasts (p. 123), moves through the countryside with hideous, ear-splitting noise (p. 172), and is altogether inimical to the flourishing of local custom. The telegraph thrusts its wire deep into the Campo, "like a slender vibrating feeler of that progress waiting . . . to twine itself about the weary heart of the land" (p. 166). The San Tomé mine lies in its mountain range like an immense ulcer.

Worked in the early days mostly by means of lashes on the backs of slaves, its yield had been paid for in its own weight of human bones. Whole tribes of Indians had perished in the exploitation; and then the mine was abandoned, since with this primitive method it had ceased to make a profitable return no matter how many corpses were thrown into its maw. (p. 52)

Later, it grew into a symbol of foreign exploitation maneuvered by ambitious politicians. It led the first group of English managers to their deaths, broke the heart of Charles Gould's father, and ate the heart out of Charles himself.

These ambiguous contributions of the new age to the well-being of Costaguana are the products of English and American capital. Conrad, frequently and inaccurately accused of being critical of all forms of colonialism except the British, had already had his say about Dutch imperialism in the Malay novels, Belgian and French imperialism in "Heart of Darkness." Faithful to his principle of skepticism, which demanded that he examine his closest, most intimately held feelings, Conrad examines Anglo-Saxon imperialism in *Nostromo* and finds it, if physically more tolerable, morally no more attractive than the others. The American millionaire Holroyd, whose special passion was the endowment of churches on a large scale in the countries where he invested his capital, expresses his views of Costaguana and of America's manifest destiny in an energetically ingenuous outburst:

Now, what is Costaguana? It is the bottomless pit of 10 per cent loans and other fool investments. European capital had been flung into it with both hands for years. Not ours, though. We in this country know just about enough to keep indoors when it rains. We can sit and watch. Of course, some day we shall step in. We are bound to. But there's no hurry. Time itself has got to wait on the greatest country in the whole of God's universe. We shall be giving the word for everything: industry, trade, law, journalism, art, politics, and religion, from Cape Horn clear over to Smith's Sound, and beyond, too, if anything worth taking hold of turns up at the North Pole. And then we shall have the leisure to take in hand the outlying islands and continents of the earth. We shall run the world's business whether the world likes it or not. The world can't help it—and neither can we, I guess. (pp. 76–77)

Sir John, the British railway magnate, is a less voluble but no less characteristic member of the same species. And Charles Gould himself, an Englishman through and through, is the most committed of all. Decoud, who understands everything all too acutely, defines the

Englishman in general and Gould in particular in these mordant terms.

> . . . he cannot act or exist without idealizing every simple feeling, desire, or achievement. He could not believe his own motives if he did not make them first a part of some fairy tale. The earth is not quite good enough for him, I fear. Do you excuse my frankness? Besides, whether you excuse it or not, it is part of the truth of things which hurts the—what do you call them?—the Anglo-Saxon's susceptibilities. . . . (pp. 214–215)

But the English tendency to sentimentalize their most self-interested actions—a tendency embraced by the Americans—does not ultimately conceal the self-interest that lies at the heart of the whole imperialist process. Abandoned mines have a strong fascination for Gould. "Their desolation appealed to him like the sight of human misery" (p. 59), filling him with an urge to reclaim them. But while he is intensely conscious of the mine, he is only dimly conscious of the natives whose welfare will presumably be advanced. The mine, not the miners or the country or the alleviation of misery, is really the center of his imaginative life. Gould finally comes to recognize that in Costaguana he is an adventurer, not a humanitarian, with something of the adventurer's "easy morality," that if it will advance his own ends he is prepared to blow the San Tomé mine sky-high (pp. 365–366) quite as though it belonged to him personally rather than leased to him as a concession by the government.

Mrs. Gould is deceived into thinking otherwise when she mistakes her husband's analogies for the objects of his interest. By the time Decoud ironically defines him for her, she already suspects the painful truth and therefore does not prevent Decoud from bluntly uttering it.[15] The mine acquires for Holroyd, also, a peculiarly feverish interest, so that though it is only a minor operation in his vast undertakings, he attends to it himself, a caprice of the great man which arouses much joking and speculation among his subordinates. The mine appears to him in the form of a man, Gould, and it is the running of the man (p. 81) which lends the whole investment its fierce and particular attraction to Holroyd. He, too, like Gould,

---

[15] His caustic remarks are echoed by Lieutenant Réal in Conrad's last completed novel, *The Rover:* "They [the English] like to have God on their side—the only ally they never need pay a subsidy to" (p. 116).

must coat his passion for things with a humane gloss—the typical
mark of the sentimental idealist. Yet the imperialism of the sentimental idealist is no less imperialist than that of the naked ex-
ploiter. Holroyd is prepared to drop Gould and his mine at the first
sign of failure, just as Gould is prepared to destroy the mine altogether if his plans for it are thwarted.

The internal politics of Costaguana is different in texture but on
no higher a plane. The constant uprisings, always in the name of
saving the country, seem to Mrs. Gould "a puerile and blood-thirsty
game of murder and rapine played with terrible earnestness by depraved children" (p. 49). Wherever she went, she heard stories of
political outrage.

. . . friends, relatives, ruined, imprisoned, killed in the battles of
senseless civil wars, barbarously executed in ferocious proscriptions,
as though the government of the country had been a struggle of lust
between bands of absurd devils let loose upon the land with sabres
and uniforms and grandiloquent phrases. And on all the lips she
found a weary desire for peace, the dread of officialdom with its
nightmareish parody of administration without law, without security and without justice. (p. 88)

One Army of Pacification, led by the Citizen Saviour Guzman
Bento, moved through the countryside with its file of emaciated
prisoners (Don José among them) dispensing justice and salvation
in about equal measure.

A lucky one or two of that spectral company of prisoners would perhaps be led tottering behind a bush to be shot by a file of soldiers.
Always an army chaplain—some unshaven, dirty man, girt with a
sword and with a tiny cross embroidered in white cotton on the left
breast of a lieutenant's uniform—would follow, cigarette in the
corner of the mouth, wooden stool in hand, to hear the confession
and give absolution; for the Citizen Saviour of the Country (Guzman Bento was called thus officially in petitions) was not averse
from the exercise of rational clemency. The irregular report of the
firing squad would be heard, followed sometimes by a single finishing shot; a little bluish cloud of smoke would float up above the
green bushes, and the Army of Pacification would move on over the
savannas, through the forests, crossing rivers, invading rural pueblos,
devastating the haciendas of the horrid aristocrats, occupying the
inland towns in the fulfilment of its patriotic mission, and leaving
behind a united land wherein the evil taint of Federalism could no

longer be detected in the smoke of burning houses and the smell of spilt blood. (p. 138)

The Monterist revolution itself lay "rooted in the political immaturity of the people, in the indolence of the upper classes and the mental darkness of the lower" (p. 387). If the masses fall victim to the claims of demagogic tyrants, it is for lack of skepticism, the quality which Conrad accused Galsworthy of not having enough of and which Decoud had altogether too much of: "The popular mind is incapable of scepticism; and that incapacity delivers their helpless strength to the wiles of swindlers and to the pitiless enthusiasm of leaders inspired by visions of a high destiny" (p. 420).

The individual personalities who rise to the surface of Costaguana politics are a fascinatingly varied but generally unappetizing lot. Guzman Bento is an illiterate peasant who commits the most shocking cruelties in the name of democracy. General Montero is cut from the same bolt. His younger brother Pedro, however, is an ambitious opportunist of another sort. Blessed with a sly intelligence, "with an apelike faculty for imitating all the outward signs of refinement and distinction, and with a parrot-like talent for languages" (p. 386), he had spent some years in Europe on the fringe of his country's consulates and legations, devouring historical novels whose heroes made their fortunes and pursued their private pleasures simultaneously. With this image of success, he returns home, seizes the occasion of his brother's successful uprising to play his own game, and by a series of bold actions almost carries the day. When the Monterists are overthrown, Pedro flees for his life into exile and is last seen "arrayed in purple slippers and a velvet smoking-cap with a gold tassel, keeping a disorderly house in one of the southern ports" (p. 487). With this exit of the most talented native politician, Conrad makes his final ironic comment on the quality of the revolutionary leadership.

He finishes off his Costaguana gallery with a series of brilliant flourishes. Father Corbelàn is another impassioned patriot, but "the idea of political honour, justice and honesty for him consists in the restitution of the confiscated Church property" (pp. 188–189). The two Sulaco deputies, Gamacho and Fuentes, tribunes of the people as it were, who leap from faction to faction as expediency dictates, have their hour of glory when Pedro arrives from over the mountains at the head of his Monterist band. One lean, one fat, they are savage cartoons of greed, vanity, stupidity, and, in terms of their own interests, imbecile behavior. But they are only trial runs en route to the creation of Sotillo, one of the superbly drawn minor villains in literature, no Lucifer certainly, but every inch a bush-league Beelzebub. He, too, had been a Blanco when the Blancos were in the saddle, but now with Montero on the rise had no diffi-culty switching sides. His hunger for the silver shipment works in him like a malignant fever. It drives him to Sulaco at the head of a troopship in the dead of night, unhinges his temper when the treasure does not fall into his hands, persuades him against his bet-ter judgment to kill Hirsch, and makes it possible for Dr. Monyghan to bamboozle him into thinking that the silver has been sunk within reach in the harbor. While on this wild-goose chase, he neglects to join forces with Pedro, a fatal misstep that permits Barrios to put both of them to rout. Sotillo is a variation on the Willems type, the man driven to self-destruction by the working of a single uncontroll-able impulse. By catching him in a characteristic moment, Conrad lights up his whole psychic landscape in a sudden flash.

Every time he went in and came out with a slam of the door, the sentry on the landing presented arms, and got in return a black, venomous, unsteady glance, which, in reality, saw nothing at all, being merely the reflection of the soul within—a soul of gloomy hatred, irresolution, avarice, and fury. (p. 448)

Well-intentioned figures like Don José do appear, but they are curiously ineffectual. Don José's courage under ill-treatment by Guzman Bento, Don Pépé's unwavering loyalty to Charles Gould, the naïve goodness of Father Roman are admirable traits; yet they do not alter the rush of events, and are only small islands in an eruptive sea. Political and social life in Costaguana encourages flexibility, change, and suppleness of conduct, rewarding those who embody these traits most pliantly. But even their success is irresist-ibly temporary, soon to be swallowed up in the unceasing flux. Since society in its political aspect does not encourage virtue, virtue never appears in a powerful enough form to redeem expediency, and Don José's memoir *Fifty Years of Misrule,* while assuredly accurate, highly civilized, and no doubt excellently written, is scarcely a bulwark in the Costaguana storm. Primitive nationalism, uncouth, unthinking, undisciplined, is an ugly phenomenon. The tragedy is that contact with advancing industrialism may sophisticate it, but renders it no less ugly by failing to endow it with any moral imperative. The whole record of society in *Nostromo,* on the political as well as the personal side, is thereby turned into a complex and heartbreaking failure.

Even so, life goes on, under its own momentum, requiring no justification other than its own continuance. This to Conrad is the great mystery, the impenetrable first cause, though as in the singular instance of Decoud not without its mysterious lapses. After all supports have been stripped away, all illusions dispelled, it is nevertheless possible for Dr. Monyghan to continue in a state of self-abhorrence, Nostromo to function without adulation, Mrs. Gould to carry on without idealism, Gould to proceed with the mine without belief in its magical powers, and the Garibaldino to survive the total destruction of his republican hopes. It even wells up in Hirsch when, hanging in mid-air, beaten, abused, humiliated, in a state of almost total shock, he spits in his tormentor Sotillo's face in a last spasm of outraged dignity, though this immediately provokes the shot that kills him.

Nostromo may be devoted to the theme of social dissolution, but it is also an account of the persistence of man. After the slogans have been exploded, the ideologies abandoned, the illusions discarded, when Conrad's determined skepticism cuts through to the naked uncomforting face of things, the power and the will to endure remain. All this is more relevant to men deep in the twentieth century than at its start. Conrad is never more out of his own time and more prescient of ours than in his affirmation of life on terms that are deliberately purged of sentiment, freed from the coloration of nineteenth century idealism, and beaten into a hardness designed to withstand the corrosiveness of wishful thinking. Here, too, his deliberate "coldness" of manner, his flat refusal to allow us to "love" his characters—the sort of emotion pervasive in Dickens and rampant in Dostoevsky—supports his unsoftened, unflinching view, a view that would only be masked or muted by too close an attachment. As in *Lord Jim,* Conrad holds us off at arm's length from too close a fraternization with his figures. It is not warmth of feeling but depth of understanding he is after. The *valeurs idéales* of his art, which he referred to so often, were a massive attempt to illuminate existence, not to supply the reader with the warm glow of personal identification. Of the major personages in *Nostromo*, not one, not even the admirable Mrs. Gould, is allowed to touch our hearts or linger very long in our affections. Conrad's skepticism keeps them at a calculated and astringent distance.

The whole life-death cycle in Costaguana is treated in the same way, and given a final definition when Conrad questions the reality of reality. Everyone in the novel is faced at some point or other with unhingement from his accepted moorings, with a sense of life, familiar life, coming to an end. This reaches Captain Mitchell in a muffled form and, at the other extreme, reaches Decoud with radical finality. Nostromo himself feels as though he has died and been reborn into another life, the same sensation that afflicts Dr. Monyghan after his torture. With this generic passage through a kind of death, the illusory nature of being is called into view, and the uncertainty of what is real suggested.

Conrad had used as the epigraph to *An Outcast of the Islands* a somber quotation from Calderón's tragedy *La Vida Es Sueno* (Life Is a Dream). Sitting in the Casa Viola just before taking off on the fateful journey in the lighter, Decoud concludes a long letter to his sister with a reference to the theme sounded in Calderón's title: " '. . . the whole thing, the house, the dark night, the silent children in this dim room, my very presence here—all this is life, must be life, since it is so much like a dream.' With the writing of the last line there came upon Decoud a moment of sudden and complete oblivion. He swayed over the table as if struck by a bullet" (p. 249). He recovers from this sensation of oblivion, but later that night, aboard the lighter in the silent, windless Gulf, he has his second psychic brush with death. It appears, appropriately, in one of *Nostromo*'s magnificent passages:

. . . the enormous stillness, without light or sound, seemed to affect Decoud's senses like a powerful drug. He didn't even know at times whether he were asleep or awake. Like a man lost in slumber, he heard nothing, he saw nothing. Even his hand held before his face did not exist for his eyes. The change from the agitation, the passions and the dangers, from the sights and sounds of the shore, was so complete that it would have resembled death had it not been for the survival of his thoughts. In this foretaste of eternal peace they floated vivid and light, like unearthly clear dreams of earthly things that may haunt the souls freed by death from the misty atmosphere of regrets and hopes. Decoud shook himself, shuddered a bit, though the air that drifted past him was warm. He had the strangest sensation of his soul having just returned into his body from the circumambient darkness in which land, sea, sky, the mountains, and the rocks were as if they had not been. (p. 262)

This second encounter is more acute and powerful than the first. Both are preliminary to Decoud's suicide, which is the physical climax to his third severance with reality, a severance at last too overwhelming for him to withstand.

This structural arrangement illustrates what Conrad and Hueffer meant in their literary confabulations by a *progression d'effet,* during which a theme acquires a cumulative meaning by being struck at different times in differing contexts. Conrad adds enormously to its range by introducing a given theme not simply inside the experience of a single character but laterally over his entire cast. The theme of lost identity, the sudden sharp sense of separation from life with its accompanying loss of conviction about reality, reaches its most spectacular point with Decoud, but it is sounded on various levels of intensity with the other figures as well. He uses the same strategy in the other novels. Conrad's narrative art is surcharged with leitmotifs, whose progression serves to bind together the materials of each story.

In *Nostromo* the device assumes a highly developed form. The themes of historical mutability, political dissolution, and the treacherous fabric of society interpenetrate the personal themes of idealism, vanity, and love. All are contained within the ultimate cycle of life and death which turns Costaguana, that typical and prophetically relevant South American republic, into an intensely yet delicately wrought microcosm of the human situation.

IX

The Ecology of Art

CONRAD'S OWN SITUATION DID NOT VISIBLY CHANGE WITH THE COM-
pletion of his monumental work. Nothing remotely resembling
Nostromo had appeared in English fiction. But the book-buying
public could not have cared less, and popular success remained
as remote as ever. The failure of his works to sell ground into his
spirit. He felt permanently condemned to play the role of Sisyphus, but characteristically saw himself as even worse off, because
his stone never seemed to move at all. In a letter to the Gals-
worthys on August 14, 1906, he wrote: "Sisyphus was better off.
He did not get periodically his stone on the top. That it rolled
down again is a mere circumstance and I wouldn't complain if I had
his privilege. But I roll and roll and don't seem to gain an inch
up the slope. And that is distinctly damnable." [1]

His discouragement in the period following *Nostromo* can be
gauged from his bitter remark to Ada Galsworthy that in the
whole of 1908, with thirteen books behind him, his royalties
amounted to less than five pounds.[2] He grew increasingly soured
on the reading public. ". . . you will realize the inconceivable
stupidity of the common reader—the man who forks out the half
crown," he wrote to Norman Douglas,[3] then beginning his career.
Two years later his misanthropy had broadened.

. . . no artist can give it what it wants because humanity doesn't
know what it wants. But it will swallow everything. It will swallow
Hall Caine and John Galsworthy, Victor Hugo and Martin Tup-
per. It is an ostrich, a clown, a giant, a bottomless sack. . . . It

[1] LL, II, 36.
[2] Letter of January 17, 1909, LL, II, 94.
[3] Letter of February 29, 1908, LL, II, 68.

has swallowed Christianity, Buddhism, Mahomedanism and the Gospel of Mrs. Eddy. And it is perfectly capable . . . of looking down upon the artist as a mere windlestraw! [4]

Yet he desperately wanted this stupid public to buy his books. He persisted in hoping—without real hope—that his luck would change, in the meantime continuing to oscillate between the twin poles of his ambivalence. His unrequited courtship of the public was owing in part to his need for money, exacerbated by his falling deeper and deeper into debt to Pinker, his agent, and in part to the old persisting desire for vindication in the eyes of his Polish relatives, of himself, of the world at large. He had felt it necessary to justify by success his career as a sailor which, at the start, had aroused so much opposition. His new career as a writer had to be justified similarly. Critical success was not enough. The evidence of achievement had to be more tangible.

He threw himself into the marketing of his books with the same nervous anxiety with which he approached their writing. Before Pinker became his agent and financial backer in 1900, he had conducted all the negotiations and publishing transactions himself, relying on Garnett for advice. His correspondence in the late 1890's reveals a dense mass of pourparlers with a swarm of book publishers and magazine editors over fees, royalties, dates, advances, rights, serialization, and contractual obligations of one sort or another. Its tone is by turns harassed, eager, aggressive, self-deprecating, but held together at bottom by belief, even pride, in the high quality of the goods he was offering for sale. This belief was generally shared by the publishers, whether they tended like Fisher Unwin to be niggardly with Conrad or like William Blackwood, the publisher of *Blackwood's Magazine* ("Maga"), who was certainly generous. Their enthusiasm began to abate when his novels lost money for them, though this was offset to some degree by the magazine serializations which could not so easily be measured in gain and loss. Even after Pinker's appearance on the scene, Conrad continued to involve himself in the commerce and tradesmanship of his art. A chronic inability to write on schedule, to deliver copy when promised, entangled him in endless arguments with publishers and, since Pinker had advanced him large sums of money

[4] Letter to Galsworthy, November 1, 1910, LL, II, 121–122.

on account, with Pinker himself. The crisis in their relationship came in 1909 when Pinker, irked by Conrad's slowness in writing *Under Western Eyes,* threatened to advance him no more money until more copy was forthcoming. Conrad flew into a rage, which he poured out in a letter to Perceval Gibbon on December 19, 1909.[5] But there was too much at stake on both sides for the quarrel to break out into an open rupture. Relations were patched up and went on as before. Conrad's publishing activities were supplemented by business investments which usually failed and by the drawing up of complicated personal insurance schemes as a means of acquiring ready cash which, for one reason or another, never came to anything either.

Conrad was not a stoic who bore his burdens uncomplainingly, but he bore them. He continued to do so long after he had given up believing in success or in the possibility of his lot ever being lightened. He carried on under the difficult conditions of exile, of a newly learned art, of neglect, debt, his own bad health, and the chronic illnesses of his wife. He suffered bitterly over the gap between his sense of his own achievement and the public's indifference to it. But he was prepared to continue, to the end if need be. As late as his middle fifties there was no relief in sight. There was also no flagging in his determination to maintain himself on as high a level of his own humanity as his energies allowed. The public breakthrough and popular success of his last ten years do not obscure the strength of character, the will, and the dogged tenacity with which he persisted through the previous twenty. He is one of the heroic figures of modern literature in his life performance as well as in his art.[6]

Though quick to reveal his feelings in letters, Conrad was slow to do so in his formal writing. He did compose two personal memoirs, but these are among the singularly impersonal documents of their kind. The first, a series of separate sketches collected and published in 1905 as *The Mirror of the Sea,* was begun while Conrad was still laboring over *Nostromo.* The pieces in it deal

5 Berg Collection, New York Public Library.

6 H. G. Wells thought this life performance unbearably pretentious. He could not stand the way Conrad "had gone literary," and described as ridiculous "Conrad's *persona* of a romantic adventurous un-mercenary intensely artistic European gentleman carrying an exquisite code of unblemished honour through a universe of baseness" (*Experiment in Autobiography,* New York, 1934, pp. 526, 530).

with incidents from his life as a seaman, and are miscellaneous
enough to embrace an account of his Carlist adventuring aboard
the *Tremolino* and an essay in honor of Lord Nelson. The individual chapters, severely impersonal even when concerned with personal matters, deal with a number of Conrad's favorite ideas: his
admiration for the language of sailors, succinct, precise, and spare;
his elevation of skill and technique into the realm of high morality
(he is the father of Hemingway in this respect); his disenchantment with steam as a mode of locomotion; his acerb comments on
the sea as a cruel, treacherous, unstable medium. But *The Mirror
of the Sea* is notable for a reason scarcely perceived in its time;
it embodies one of Conrad's special qualities, his abnormal awareness of place, an awareness magnified to almost a new dimension
in art, an ecological dimension defining the relationship between
earth and man.

Traces of this had appeared in the first two Malay novels. The
Pantai River, which flows from the remote interior of Borneo
past Almayer's house, incarnates both his entrapment and his
dream of liberation. At its extremities it connects the twin pegs
of his fantasy life: Lingard, his benefactor, who comes from the
sea into which the river flows (Lingard enters it through a secret
passage for a long time known only to himself) and the gold mine
at the other end, the interior end, which Almayer hopes one day
to possess. Yet all the while, in actuality, he is pinned to one tiny,
wretched trading post midway on the river, cut off from Lingard
by an immensity of ocean, and from the gold by a savage jungle
country which he cannot hope to master without help. Just as the
river is the principal feature of both the physical and psychic landscape of *Almayer's Folly*, so the jungle is of *An Outcast of the
Islands*. It embraces Willems's two characteristics, a blind sensuality and a struggle to the death for a place in the sun. As a result the three great events of his life take place in the jungle: he
sees Aissa for the first time in a jungle glade, discloses Lingard's
secret river passage to the Malays (another of his racial betrayals),
and is killed there (in a blaze of sunshine, as it happens; Willems
manages to die in the sun if not to live in it). Neither river nor
jungle is distorted to serve literary or symbolic ends; they would
still be as they are, perfectly unchanged, if Almayer and Willems
had never existed.

Conrad not only perceives nature through his senses, but is aware of the profound parallelisms that link it with men. The ecological side of his art consists of demonstrating these parallelisms according to the demands of the particular scene. In his early period this demonstration reached its climax in the baffling and powerful story, "Heart of Darkness." [7] Marlow is again the narrator, this time of an experience that happened some years after the sinking of the *Judea*. His account of a journey up the Congo in fascinated search of a Belgian trader named Kurtz begins and ends on the Thames, with his four interlocutors sprawled on the deck of a yawl waiting in the gathering darkness for the tide to turn. The process of suturing nature with the mood of Marlow's African experience begins at once. "The sea-reach of the Thames stretched before us like the beginning of an interminable waterway" (*Youth and Two Other Stories*, p. 45), a waterway, we are informed a few paragraphs farther on, "leading to the uttermost ends of the earth" (p. 49). This continuum of nature, in which the rivers of the earth flow into one another indissolubly so that what happens on the Thames happens on the Congo also, is reinforced by the comment "the sea and the sky were welded together without a joint" (p. 45). The theme of all experience being one experience, transcending time and space, underlies the story, and appears in several variations. One variation on the theme is historical, one imperialist, one personal, and all rest on a vision of the earth as a single, interpenetrating whole. Conrad continuously evokes this idea by his fusions of landscape. Again the fusion is not manufactured to suit the purpose of his fiction, but a quality of nature organic to it which the author asks us to be aware of.

The historical note allies itself to the double movement of the

---

[7] Another of the Conrad tales which have supplied critics with a field day. They have found in Marlow's journey up the Congo a parallel to Aeneas's trip to Hades, a Freudian and/or Jungian passage into the subconscious self, a disguised retelling of Passion Week, a return to the Garden of Eden, etc. Conrad invites all this sort of textual pearl-diving by his elaborate use of vaguely portentous and invitingly "significant" words like inscrutable, unspeakable, unearthly, incomprehensible, mysterious, impenetrable, inconceivable, intolerable, and incredible, for which the story has been criticized by F. R. Leavis. Other defects include a tendency to preachiness ("He must meet that truth with his own true stuff—with his own inborn strength") and an occasional disposition to the trite image ("a spark from the sacred fire"). These rhetorical and stylistic blemishes mar the text of the story without, however, diluting its impact.

tides. In Elizabethan times Drake and other raiders sailed from the light of England into the darkness of unknown seas, returning with the "round flanks" of their ships bulging with treasure. Nineteen centuries ago the incoming tide brought the Romans from the light of Rome into the darkness of England where decent young citizens in togas no doubt felt "the utter savagery" of the country closing round them. Modern imperialism is no different from ancient. "The conquest of the earth, which mostly means the taking it away from those who have a different complexion or slightly flatter noses than ourselves, is not a pretty thing when you look into it too much" (pp. 50–51). Whereupon Marlow proceeds to look into it. He goes to Brussels, a city like "a whited sepulchre," headquarters of the Congo trade, to apply for a post as captain of a river steamer. He is hired at once to replace a man just killed in a skirmish with natives over two black hens. The natives flee their village in terror, and in time grass grows through the ribs of the dead man. The Brussels street where the company is located has grass sprouting between the stones, and in the anteroom of the office sit two women (the two black hens) knitting black wool. The repetition of sensory details and of symbolic analogues—in this instance the grass and the woman-hen concord—lends the story a central pulsation and reinforces the theme of indissolubility that lies at its heart.

The darkness of Africa has bleached Brussels into a sepulchral whiteness. Other death images of imperialism appear. On the trip down, Marlow's ship passes a French man-of-war firing into the empty bush. No sign of life is visible anywhere but "there she was, incomprehensible, firing into a continent. . . . There was a touch of insanity in the proceeding . . . not dissipated by somebody on board assuring me earnestly there was a camp of natives—he called them enemies!—hidden out of sight somewhere" (p. 62). After landing at the mouth of the Congo, Marlow runs into a grove filled with dying Negroes, too broken in health to work on their chain gangs any longer. Farther on, at the Central Station, he meets the manager and his henchmen, crassly devoted to extracting as much ivory as possible out of the country: "To tear treasure out of the bowels of the earth was their desire, with no more moral purpose at the back of it than there is in burglars breaking into a safe" (p. 87). Their naked rapacity fills Marlow with loathing, and this quickens his interest in Kurtz, who came to Africa with the "higher" aim of civilizing the natives and whom even his enemies acknowledge to be remarkable. He, too, is an imperialist trader (he sends out record-breaking quantities of ivory) but of a different sort, and Marlow is now confronted with "a choice of nightmares," between the systems of values represented by the manager and by Kurtz. The imperialist theme merges with the personal, and Marlow the observer-traveler now changes into Marlow the moral participant.

What redeems imperialism—it is again characteristic of Conrad that he should examine a generally repulsive process with an eye to salvage—is "an idea at the back of it; not a sentimental pretence but an idea; and an unselfish belief in the idea—something you can set up, and bow down before, and offer a sacrifice to . . ." (p. 51). Kurtz has such an idea, of elevating the native, and the manager has not. Both are in the African darkness but on different levels of morality, and Marlow allies himself at once with Kurtz. If darkness it is to be, it had better be Kurtz's. His at least has intelligence, a noble purpose, and a touch of grandeur, while the manager's is rooted in a grubby, mean-spirited avarice. No matter that Kurtz has lost his footing and plunged into an abyss of degradation, that he has engaged in unspeakable rites, allowed the tribesmen to deify him, taken a savage mistress, slain Africans whose heads he awesomely impaled on posts outside his lodging, could exclaim "exterminate the brutes" after all his early intentions to civilize, and die with the cryptic words "the horror! the horror!" on his lips. If he has fallen, he has fallen from a formidable height, and Marlow finds in his fall a sign of his superiority. The manager, by contrast, is never ill, never varies his dead-level routine, never displays the slightest sign of humanness, has, in fact, nowhere to fall to. Marlow embraces the inescapable darkness of life, but it is a mark of his humanity that he maintains his powers of discrimination within it.

He discovers, also, that it is possible to function in darkness without falling satanically into its bottomless pit like Kurtz, or existing, like the manager, without the slightest awareness of light. He maintains himself by continually making moral judgments about the experience before him. The young Russian who is attached to Kurtz he recognizes as an admirable incarnation of youthful adventurousness, just as the manager's assistant, with his nose for influential connections back home, is a "papier-mâché Mephistopheles," a villain of the second grade ("it seemed to me . . . I could poke my forefinger through him, and would find inside nothing but a little loose dirt . . ." [p. 81]). The Company's chief accountant who, in the grueling heat of Africa, appears in starched collar, white cuffs, and snowy trousers, may look like a hairdresser's dummy, but he elicits Marlow's admiration: ". . . in the great demoralization of the land he kept up his appearance. That's backbone. His starched collars and got-up shirt-fronts were achievements of character" (p. 68). Marlow finds the physical act of refloating the sunken steamer a preservative in the jungle, as he does the unexpected discovery of a manual of seamanship in an abandoned hut up-river. The darkness of Africa embraces both demoralizing savagery and burgeoning life. Along the coast Marlow observes a boat being paddled by blacks: ". . . they had faces like grotesque masks—these chaps; but they had bone, muscle, a wild vitality, an intense energy of movement, that was as natural and true as the surf along their coast" (p. 61). In the end, Marlow returns to Europe and seals his commitment to Kurtz by lying to his fiancée. She wants to know what his last words were, and it seems to Marlow too dark altogether to tell her the truth. He tells her instead what she wants to hear, that the last word Kurtz uttered was her name. The lie, like the imperialism to which even Kurtz is allied, is an evil thing (lying makes Marlow "miserable and sick, like biting something rotten would do" [p. 82]) but is redeemed, as Kurtz's ivory activities were, by a benevolent and idealistic motivation. The truth would only have plunged her into needless disillusionment and pain. Marlow thus finally displays his heightened powers of discrimination, perhaps the ultimate benefit accruing from his trip to Africa.

If the historical theme expands into the imperialist, the imperialist into the personal, all of them are held aloft by the frame of external nature rooted at the bottom of the story. The Congo appears as "an immense snake uncoiled, with its head in the sea, its body at rest curving over a vast country, and its tail lost in the depth of the land" (p. 52). Its banks are lined with contorted mangroves; the water exudes the smell of primeval mud. And the wilderness in back waits in silence for the departure of rapacious men, a silence that "went home to one's very heart" (p. 80). For those outsiders who linger in it too long, or invade it too deeply, it is sure to exact a terrible vengeance by exposing them, as it does Kurtz, to unbearable temptations. In the end it stamps the very flesh with its imprimatur, so that Kurtz's bald skull looked exactly like an ivory ball. The Thames, which seems at the start to be a waterway leading to the uttermost ends of the earth, merges into the Congo, which flows not so much in space as in time, "travelling back to the earliest beginnings of the world" (p. 92). The perils of such a journey are highlighted by the wreckage en route: an undersized railway truck lying on its back with its wheels in the air, looking "as dead as the carcass of some animal" (p. 63); the steamer Marlow drags up from the bottom, resembling "the carcass of some big river animal" (p. 81); finally Kurtz himself, "lying at the bottom of a precipice where the sun never shines" (p. 149), a precipice into which Marlow himself nearly falls but is saved at the last moment.

All the while, Marlow tells this story, which he announces as "the farthest point of navigation and the culminating point of my experience" (p. 51), looking like a Buddha dressed in European clothes. The combination of east and west underlines the universality of his theme, linking the Thames and the Congo, Africa and Europe, the ancient Romans and latter-day British, streets in Brussels and mud paths in the heart of the wilderness. Kurtz as a pan-European figure, not simply a Belgian, is emphasized by the details of his parentage: "His mother was half-English, his father was half-French. All Europe contributed to the making of Kurtz" (p. 117). The spear, which to the astonishment of the natives "went quite easy between the shoulder-blades" of the white captain whom Marlow replaces, is the same spear which later passes through the body of the black helmsman, to the astonishment of Marlow himself. He compares the far-off drums of Africa to "the sound of bells in a Christian country" (p. 71). The disappearance of the Africans before the onslaught of the white men is described in terms of the emptying of farms in England "if a lot of mysterious niggers armed with all kinds of fearful weapons suddenly took to travelling on the road between Deal and Gravesend, catching the yokels right and left to carry heavy loads for them" (p. 70).

Throughout, Marlow pronounces the kinship between the howling, screaming Congolese and the rest of humanity, climaxed by the look given him by the dying Negro helmsman, a look creating a "subtle bond" between them: "And the intimate profundity of the look he gave me when he received his hurt remains to this day in my memory—like a claim of distant kinship affirmed in a supreme

moment" (p. 119). The match which the Buddha-like Marlow lights
in the Thames night toward the end of his tale affirms not only the
contrast between light and darkness but the flow between them, a
flow establishing their subtle bond. The earth itself, with its rivers
and continents, its jungles, seas, and peoples, covering its immense
range in space and time, supplies "Heart of Darkness" with an ultimate source of reference. Behind the movement and symbolism of
the story lies its ecology. Leaving the protective comforts of civilization for his plunge into barbaric darkness, Marlow learns to make
his way about in it, to distinguish its noble and ignoble qualities,
and by exposing himself to its pressures, he embraces the indivisibility of experience, reflected at every point by the indivisibility of
the earth itself in all its manifestations. He and it are in the end
"welded together without a joint."

A similar attention to the psychophysical joining of men and objects is evident in *The Mirror of the Sea*. There is, throughout, a
persistent interfusion of ships and human beings: "To deal with men
is as fine an art as it is to deal with ships. Both men and ships live in
an unstable element, are subject to subtle and powerful influences . . ." (p. 27). Ships themselves are approached with humanizing delicacy. Docked in London they "seemed lost like bewitched
children in a forest of gaunt, hydraulic cranes" (p. 113). At sea they
demand of their masters the most exacting skill: "Of all the living
creatures upon land and sea, it is ships alone that cannot be taken
in by barren pretences, that will not put up with bad art from their
masters" (p. 35). Conrad's distaste for steam lies in its breaking the
tie between ships and men. Science, not men, guides the steam vessel,
and in fact removes men from the forms of nature and an intimate
personal wrestling with it. Nature is one of the great proving
grounds of self; anything which denies us the opportunity to test
our powers in her arena reduces our life intensity. Taking a steamship about the world "has not the artistic quality of a single-handed
struggle with something much greater than yourself; it is not the
laborious, absorbing practice of an art whose ultimate result remains
on the knees of the gods. It is not an individual, temperamental
achievement, but simply the skilled use of captured force . . ." (p.
31). Conrad does not share Wordsworth's quasi-mystical worship of
nature as the spring that awakens one's most deeply submerged feelings. Yet the intimacy between man and nature makes sailing an art

that arouses affection and excitement, while the impersonality of **steam** reduces it to a science that stimulates only a sense of duty.

A wide miscellany of other phenomena within the orbit of life at sea emerge in a series of miniature, delicately contoured essays. Gales are evoked, classified into types, marked for individual variations, and replaced onstage by the four winds. These are gauged with singular exactness, and launched in sentences whose gait, sound, and rhythm suggest the movement of each particular wind. Equally careful attention is paid to anchors and river estuaries, falling spars that endanger the lives of hapless seamen, the pitch and roll of a yacht in full racing maneuver, the dark faceless jungle of the London waterfront. Amid this ceaseless multiplicity a close-range harmony appears, binding together the processes of men and nature in ties that are no less indissoluble for appearing in the fragile proportions of *The Mirror of the Sea*.

The last chapters of the book are dominated by the personalities of Dominic Cervoni—a leading figure in Conrad's youthful adventures in France—and Lord Nelson, two Conradian heroes marked by the indefinable quality of presence. Though a rough-hewn, untutored Corsican seaman, Cervoni was perfectly at home in Doña Rita's salon. On the sea, in jousts with the law, in taverns on the Marseilles waterfront, through painful moments when he feels himself and his honor betrayed by the treachery of his nephew César, he maintains an unshakable poise. Its source is an instinctive belief in his own powers and an unswerving acceptance of a moral system that is all the more deeply rooted in him because it is so medieval. His blood feuds and family pride, arising as they do from a primitive sense of life and death, free Cervoni from the gnawings of self-consciousness and enable him to function as a force in nature. Aboard the *Tremolino*, he is an organic part of ocean, sky, wind, boat, the very coloration of the air, whose primal energies flow into him and are reinfused by the current of controlled and powerful will flowing from him in turn. To the Conrad of 1875, freshly and deliberately torn away from the confused myths and moralities of his own country, Cervoni must have seemed the ideal of heroic integration. To the Conrad of 1905, caught in the mazes of a new existence, he appeared as the archetype of forthright action.

Lord Nelson is a more remote creature, whom Conrad must cull out of books and the comments of others, but he too stands as a controlling figure poised at a crowded intersection of men, ships, nature, and history. Note is taken of his "frank and conciliatory manner to his subordinates," the valor of his adversaries, the trickiness of the wind at Trafalgar, his rejection of traditional concepts of naval warfare, the loyalty he aroused in all ranks from deckhands to lords of the admiralty. Nelson does not emerge from the resistant past with the clarity and immediacy of Cervoni. Yet he, too, is a force unifying the energies of nature and the purposes of men, and by establishing a harmony between them impresses his genius upon us.

Behind Nelson, behind Cervoni, behind the ships, the skippers, the distant ports, the fogged wilderness of the London docks, behind the savage remarks on the treacherous sea and the tender ones on the obscure valor of the seaman's life, we hear the voice that informs *The Mirror of the Sea,* the voice of Conrad himself. It is deliberately, almost self-consciously restrained. Conrad plainly dreads laying bare his soul or approaching his memoir as though it were a confessional. He cannot be cheerfully frank like Shaw or engagingly personal like Cellini. He is unable to empty his mind and heart of all their contents as though they were Aristotelian tubs, in the style of H. G. Wells. The only moment of private emotion he allows himself comes when, after romping with him in her salon, Doña Rita assures the jealous J.M.K.B. (the Mr. Blunt of *The Arrow of Gold,* the man with whom the young Conrad was supposed to have fought a duel): *"Vous êtes bête, mon cher.... Ça n'a aucune conséquence"* (*Mirror,* pp. 161–162). Only this one personal revelation in a volume of reminiscences that stretch back over thirty years. Conrad's sense of privacy was morbidly intense. Though he craved the fruits of publicity, he objected to submitting photographs of himself in connection with his writing. ". . . my face has nothing to do with my writing," he exclaimed indignantly on one occasion.[8] He felt the reader's interest should be entirely in the work and not at all in the author as a man. "Once the last page is written the man does not count. He is nowhere," he observed in a letter to Arthur Symons.[9]

Yet the very sharpness of the line that he drew to separate the pub-

[8] Letter to David S. Meldrum, November 27, 1902, *Letters of Joseph Conrad to William Blackwood and David S. Meldrum,* ed. by William Blackburn (Durham, N. C., 1958), p. 171.

[9] August, 1908, LL, II, 73.

lic and private, the writer and the man, was in itself revealing. It was a judgment against a gossip-hungry public eager for sensation and colorful personalia, already evident in Conrad's time with the rise of the tabloid newspaper. It registered his distaste for the democratic process that helped to equate all men by making everything known. It also marked the exile desperately unsure of himself on alien soil, seeking to create a new personality, an impersonal personality as it were, that might fit more easily into the new environment than the differently articulated self formed during the far-off years in Poland. An aloofness, a fastidious self-protectiveness had begun to encrust Conrad during his years in the British merchant service and increased visibly after he settled down in England.

There is a curious contrast between his novels, crowded with characters who are perpetually confessing, and his memoirs whose tone is studiedly antipersonal. One might say that a bridge exists between the writer and his imaginative work, which is lacking in his direct literary statements. Paradoxically, in *The Mirror of the Sea,* Conrad glorifies the very ideals, like fidelity, courage, and craftsmanship, whose adequacy he challenges in his fiction.[10] It is as though he will not examine ideas with ruthless skepticism unless they are cloaked in the camouflage of storytelling. Cervoni and Nelson, with their total fusion of inner capacities and outward actions, would never have been allowed to stand with such unquestioned simplicity in a major Conrad novel.

In 1908, three years after the appearance in book form of *The Mirror of the Sea,* Conrad began writing for Hueffer's new magazine, *The English Review,* the reminiscences which were eventually published as a book in 1912 under the title *A Personal Record.* This was Conrad's second and final volume about himself. At a cursory glance it appears to be considerably more intimate than the first. Conrad

10 This is the underlying theme of Douglas Hewitt's brief critical study, *Conrad: A Reassessment* (Cambridge, England, 1952). But Hewitt allows himself to become ensnarled in the complex relationship of Conrad and his work. After insisting that Conrad's life, while interesting, is irrelevant to an understanding of his novels, he proceeds to make frequent references to the life in his account of Decoud, in his speculations about Conrad fighting against his own secret doubts about the morality of the universe, and elsewhere. A better approach to this involved and necessarily tenuous question is to regard Conrad, under the stresses already indicated, as revealing his formal Anglicized self in his essays, sketches, and memoirs, while reserving privacies of soul for his fiction. The circumstances of his deracinated life made this division inescapable.

describes how *Almayer's Folly* came to be written. He deals with relatives in Poland, the political position of his father, his own feeling and instinctive preference for English as the language to write in, the nature of art, and the character of the universe. But we are informed very early that "there are some of us to whom an open display of sentiment is repugnant" (p. xviii). And farther on, Conrad announces his desire "to keep these reminiscences from turning into confessions, a form of literary activity discredited by Jean Jacques Rousseau . . ." (p. 95).

There is no doubt that he succeeds. Private sentiment is subdued to public statement. Personal experience is objectified to the point where the "I" of the story is less Conrad than an autobiographical narrator invented by Conrad to screen the material flowing from author to reader. *A Personal Record* proceeds at a measured, solemn pace which gives each incident a finished quality more in keeping with a memorial or commemorative volume than a self-revelation. He describes in great detail the physical conditions under which he began writing his first novel, the way in which the unfinished but slowly accreting manuscript was hauled about the world, the original of Almayer as Conrad knew him in the Far East—all with a view to establishing the resonant fusion of his lives as seaman and author. The fusion is there. We see clearly the connection between the two, and beyond that the connection between the peculiarly literary upbringing of Conrad as a boy under the intimate tutelage of his highly literary father, and his eventual if dramatically postponed career as a novelist. But the emotional current that accompanied these events, the barometric readings of the inner spirit, the flow of feeling and psychic response that clusters about every experience and surcharges it have been impersonalized to the point of marmoreal gravity. One reviewer, put off by this gravity, despaired of ever discovering the "real" man: "A glance at the Conrad of the photographs, remote, proud, and wooden, is enough to show the hopelessness of such inquiry." [11] But the very act of concealment is revealing. It exposes Conrad's Flaubertian cult of artistic objectivity and indicates the depth of his hypersensitiveness and defensiveness about his submerged self (which he in part rationalizes into an aristocratic contempt for the confessionalism of a democratic age). It is a record

11 Richard Mayne, *The New Statesman*, February 21, 1959.

of detached impressions and opinions he is presenting, not an exploration of his intimate, personal being.

The result is rendered all the more striking by Conrad's straight-faced announcement of traditional intentions. In the preface he proclaims his hope "that from the reading of these pages there may emerge at last the vision of a personality; the man behind the books so fundamentally dissimilar as . . . 'Almayer's Folly' and 'The Secret Agent,' and yet a coherent, justifiable personality both in its origin . . . and action" (*A Personal Record*, p. xxiii). A personality does emerge, but it has its back instead of its face turned toward us. We see it after a fashion and acknowledge its presence, but it is altogether too veiled to explain the authorship of fundamentally dissimilar novels or to emerge into coherence and justifiability. Later in the same paragraph a second statement is made which prepares the way for another reversal of expectations. Conrad describes as his immediate aim the presentation of "the feelings and sensations connected with the writing of my first book and with my first contact with the sea" (p. xxiii). But feelings and sensations are rarely invoked in the pages that follow, and indeed the narrative tone remains dry and unemotional, and pitched in the same key throughout. The gnawing sense of guilt at leaving Poland, the anecdote about the ancestor who during Napoleon's retreat from Moscow was forced to eat a Lithuanian dog to keep from starving, the atmosphere of Conrad's room in Bessborough Gardens on the morning that he sat down to the blank first page of *Almayer's Folly,* the encounter with the original Almayer in Borneo, and the celebrated passage dealing with life as a dramatic spectacle—all these are presented with the same sober, understated detachment.

The book is intentionally unvaried. By eliminating gradations, it manages to protect the intimacy, the particularity, the special tonality of the private self. Conrad's feat in depersonalizing the personal statement can only arouse admiration, for he manages to do so while dispensing information and shedding light on those affairs of his life that he chooses to discuss as though he were telling all. The total effect is of a controlled deliberative mind, carefully objectifying the memories selected for discussion. Along this line *A Personal Record* achieves its most notable success.

The passing years reinforced Conrad's view of his obligations to his private self. In 1921 he assembled his random essays and published them as *Notes on Life and Letters*. The Author's Note prefacing it restated his credo with finality. "The only thing that will not be found amongst those Figures and Things that have passed away, will be Conrad *en pantoufles*. It is constitutional inability" (p. vi). By this time his faithful readers have gathered that they would never see the Master in bedroom slippers, yet he feels impelled to make a point of it again this late in the day. On the same page he amplifies the image: "This volume . . . is as near as I shall come to *deshabille* in public; and perhaps it will do something to help towards a better vision of the man, if it gives no more than a partial view of a piece of his back . . ." (*Notes,* p. vi). How to get a better vision of a man by gazing at his back would seem a baffling question. But in Conrad's case, the gesture of turning away from us emphasizes his insistence upon distinguishing between public and private, a distinction increasingly blurred in our own time. The result is that in order to get at Conrad, a leap must be made from the memoirs to the man, with very little help from Conrad himself.

However hesitant he may be at revealing himself, Conrad is eager to illuminate external incident, and as long as the current of his life flows outward, he is as frank and detailed as even the most demanding reader could wish. Since his written recollections stop with the end of his career at sea, they concentrate inevitably on the movements and physical geography of his wanderings about the earth. David Daiches observes that geography rather than economics and the structure of society is Conrad's special medium.[12] This is not a wholly accurate statement, as a glance at his three political novels reveals. It is true, however, that Conrad has dramatized and psychologized geography in the remarkable way that roots his art in its deeply grounded ecology. Conrad was the most notable and far-ranging traveler among English writers since Byron. Countries and places as points in space give off particular emanations that infuse his consciousness and vibrate in his prose. Moreover, he orchestrates nature in a variety of keys. It is the element that tests MacWhirr and Jim. It embodies the sensual destructiveness of Willems. It embraces the primitive, prehistoric past to Marlow, and represents to Decoud the chaos of unformed, unfixed, undifferentiated matter flowing in the mindless stream that numbs identity. To Conrad himself, it is the

12 *The Novel and the Modern World* (Chicago, 1939), pp. 48–49.

frame that encloses man, imposing upon him fixed rules of action and at the same time protecting him from the terrors of infinity that so afflicted Pascal. We cannot penetrate beyond it—a chafing fact. Yet this is a blessing too, for beyond it there may be nothing but the quite unencompassable and therefore unbearable prospect of endless emptiness.

In his two autobiographical narratives Conrad throws himself into a series of personal collisions with nature—at sea, on inland rivers, along the dangerous islands of the Malay Archipelago, in the jungles of Borneo and Africa—obscurely moved by a search for experience, but moved also by a need to escape the restrictions and sorrows of early youth, by a natural love of adventure, by restlessness, ennui, and at times the sheer, seemingly aimless momentum of chance. Surveying all this with the retrospective eye of his middle years, Conrad finds in his past the evidence not so much of an organized pattern as of "a subtle accord," less the emergence or unfolding of a purposive plan than the progress of a temperament. It is the evolution of a temperament, his own, that keeps Conrad's recollections of his own past from breaking up into miscellaneous fragments and turns them into his own special kind of personal record.

In it he never allows us to forget what we have already discovered in the novels, that he, like his characters, was sharpened to a fine edge by a ceaseless intimacy and penetrative contact with nature in her changeless and multiple forms. His personal record is, at bottom, an ecological one as well.

X

Dark Vision of Megalopolis

AT THE BEGINNING OF 1905, WITH THE LABORS OF "NOSTROMO" BEHIND him, Conrad took his son and ailing wife for a holiday to Capri. In keeping with the general tone of his life during this period, the holiday was a disaster. He did little writing. His chronic ailments returned to plague him. His wife spent most of her time in a wheel chair recuperating from an operation on an injured knee. Even the weather was bad. During the whole of their stay in southern Italy, from January to May, only the news that the King was awarding him a grant of five hundred pounds in acknowledgment of his services to literature broke the gloom. The money was painfully welcome, yet it did not take Conrad's mind off his troubles for long. In a letter thanking Edmund Gosse, one of the men who recommended him for the award, Conrad returned to a subject that clung to him almost obsessively, the agonies of writing. He speaks of

. . . those difficult moments which Baudelaire has defined happily as *"les stérilités des écrivains nerveux."* Quincey too, I believe, has known that anguished suspension of all power of thought that comes to one often in the midst of a very revel of production, like the slave with his *memento mori* at a feast.[1]

The fear of literary sterility was now his constant psychic companion. The act of creation had always been uncertain and spasmodic with him. "I prefer to dream a novel rather than write it," he confessed to Mme. Poradowska. "And English is . . . still a foreign language to me, requiring an immense effort to handle." [2] But ten years of unsuccess, complicated by domestic pressures and financial

---

1 March 23, 1905, LL, II, 14.
2 Letter of January 5, 1907, *Letters to Marguerite Poradowska,* pp. 108–109.

stress, had added to these troubles a hazardous tension that he found increasingly difficult to bear. A period of blank impotence would be followed by a spurt of feverish writing. Whenever this came to an end, Conrad feared that it had ended for good. His favorite image for his art was that it was like quarrying in the depths of a coal mine. ". . . I had to work like a coal miner in his pit quarrying all my English sentences out of a black night," he wrote to Garnett on August 28, 1908.[3] A day later, in a letter to Arthur Symons, he repeats the figure and extends it: "I have been quarrying my English out of a black night, working like a coal miner in his pit. For fourteen years now I have been living as if in a cave without echoes."[4] By very definition, a mine is something that peters out, and Conrad was gloomily certain that his particular vein of aesthetic ore would peter out, too. He waited in dread for it to happen at any moment.

The moments came and went, and it did not happen. In time Conrad learned to live with his capricious muse. He did not cease complaining about it or filling his letters with lamentations, or give up his deep-seated fear that the whole writing machine in him would abruptly grind to a halt. He did, however, abandon hope that the difficulties would go away of their own accord, that he would wake up one day to find himself a changed man, freed from the weight of the burden. More wishful thought than realistic judgment, this hope died hard, but die it did, leaving him free to embrace the hard irreducible fact that his particular nature, habits, and procedures as a writer were fixed objects beyond his power to alter. The stoical face of Conrad's universe was thus reinforced by the embracing of his own identity. Once he surrendered the idea that he could alter it, he was left free to cope with the task, difficult enough in all truth, of enduring it.

Having left the underground of Poland in his youth, he now entered another underground, "the cave without echoes," as he put it, of his own hagridden creative life. Every day as he sat down at his desk to write he sank into it, remaining there until his stint was over and he could come up again into the outer air of ordinary life. Below, he was alone with his ideas, imaginings, scenes, characters, fictional problems, and the paralyzing blankness into which all of them

[3] Garnett, p. 214.
[4] Letter of August 29, 1908, LL, II, 84.

frequently lapsed. This double existence became his natural mode after a time, and supplied him with the psychic frame for his next two novels, *The Secret Agent* and *Under Western Eyes,* which dealt with political undergrounds and the double lives of men caught up in them. His astonishing familiarity with anarchist circles in London and Russian émigré centers in Geneva came not from any expertise in political matters—Conrad disclaimed this from the start—but from an inward knowledge of how human beings felt, thought, and behaved when thrust into a split-level existence. Having embraced his own underground, Conrad came to regard it as an intenser, perhaps even superior form of life, and, like so many men, learned to make a virtue out of his necessity. Just as he never got over a slight feeling of contempt for persons who never emerged from the protective shelters of Western Europe and exposed themselves to the dangers of life in the Malay Sea,[5] so he never quite succeeded in avoiding a patronizing attitude toward those who were content to live on the comfortable surface.

This attitude is sharply expressed in his story "The Informer," written in December, 1905. Its dominating figure is Mr. X, a famous revolutionist, organizer of underground conspiracies, and author of fire-breathing tracts against the bourgeoisie which are enormously popular with the middle classes. As a result, he is rich and can indulge his taste for Chinese porcelain and for eating in expensive restaurants. In the story he is dining with the narrator, a dealer in Chinese curios, who listens in frightened fascination to a tale by Mr. X about a police informer planted as a spy among the anarchists in London. The tale is of no great consequence, but the relationship between Mr. X and the narrator is. The narrator sees him as in many ways like himself, sharing his taste in art, good living, fine clothes, the cultivated life. But there is the other side to him, the

5 In "Heart of Darkness," Marlow accuses his listeners of buying their civilized protections with too heavy a price in ignorance: "You can't understand. How could you?—with solid pavement under your feet, surrounded by kind neighbours . . . stepping delicately between the butcher and the policeman, in the holy terror of scandal and gallows and lunatic asylums. . . . These little things make all the great difference. When they are gone you must fall back upon your own innate strength, upon your own capacity for faithfulness" (*Youth and Two Other Stories,* p. 116). This is what he himself has to fall back on in Africa, and feels the richer for it. Marlow does not fail to irritate his audience aboard the *Nellie* (and ourselves as well) by his excessive awareness of having lived more deeply than they.

hidden underground side, which the narrator looks upon with loathing, yet not without a certain morbid interest, too. The man was a monster, to be sure. Still,

He was alive and European; he had the manner of good society, wore a coat and hat like mine, and had pretty near the same taste in cooking. It was too frightful to think of. ("The Informer," *A Set of Six*, p. 76)

But he does think of it, and not so much because Mr. X is a ferocious example of a split personality but because he causes the narrator to worry about himself. When a mutual friend laughs off Mr. X's tale as a joke, the narrator cannot dismiss the matter so lightly. It is no joke to him. The whole affair with Mr. X, who is his possible other self, has been too disturbing, altogether too disturbing. The narrator is cut off from his deeper, more primitive self, the self which, in Mr. X's words, accepts terror and violence as the only means of amending mankind, by his single passion for collecting *objets d'art*, for regarding interesting human beings as collectors' items, for regarding himself as "a quiet and peaceable product of civilization." Mr. X may be a monster, but he is a living monster (just as Kurtz became a monster but an intensely alive one), while the narrator, utterly refined and "civilized," is almost as dead as the Chinese bronzes and porcelain he so lovingly assembles.[6]

If this man exists on the careful surface of things and never gets below it, he is no worse off than men who live below and never get to the surface. In the story "An Anarchist," that might almost be a companion piece to "The Informer" and was indeed written the month before, Conrad explores this reverse situation. The tale serves him as a brief rehearsal for *The Secret Agent* where the theme of human beings trapped in an iron underground is given a full orchestral treatment. In "An Anarchist" a young French mechanic, with a warm heart and a weak head as he describes himself, is arrested for shouting anarchist slogans while drunk one night. He has no interest in anarchism or in ideology of any kind. But he serves a

---

[6] In his book *Conrad's Measure of Man* (Madison, Wisconsin, 1954), Paul Wiley observes that aestheticism is used by Conrad in his later work as an armor of death. The painter Henry Allègre in *The Arrow of Gold* and the two central characters in the story "The Planter of Malata" are death figures insulated from life by art and compared in imagery to statues whose cold, pallid beauty denotes the absence in them of vital emotion.

jail sentence as a dangerous radical, is blacklisted, forced into the anarchist movement against his will, and finally shipped off to prison in the West Indies. We see him at the end working as a mechanic on a Caribbean plantation, back in civilian life physically but still functioning psychically in a melancholy limbo of his own. He has been too deeply injured to return to normal under his own power and is dying slowly for lack of air. The double life may be necessary in Conrad for a full discovery of self. But nothing is worse than living only half of it at a time. It does not matter which half. Exclusive submersion below is as damaging and self-limiting as a timid or complacent clinging above. This dichotomy lies at the center of Conrad's moral definition of human nature. It is this that he legates to T. S. Eliot, who changes Conrad's prepositions from above-below to inward-outward and installs Kurtz as a life figure in the epigraph to "The Hollow Men."

The interregnum between *Nostromo* and *The Secret Agent*, the next of Conrad's great imaginative efforts, was almost over. He had written the first of his autobiographies in *The Mirror of the Sea* and was soon to complete the last of the stories to appear in the collection *A Set of Six* (1908). The two most significant of these, "The Informer" and "An Anarchist," were flanked by four others of lesser consequence. One, "Gaspar Ruiz," was the last of his South American tales, an account of a simple-minded giant driven by love to political and military adventures beyond his power to control—reduced to pedestrian melodrama by an excess of action over character. A second, "The Brute," dealt with a malevolent ship which always killed someone on each of its voyages, a thin-textured tale redeemed briefly in the startling scene of the young woman dragged to her death by the "great, rough iron arm" of the anchor. A third, "The Duel," is a small anecdote extended to inordinate length of a feud between two officers in Napoleon's army. Garnett admired this story greatly—one of his rare errors in critical judgment—but it stands largely as an early indication of Conrad's almost dynastic interest in writing a novel about Napoleon (Conrad's ancestors on both sides were officers in the Grande Armée), an interest to be tediously and unsatisfactorily gratified in his final novel, *Suspense*, left unfinished at his death. The fourth, "Il Conde," describes the painful case of an elderly foreign visitor to Naples condemned to death by the ugly malevolence of an aristocratic Italian hoodlum; here again a tiny incident is forced to stand on its own feet, unsupported by the overtones with which Conrad invests his significant work. On the purely narrative level, these half-dozen stories are managed with skill, and serve as technical exercises on the road to Conrad's next great effort.

This work, _The Secret Agent_, was to be neglected even more grossly than the others. When the novel appeared in 1907, it aroused an almost universal chorus of disapproval mainly "on the ground of the sordid surroundings and the moral squalor of the tale." In the Author's Note, written in 1920, Conrad himself was moved to defend not only the book but his intentions in writing it.

. . . the thought of elaborating mere ugliness in order to shock, or even simply to surprise my readers by a change of front, has never entered my head. In making this statement I expect to be believed, not only on the evidence of my general character but also for the reason, which anybody can see, that the whole treatment of the tale, its inspiring indignation and underlying pity and contempt, prove my detachment from the squalor and sordidness which lie simply in the outward circumstances of the setting. (p. viii)

With rare exceptions its critical reception after Conrad's death was equally unfavorable. Virginia Woolf classified it with those later works of Conrad that she felt suffered from ambiguity, uncertainty, and disillusionment; she preferred the early Conrad of "Typhoon," _The Nigger of the "Narcissus,"_ and _Lord Jim,_ tales of simple heroism, which she regarded as classics. Albert Guerard, devoted to the thesis that Conrad fails when he does not have a narrator to express his view,[7] admired isolated items in the novel but concluded that the work as a whole was "a _tour-de-force,_ and a rather unsuccessful one at that." Irving Howe attacked the book on political grounds: it failed to present a historically accurate view of the anarchist movement.[8]

Even the occasional sympathetic views, when they dealt with the novel at any length, concentrated on particulars. In a preface to the German edition of _The Secret Agent,_ Thomas Mann thought of it only as a thrilling crime story which expressed Conrad's anti-Russian

[7] This dubious argument is developed in Guerard's 1947 monograph on Conrad. Ten years later, in _Conrad the Novelist,_ he modified it to the point of almost abandoning it altogether.

[8] _The Kenyon Review,_ Winter, 1954.

feeling.[9] Walter Allen, in his *Short History of the English Novel,*
commended the novel in a brief sentence but gave his critical space
to *Nostromo.* It remained for F. R. Leavis to recognize its importance, and the ten pages devoted to the novel in *The Great Tradition* examine it sympathetically. While Leavis, however, has a
shrewd eye for the power of individual episodes, he does not penetrate to the heart of the novel where the meaning that binds together
its separate parts awaits description.

The reasons for the unpopularity of *The Secret Agent,* for the
distaste it aroused and the neglect into which it sank, are not hard
to find. Aside from its "sordid surroundings" and "moral squalor"—
conditions less likely to discourage the contemporary reader than
the English public before the First World War—it is a novel without
a hero. It is the only such novel ever written by Conrad, and one of
the few of its kind in the whole history of fiction. There is no dearth
of characters; no fewer than eight sit to full-length portraits. But
there is no "central" figure, around whom either the action or the
meaning of the story revolves. It revolves about them all. Moreover,
there is no main character in terms of sympathy, liking, or identification. Once again Conrad deliberately cultivates an emotional gap
between the reader and his fictional figures, a gap that his formidable
irony prevents us from bridging. He thereby forces us into a position
of detachment, though our instincts as readers and as human beings
cry out for close communion. By driving the reader away from his
normal self, *The Secret Agent* became "unpalatable," "unpopular,"
"not to the general taste."

This condition was not capricious. On the contrary, it stemmed
from Conrad's deepest intention. This intention not only determined the shape, the form, the ruthless and unbridgeable detachment, the absence of a hero, but indeed made them unavoidable.
Conrad was driven by his theme to embrace the structure that he
did.

Traditionally, the theme of *The Secret Agent* was thought to be
anarchists and the anarchist movement. Comparisons were hence
frequently drawn with Dostoevsky's *The Possessed,* Turgenev's
Virgin Soil, and James's *The Princess Casamassima,* earlier novels
dealing with anarchism. *The Secret Agent* was thereupon examined

[9] *Past Masters and Other Papers,* tr. by H. T. Lowe-Porter (London, 1933), pp.
234–235.

historically: Were Conrad's rather shabby lot of anarchists true to life? Did not the actual anarchist movement produce powerful figures like Bakunin and Kropotkin for whom there are no equivalents in the story? Were not Conrad's political insights therefore inferior to Dostoevsky's? On the factual level the novel is, of course, crowded with details about the activities of the anarchists, and the explosion in which the half-witted Stevie is blown to pieces is a counterrevolutionary stroke designed to discredit them. The fortunes of many of the characters are involved with the anarchist movement. Verloc is its traitor, the Professor its ferocious logician, Michaelis its idealistic if impractical spirit, Ossipon its unprincipled sensualist, Inspector Heat and the Assistant Commissioner its official enemies. Conrad comments frequently and shrewdly on the nature of revolution and the reasons that drive men to become revolutionaries. Little wonder that the main current of the novel should be regarded as political.

The only man to challenge this interpretation in any way was Conrad himself. "I had no idea to consider Anarchism politically, or to treat it seriously in its philosophical aspect," he wrote to John Galsworthy on September 12, 1906.[10] A year later, in a letter to Cunninghame Graham, he remarked: ". . . I don't think I've been satirizing the revolutionary world. All these people are not revolutionaries,—they are shams." [11] To Mme. Poradowska he had written: ". . . you well know that anarchy and anarchists are outside my experience; I know almost nothing of the philosophy, and nothing at all of the men. I created this out of whole cloth." [12] His formal research for the book amounted to little more than a scanning of the newspapers. The idea for Verloc's assault on science was derived from an actual attempt to bomb Greenwich Observatory. The Assistant Commissioner was suggested by the memoirs of a Scotland Yard Inspector. Conrad's knowledge of anarchism was "popular" in character; he knew no more than any educated man of the day who had made no special study of it.

Conrad was gratified, but also surprised, when assured by readers that Mr. Vladimir and the anarchist refugees were perfectly recognizable types known to anyone who had anything to do with the movement. This success he ascribed to the triumph of imagination

---

10 LL, II, 37.
11 October 7, 1907, LL, II, 60.
12 Letter of June 20, 1912, *Letters to Marguerite Poradowska*, p. 116.

over research, to his immersion in his characters as human beings rather than as embodiments of political doctrine: "I have no doubt . . . that there had been moments during the writing of the book when I was an extreme revolutionist, I won't say more convinced than they but certainly cherishing a more concentrated purpose. . . . I don't say this to boast. I was simply attending to my business. . . . I could not have done otherwise. It would have bored me too much to make-believe" (*The Secret Agent*, p. xiv).

Plainly, then, the anarchist theme supplies the novel with its physical scaffolding. But no more. Underneath lies the heart of the book, the dominant idea that determines its movement and is responsible in the first place for the selection of anarchism as the sheath of the plot. That heart is London, and the idea stemming from it is the life of man in the great city. Because of Conrad's conception of that life, *The Secret Agent* cannot have a hero. Because of that conception, Conrad selects the anarchist movement as the novel's formal center without making a serious political or historical study of it. Because of it, too, the characters without exception are split away from their ideal selves, as are all of Conrad's figures, but are prevented from summoning the moral energy to overcome their difficulties, the very energy that gives Conrad's other novels their heroic dimension.

We have seen how Conrad was throughout his career peculiarly sensitive to place, and associated human possibilities with various types of places. Of the great modern novelists, he developed to the fullest an ecological *mystique*. The sea was more than a broad expanse of water, more than an exciting physical arena, more than the stage on which the human drama was played out. It was also an agent whose powers and qualities made it possible for human beings to behave in certain ways, and drew from them particular responses. The same is true of rivers, and the rivers on which Lingard, Kurtz, Marlow, and Lord Jim sail, place their stamp on the ultimate experiences of these men. The same is true of islands (Axel Heyst lives on one in *Victory*), of mountain masses ("The Secret Sharer" and *The Shadow-Line* are brought to their climax by them), of the jungle (the sexual corruption of Willems in *An Outcast of the Islands* occurs there), and of the great cities of the Western world. The impact and spiritual infusions of the physical environment, whether natural or man-made, have always been strongly felt in the reading of Conrad, but little explored. The controlling role of the Conradian city is given its only major definition in *The Secret Agent*. An examination of this role not only will compel us to approach the meaning of the novel in a new way, but will define the relationship between earth and man underlying the whole of Conrad's art.

The scene of *The Secret Agent* is in dramatic contrast with *Nostromo,* the novel immediately preceding it. Conrad himself makes this contrast explicit: "One fell to musing . . . of South America, a continent of crude sunshine and brutal revolutions, of the sea, of the vast expanse of salt waters, the mirror of heaven's frowns and smiles, the reflector of the world's light. Then the vision of an enormous town presented itself, of a monstrous town more populous than some continents and in its man-made might as if indifferent to heaven's frowns and smiles; a cruel devourer of the world's light. There was room enough there to place my story . . . darkness enough to bury five millions of lives" (*The Secret Agent,* p. xii). London appears in the author's mind, even before the novel is imagined, as monstrous, indifferent, a devourer of light, a center of darkness burying its inhabitants.

These are the very terms in which the city is referred to in the novel.

. . . the enormous town slumbering monstrously on a carpet of mud under a veil of raw mist. (p. 300)

. . . the whole town of marvels and mud, with its maze of streets and its mass of lights, was sunk in a hopeless night, rested at the bottom of a black abyss. . . . (pp. 270–271)

His descent into the street was like the descent into a slimy aquarium from which the water had been run off. (p. 147)

. . . enveloped, oppressed, penetrated, choked, and suffocated by the blackness of a wet London night . . . . (p. 150)

Envelopment, oppression, suffocation, and a blackness through which its inhabitants are forced to grope express the soul of the city and define the conditions under which the characters in *The Secret Agent* are compelled to live. They are hemmed in by the anonymous urban swarm, and emotionally strangled.

. . . but all round him, on and on, even to the limits of the horizon hidden by the enormous piles of bricks, he felt the mass of mankind mighty in its numbers. They swarmed numerous like locusts, industrious like ants, thoughtless like a natural force, pushing on blind and orderly and absorbed, impervious to sentiment, to logic, to terror, too, perhaps. (pp. 81–82)

Beginning with this conception of London, Conrad arranges his story in accordance with it. The anarchist movement is its perfect political equivalent. The anarchists, feeling oppressed by the social order, seek to overthrow it by violent means in order to usher in an era of human brotherhood. They are not against people or classes, but against institutions, which gives their bomb-throwing an abstract quality unique in nineteenth century radicalism. This is why Mr. Vladimir orders Verloc to blow up not the Prime Minister or the Archbishop of Canterbury but Greenwich Observatory; that embodiment of pure science suggests the ultimate target of anarchism far better than any individual, however powerful. The Professor wants to goad the police into shooting the anarchists down in broad daylight with the approval of the public, for only by encouraging the defenders of law and order to embrace illegal and immoral means can the principle of legality and the system based upon it be undermined. The almost dehumanized preoccupation of the anarchists with principles, systems, and abstractions is the analogue of the impersonal, dehumanized city—that immense abstraction— where the anarchists feel their social targets to be most heavily concentrated. By sheathing his novel in the anarchist apparatus, Conrad creates at once the air of conspiracy and desperation, of individual men and women struggling vainly to assert their identity, to make themselves felt, their presence known, amid the overwhelming anonymity of city life, which to him was the essence of human existence in London.

The theme of duality, one of the keys to *The Secret Agent,* expresses the split in the lives of the characters who are forced apart by their inability to maintain their wholeness amid the antihuman pressures of the great city. Mr. Vladimir is both a drawing-room dandy and a ruthless instrument of Russian Czarism. Winnie Verloc is a placid wife but also a murderess. Verloc is a domesticated storekeeper and a secret agent. The Professor is a fanatical logician of pure terror devoting his life to developing a perfect detonator, yet he is frightened silly by the mere thought of the endless swarms and crowds of people in London. The police are officially respectable but they are morally no better than the thieves they pursue. Conrad has a remarkable passage on this subject:

. . . the mind and the instincts of a burglar are of the same kind as the mind and the instincts of a police officer. Both recognize the same conventions, and have a working knowledge of each other's methods and of the routine of their respective trades. They understand each other, which is advantageous to both, and establishes a sort of amenity in their relations. Products of the same machine, one classified as useful and the other as noxious, they take the machine for granted in different ways, but with a seriousness essentially the same. (p. 92)

All the characters are forced by circumstances to commit actions hostile to their own natures. Verloc, an indolent man, is compelled to bomb the Observatory. Inspector Heat is driven out of his familiar police methods by pressure from the Assistant Commissioner. The Assistant Commissioner feels himself cramped by the immense police bureaucracy of London after his years in the Colonies where there was room for individual maneuvering. Mrs. Verloc, wrenched out of her relationship with Stevie, is driven to murder and suicide. Michaelis, by temperament a childlike idealist, goes to jail for assaulting a prison van in a courageous attempt to free a political prisoner. Ossipon, an easygoing lecher, is thrust into a current of passion that threatens to drown him, and leaves him in the end with shattered nerves.

The images of the novel suggest dislocation and doom. The bell over Verloc's shop is cracked. The prison from which Michaelis has been paroled is "a colossal mortuary for the socially drowned" (p. 44). Stevie sits in the room back of the shop drawing an endless number of circles, "a mad art attempting the inconceivable" (p. 45)—this is subtly juxtaposed with the talk (equally mad) of the anarchists in the front parlor. In the Embassy scene, the first emissary of spring is a fly buzzing on the window—a squalid symbol for the new season. The carving knife, which is eventually thrust into Verloc's bosom, makes its appearance early in the book and serves as a somber portent of coming events.

But the most drastic analogue to the life of man in the swarming city is the persistent failure of the characters to understand and communicate with one another. Neither Verloc nor Winnie, though married, has the faintest notion of what the other is thinking and feeling. Indeed, Winnie's philosophy is summed up in the melancholy line, "She felt profoundly that things do not stand much looking into" (p. 177). This conviction makes the final tragedy possible. The Assistant Commissioner and Inspector Heat are in the closest professional contact, but they remain almost total strangers even in the matter of police tactics and procedures. Stevie looks up to Verloc with reverence and trust; but it is precisely Verloc who, ignorant of his wife's deep attachment to her brother, places a bomb in his hand and sends him to his death. Misunderstanding reaches its most eloquent statement, grimly comic under the macabre circumstances, when Ossipon and Mrs. Verloc join forces after Verloc's murder with grotesque illusions about each other's motives and intentions.

The principal scenes are built on the basis of deliberate duality. While Mr. Vladimir is giving Verloc his new instructions in tones that scarcely conceal his contempt for the agent, Verloc feels a growing hatred for his new employer, which he must make every effort to conceal. The effort leaves him half-choked with frustration and consumed with a slow rage at his entrapment. In the novel's one act of pure unselfish love, Winnie's mother removes herself to an almshouse in the hope of strengthening her son's position in Verloc's house; she feels it likely that he will be more willing to support one of his wife's relatives than two. But her removal is exactly what precipitates Stevie into Verloc's company and leads straight to his doom. The Assistant Commissioner, urged to arrest Michaelis as the man probably responsible for the bombing, becomes reluctant to do so when he sees the veteran anarchist taken up by the great society lady to whom his wife feels obligated. Stevie himself, who shrinks at the thought of living creatures suffering pain and quarrels with coachmen who abuse their horses, is blown to bits with a concussiveness so disintegrating that his remains have to be swept together with a broom and dustpan. The total split that exists between the anarchists and the society they seek to overthrow is matched by the split that exists within the lives of the individual characters. In the structure of the novel the great, teeming, grimy city is the appropriate format for this incohesiveness and the image which supplies it with an ultimate source of reference.

Sloth, too, hangs heavy over the novel, more so than usual in the work of a writer who studied and exploited this emotion throughout his career. It is introduced with Verloc almost at once. ". . . he had an air of having wallowed, fully dressed, all day on an unmade bed" (p. 4). And a little later: ". . . he had embraced indolence from an impulse as profound, as inexplicable, and as imperious as the impulse which directs a man's preference for one particular woman in a given thousand" (p. 12). Mrs. Verloc, much younger than her husband, is trapped in an inertia equally profound. We see her sitting at the counter of the store, immobile, expressionless, hour after hour, not a thought or sensation marring the passionate silence of her consciousness. This passivity lends her a mysterious air, even an air of sensual promise, which causes Ossipon to covet her, but Conrad does not allow us the comfort of romantic indulgence. He links Mrs. Verloc's air of mystery to her lack of curiosity. "Curiosity being one of the forms of self-revelation, a systematically incurious person remains always partly mysterious" (p. 237).

The psychic indolence of the Verlocs extends to the other figures. Inspector Heat is anxious to follow established lines. They require no new effort. They have worked before, in the sense, at any rate, of having earned him rapid promotion. He listens cynically as the Assistant Commissioner outlines a new course of action; he has, after all, seen Assistant Commissioners come and go. The ethical issue does not exist for Heat; it would make the practice of his profession too unsettling. His solution to the bombing is the arrest of Michaelis, a known anarchist, a paroled prisoner, easy to lay hands on. Whether Michaelis was responsible for the bombing is beside the point. His arrest would quiet the public outcry. The Inspector looks for no more. It is not justice he is after, but success, and success is based on the tenacious pursuit of routine. Any departure from the line of least resistance threatens his position. In the remarkable scene when he meets the Professor in a deserted street, Inspector Heat, though loathing the anarchist with all his heart and aching to arrest him, never for a moment contemplates doing so. The Professor has enough dynamite on his person to blow to smithereens anyone within sixty yards, including, of course, himself. The Inspector is very anxious to lay his hands on this grimy zealot, but he is even more anxious to remain alive. The two circle each other warily, exchange a few caustic remarks, then go their separate ways. The Inspector is not a coward; he is simply a man who has mastered the principle of inaction. Within the vastness of the bureaucratic police structure, he recognizes the futility and folly of attempting to assert himself as an individual. Much better to do the safe, the easy, and the usual.

This aggressive inertia is found elsewhere. The anarchists themselves lead passive and parasitical lives, punctuated by irregular and infrequent outbursts of political violence. Yundt and Michaelis are dependent on women for their care. Ossipon preys on women, especially those with savings bank books. The Professor commutes between his shabby room and his equally shabby favorite restaurant, doing nothing. Conrad is led to remark that all revolutionists are lazy since they are unwilling to summon the disciplined effort necessary to live by the rules laid down by society.

Nearly all the characters fall back upon their natural passivity, encouraged by the immense and forbidding facelessness of London. Verloc, forehead pressed against his bedroom window, sees only "the enormity of cold, black, wet, muddy, inhospitable accumulation of bricks, slates, and stones—things in themselves unlovely and unfriendly to man" (p. 56). He recoils from this sight, feeling "the latent unfriendliness of all out-of-doors with a force approaching to positive bodily anguish" (p. 56). The recoil of the characters from the grim, dehumanizing ugliness of the city is one of the novel's persistent phenomena. Even Stevie finds in it only scenes of pain and shock: cabbies who abuse their horses, crowds moving about with a disturbing, frenzied speed, and finally the bomb that annihilates him altogether.

Outside *The Secret Agent* Conrad seldom lingers in London. When he does, the result is the same. The closing scene of "Karain: A Memory," one of the stories in the early *Tales of Unrest* (1898), occurs in the great metropolis. The view is dispiriting.

. . . the broken confusion of roofs, the chimneystacks, the gold letters sprawling over the fronts of houses, the sombre polish of windows, stood resigned and sullen under the falling gloom. The whole length of the street, deep as a well and narrow like a corridor, was full of a sombre and ceaseless stir. Our ears were filled by a headlong shuffle and beat of rapid footsteps and an underlying rumour—a rumour vast, faint, pulsating, as of panting breaths, of beating hearts, of gasping voices. Innumerable eyes stared straight in front, feet moved hurriedly, blank faces flowed, arms swung. Over all, a narrow ragged strip of smoky sky wound about between the high roofs, extended and motionless, like a soiled streamer flying above the rout of a mob. (pp. 54–55)

In "Heart of Darkness" Marlow refers to London as "the monstrous town," and in *The Mirror of the Sea* Conrad himself compares it to a dark, twisting jungle. On one occasion in *Chance,* a much later novel, another major scene takes place in London. Once again it is the demoralizing side of the city that greets us.

. . . the great perspective of drab brick walls, of grey pavement, of muddy roadway rumbling dismally with loaded carts and vans lost itself in the distance, imposing and shabby in its spacious meanness of aspect, in its immeasurable poverty of forms, of colouring, of life —under a harsh, unconcerned sky dried by the wind to a clear blue. It had been raining during the night. The sunshine itself seemed poor. (p. 204)

The people who inhabit this dreary landscape are akin to it.

Every moment people were passing close by us singly, in twos and threes . . . with sallow faces, haggard, anxious or weary, or simply without expression, in an unsmiling sombre stream not made up of lives but of mere unconsidered existences whose joys, struggles, thoughts, sorrows and their very hopes were miserable, glamourless, and of no account in the world, and when one thought of their reality to themselves one's heart became oppressed. (p. 208)

Appropriately, the chromatic movement of *The Secret Agent* is from light to darkness. The two scenes in the bedroom of the Verlocs reach their climax in this way. Taking his cue from Othello's "Put out the light, and then put out the light," Conrad closes each scene with the extinguishing of the lamp by the Verloc bed. The light cast by this lamp is, of course, deceptive; it simply throws the spiritual darkness in which the married couple grope into sharper relief.

In the first scene Verloc, badly shaken by the upsetting assignment he has received from Mr. Vladimir, dreads going to sleep. ". . . he felt horribly wakeful, and dreaded facing the darkness and silence that would follow the extinguishing of the lamp" (p. 58). At last, Mrs. Verloc, already in bed, asks him "in a faint, far-away voice. 'Shall I put out the light now?' The dreary conviction that there was no sleep for him held Mr. Verloc mute and hopelessly inert in his fear of darkness. He made a great effort. 'Yes. Put it out,' he said at last, in a hollow tone" (p. 60). The hollowness of his tone, in keep-

ing with the faint, faraway voice of his wife, suggests the nature of
their relationship, which begins in ignorance and ends in the darkness not only of extinguished lamps but of death itself.

On the second occasion the psychic pressure of his assignment has
eaten more deeply into Verloc's nerves. The sensory framework of
the scene conveys a heightened sense of foreboding. Mrs. Verloc
"let the lonely clock on the landing count off fifteen ticks into the
abyss of eternity, and asked: 'Shall I put the light out?' Mr. Verloc
snapped at his wife huskily. 'Put it out' " (p. 181).

The extinction of a third and final light is yet to come. Mrs.
Verloc murders her husband, then flees the house. In her panic she
forgets to turn off the light in the parlor and to close the door of
the shop. In the Soho darkness outside she runs into Ossipon and to
his astonishment throws herself into his arms. He takes her money,
accepts her embraces, and returns with her to the shop in Brett
Street. There to his horror he sees Verloc's body. "Mr. Verloc did
not seem so much asleep now as lying down with a bent head and
looking insistently at his left breast" (p. 285). The scenes that follow
are described by Conrad with a paralyzing dramatic tension. They
are climaxed by the heart-stopping moment when the constable on
his rounds rattles the doorknob, followed by Mrs. Verloc begging
her terrified companion to turn off the light. This he finally does,
and the two, psychically shattered, stagger off into the London darkness to their last fateful parting. There is nothing in Conrad's fiction
to equal the excitement, terror, visual realization, and handling of
sensory detail of the eleventh and twelfth chapters of *The Secret
Agent*, which bring to a powerful climax the dominant movement
of the novel toward the destructive obscurity of night.

The circumstances surrounding the writing of the novel intensify
the desperate view Conrad took in it. The creation of *Nostromo* had
chained him to his desk for eighteen months, and when that immense novel, as Mrs. Conrad put it, "turned out a black frost as far
as the public went, Conrad was bitterly disappointed." [13] His earlier
books had been failures too, but he had nourished the secret hope
that he would at last succeed with this one. When he took up *The
Secret Agent*, it was in a mood of deep frustration and defeat. Mrs.
Conrad, who was pregnant at the time, remarked on his facial ex-

[13] *Joseph Conrad As I Knew Him* (New York, 1926), p. 53.

pression during the writing: "As I did not know in the least what the book was about, I could not account to myself for the grimly ironic expression I used often to catch on his face, whenever he came to give me a look-in. Could it have reference to the expected baby? No! It was only a reflection of the tone of the book's." [14] At this time, too, Mrs. Conrad had to undergo a serious operation on an injured knee. In Geneva, where the novel was finished, both of Conrad's sons fell very ill, which led their mother to write: "I cannot recall that time . . . without a shudder, for . . . it was by the merest chance that either of the boys lived to return to England." [15]

These several circumstances drove Conrad to search for an arresting symbol of the life of failure. He finally settled upon the image of London. It was the center of the country that he had adopted, but which had not adopted him. It was the center of the world of letters that he had embraced as a second profession, without success. It was the center of money, and money was precisely what he had not been able to earn enough of to pay his family's expenses out of his own labor. London, in short, was the living embodiment of all the worldly values that he felt himself, in the deepest personal sense, to have failed in. When these feelings were most acute, Conrad wrote *The Secret Agent,* a novel dealing with people who fail and with the life of failure. He pressed them into the iron clamp of the great city, whose hugeness and multiplicity made vain the efforts of men to reach out and conquer. If Verloc is the political agent whose activities supply the plot with its motion, the megalopolis that he inhabits is the psychological agent that invests the characters with their somber coloration and their melancholy destiny.

Like *Nostromo, The Secret Agent* failed with the public. But it records with harsh and singular power Conrad's savage vision of life at a dark time in his career.

14 *Ibid.,* pp. 53–54.
15 *Ibid.,* p. 125.

XI

The Russian Colossus

THOUGH CONRAD WAS NEVER TO WRITE A NOVEL ABOUT POLAND, HE FELT driven to write one about Russia. In all of his fiction there is but a single Pole to be found: the vaguely drawn aristocrat in the story "Prince Roman" (1911), in substance scarcely more than a family-album anecdote. There is no lack of Englishmen, Frenchmen, Dutchmen, Italians, and Germans. A Russian turns up in "Heart of Darkness," of all unlikely places, and Conrad's Russian novel, *Under Western Eyes,* is, of course, crowded with them. But only a single Pole. The Yanko Gourall of "Amy Foster" is a Carpathian from somewhere in Central Europe. Even *Nostromo,* that smorgasbord of nationalities, colors, and religions, does not include any Poles. The separation between his native country and his art was almost total.

Whatever private inhibition barred the Poles from his fiction, no such restraint operated in the case of Poland's traditional enemies. Two of the three Germans who appear in Conrad are villainous types, though Germany by no means aroused in him the formless dread evoked by Russia. One was the German captain of the *Patna,* consumed by the single passion of self-love, given to comically violent rages when his safety is threatened, a grotesque incarnation of animal vulgarity and xenophobic meanness summed up by his characteristic exclamation, "I shpit on it." The other is the hotelkeeper Schomberg, who appears briefly in *Lord Jim,* at greater length in "Falk," and blossoms into a major figure in *Victory.* He, too, loves himself with a hotly exclusive passion, yields without resistance to fits of outraged vanity, and ferociously envies men more finely grained than himself whom he then seeks to pull down. He regards their very existence as a personal affront.

These two embody Conrad's view of the German character: energetic, aggressively self-centered, paranoiac, volatile, physically unlovely, and morally unlovable. In his essay "Poland Revisited," he described the German genius as having "a hypnotising power over half-baked souls and half-lighted minds," and Germany herself as a "highly organised mediocrity" (*Notes on Life and Letters*, p. 159). Her mediocrity is embodied in Conrad's third German figure, Captain Hermann in the story "Falk." He is a good-natured, thickheaded burgher, totally incapable of responding to feelings outside his narrow emotional orbit. It was Prussia's organization and aggressiveness that in Conrad's eyes made her menacing, and her mediocrity that made her uninteresting. Schomberg, Hermann, and the *Patna* captain are, in the end, highly colored caricatures. Like their compatriots in the cartoons of George Grosz, they are alive in a limited frame.

Russia was another matter. Germany meant very little to Conrad, one way or another, but Russia affected him deeply. In his essay "Autocracy and War," composed in 1905 as a comment on the Russo-Japanese War, Conrad reserved his more inflamed rhetoric for Russia, though Germany appeared to him the greater immediate menace to the safety of Europe. His epithets for the Czarist empire suggest a nightmare view: blind Djinn, Old Man of the Sea, ravenous Ghoul, a country "armed with chains, hung over with holy images," ruled by a blind despotism scourging and slaughtering its subjects. Russia has not done "a single generous deed" or rendered a single service "to the polity of nations," though all the while laboring under a delusion of universal conquest, tainted "by a half-mystical, insensate, fascinating assertion of purity and holiness" (*Notes on Life and Letters*, p. 98). The Japanese laid to rest the myth of Russian power, a myth Europe had mistakenly labored under for centuries. Conrad insists on Russia's weakness as he does on her ferocity, and regards her with a mixture of contempt and horror. Since it was Russia that had annexed the section of Poland in which Conrad was born, the intimacy of enslavement had produced upon him a violent reaction which remained with him permanently. The hypnotic spell of that vast empire, which he always saw in primeval terms, held him transfixed, and none of his frequent exclamations that he and Poland belonged to the West could release him from it. Nor did his protestations that he knew not one word

of Russian, not even the alphabet, that as a boy he had no contact
with Russians, that the Poles kept themselves strictly apart and
even in Russian exile held themselves aloof from the oppressor,
conceal the tie which bound him, in fascination as well as revulsion,
to the mammoth from the East.

He refused to attend meetings in England, even for worthy
causes, if a Russian were present. He would balk at magazine offers
and bridle at public grants if a Russian were even remotely involved.
The great Russian novelists of the nineteenth century aroused in
him mixed emotions. He admired only Turgeniev without reserva-
tion, no doubt because he was the least Russian and most Westernized of the lot. Tolstoy he disliked—too mystically and redemptively
Christian for his taste, too lured by abstract ideas. His chief anti-
pathy was reserved for Dostoevsky.[1] After reading *The Brothers
Karamazov* in Mrs. Garnett's translation, he wrote to Garnett:
". . . it's an impossible lump of valuable matter. It's terrifically
bad and impressive and exasperating. Moreover, I don't know what
D stands for or reveals, but I do know he is too Russian for me.
It sounds to me like some fierce mouthings from prehistoric ages." [2]
Five years later he referred to Dostoevsky as "the grimacing, haunted
creature."

It was not the Russian's perpetual descent into the torments and
pathology of the soul that repelled him—Conrad was, after all, an
explorer of the same landscape—but that he seemed to revel in it.
The journey may have been unavoidable to a serious writer, but it
always filled Conrad with horror, as it did Marlow and Kurtz.
Dostoevsky appeared to him to wallow in and enjoy the darkness
as though it were his natural element.[3] His narrative power and
demonic energy fascinated Conrad; his Russian at-homeness in the
awfulness of man shocked and disgusted him, as he was shocked and
disgusted by the same quality in the Russian state, a quality that he

1 Yet Conrad's own writing was influenced more by Dostoevsky than the others.
Thomas Mann regarded Stevie, in *The Secret Agent,* as "unthinkable" without
Dostoevsky's Idiot *(Past Masters and Other Papers,* p. 245).

2 Letter of May 27, 1912, Garnett, p. 240.

3 Curle's comment amplifies the satanic note: "Dostoievsky represented to him
[Conrad] the ultimate forces of confusion and insanity arrayed against all that he
valued in civilization. He did not despise him as one despises a nonentity, he
hated him as one might hate Lucifer and the forces of darkness" *(The Last
Twelve Years of Joseph Conrad,* New York, 1928, p. 26).

attributed to its Asiatic and Byzantine origins. Whenever anyone sought to pin a Slavonic label on him—H. L. Mencken was the last of his admirers to do so in his lifetime—he was stung to extravagant indignation, and rushed at once to dissociate himself from "Slavo-Tartar Byzantine barbarism" and reassert his ties with the West.

At the same time he insisted on the impersonal detachment of his feelings, and grew very touchy when accused of bias. His view of Russia was not the vengeful sentiment of an oppressed subject, insisted Conrad, but the plain reading of a disinterested observer. As for the Russian writers, he had read only a scattering of their works and those in translation, so he did not pretend to be an expert. But of the absolute veracity and truth of his own novel about the Russians, he had not the slightest doubt. When Garnett complained that *Under Western Eyes* revealed Conrad's hatred of Russia, the author exploded:

There's just as much or as little hatred in this book as in the Outcast of the Islands for instance. . . . I don't expect you will believe me. You are so russianized . . . that you don't know the truth when you see it—unless it smells of cabbage-soup when it at once secures your profound respect. . . . But it is hard after lavishing "a wealth of tenderness" on Tekla and Sophia, to be charged with the rather low trick of putting one's hate into a novel. If you seriously think that I have done that then my dear fellow let me tell you that you don't know what the accent of hate is.[4]

Conrad happened to be right and Garnett wrong about the novel, but Conrad's angry reaction to the charge—ordinarily he was all too prone to accept Garnett's criticism—revealed the soreness of the whole question and his raw hypersensitivity to it. He could regard the Germans with a contemptuous, almost patronizing carelessness, but the Russians brought him to a rapid boil, and aroused in him an emotional response from some deeper part of himself which in life he was never able to objectify.

Art once again came to his rescue, for he was able to achieve in fiction that control of powerful feeling that escaped him in personal experience. *Under Western Eyes* (1911) turned out to be a safety valve for the rush of angry sentiment about his country's hereditary enemy and, in however obscure or oblique a fashion, an escape hatch

4 Letter of October 20, 1911, Garnett, pp. 232–233.

for his own tangled feelings about Poland. But he maintained to the end that the novel had nothing personal about it: "Subjects lay about for anybody to pick up," he wrote in the same letter to Garnett in which he ascribed pro-Russian prejudice to his friend. "I have picked up this one. And that's all there is to it." [5] And later on: "Is it possible that you haven't seen that in this book I am concerned with nothing but ideas, to the exclusion of everything else, with no arrière pensée of any kind." [6] Both men were to some degree justified. Garnett, acutely conscious of Conrad's convictions over the years, observed the depth of feeling from which the novel emerged. But Conrad, aware of his responsibility to truth and the need for establishing characters (even Russian ones) with their own complex validity, was properly impressed with his power to create the sympathetic characters of Nathalie Haldin and her brother, Razumov, Mikulin, and Sophia Antonovna—all intensely and immediately human—to go with a monster of cruelty like Nikita and a monster of vanity like Peter Ivanovich. The man and the writer in Conrad are never more sharply separated and, at the same time, more intimately coupled than in his double vision of the Russian colossus.

There is room in *Under Western Eyes* both for Conrad's strong personal sentiments about Russia as an Asiatic despotism and his psychological interest in the Russians as individuals belonging, after all, to the human race. Indeed, the first conception contributes to the second. The image of Russia hanging over its subjects like a menacing cloud drives them to extremes of passion, to outbursts of energy that make them, paradoxically, more intensely, violently human than other peoples. Certainly more so than the novel's intermittent narrator, the Englishman who teaches languages in Geneva and is thrown into contact with the Czarist exiles. He is a typical West European, prudent, restrained, democratic, and at the same time shallower and with a smaller capacity for emotion than the Russians. They may be driven too far, but he, plainly, is not driven far enough. There again rises in Conrad the question of the price paid by civilization. In its comforts, in its civilities, the West has made life agreeable, perhaps too agreeable, for it threatens to cut its citizens off from the self-knowledge and self-

5 Garnett, p. 232.
6 *Ibid.*, p. 233.

exploration that can come only when they are exposed to pressure. The main object of civilization is to reduce the pressure of life or to deflect it, necessary if men are to rise from the level of primitive survival. But when carried too far—and under the spur of its own momentum this can scarcely be avoided—the process will extract an increasingly heavy price in complacency, the atrophy of emotional response, and the superficialization of human nature itself. The professor of languages suffers from these tendencies, though not so much but that he recognizes in the Russians, amid his loathing of them, a capacity that he does not possess. The Russians, closer to primitivism, maneuvered by a grossly primitive government, are given to the excesses that destroy them, but they seem somehow more alive in their death thrashings than does the Englishman in his prudent and mannerly self-control.

Conrad allies himself with the West, insists that Poland is a Western country, flaunts her Latin credentials on all occasions, yet is close enough to Russia—at least the artist in him is—to feel her hot, if morbid vitality. Hence the disquietening fascination Dostoevsky exercises over him, akin to Mr. X's effect on the nameless narrator of "The Informer." His special position as a Pole enables Conrad to approach Russia at point-blank range while at the same time freeing him from a slavish embracing of Western values. *Under Western Eyes* underlines Conrad's psychological mastery of the European scene, his organization of East and West into a unified imaginative structure.

The central figure of *Under Western Eyes* is another of Joseph Conrad's unfilled men. Razumov measures his descent from Lord Jim and Nostromo, and is himself continued in later novels by Axel Heyst and the young captain of *The Shadow-Line*.

Most of these men are unfilled because they are without psychological content to begin with, and acquire their personalities, if they acquire them at all, as a result of their experiences in the story or from the conceptions read into them by the commenting characters. Indeed, one of the primary functions of Conrad's narrators—Marlow is the best known but by no means the only one—is to midwife these as yet unformed heroes into life and then attend their materialization.

Their blankness assumes various forms. Jim is a raw youth who for many chapters remains paralyzed before his opportunities; an irritating enigma to himself, he is a source of endless speculation to others, each of whom reads into the tantalizing void of Jim the necessities of his own nature. The youthful captain of *The Shadow-Line*, bored and impatient, waits for experience to come to him; his personality slowly emerges inside the chrysalis of his first command. Nostromo and Heyst are older men. We see Nostromo as a heroic leader capable of any exploit, iron-nerved and absolutely reliable in emergencies. But when the society in which he functions is overthrown, he crumbles all at once, and is revealed as a man without inner resources, deriving his strength from external approval like a basketball which swells to its proper shape only when enough air is pumped into it from the outside. He is full to start with, and emptied at the end. Heyst, a pale carbon of a philosophically dominating father who preaches isolation from life, drifts wraithlike on the edge of events. When drawn into action by the weaknesses of pity and the temptations of sex, the substance of his own self, hitherto held in check, is released into being. The figures who open and close in this fashion supply the physical motion of Conrad's novels with its psychological equivalent.

Razumov is Conrad's richest achievement in the uses of the unfilled man. He is introduced as a youth without personal ties of any kind and without an acknowledged family. Among eighty million Russians he "had no heart to which he could open himself" (*Under Western Eyes*, p. 39). The natural son of Prince K, he is cut off from a normal upbringing by the fact of his illegitimacy. Even his face lacks individual distinctness: "It was as if a face modelled vigorously in wax . . . had been held close to a fire till all sharpness of line had been lost in the softening of the material" (p. 5). An obscure, not altogether respectable lawyer hands him an allowance at periodic intervals, a sum large enough to pay his living expenses at the university. Though a student for some years he has made no friends, his air of forbidding aloofness discouraging contact. Paradoxically, this very air is taken by his fellow students as a mark of intellectual profundity and moral purity, as the sign of "an unstained, lofty and solitary existence." Unknown to himself, Razumov has acquired a reputation as a man in whom one could have confidence: "He had been made a personage without knowing anything about it" (pp. 82–83). When he discovers this, he is moved to remark wryly, "The scoundrels and the fools are murdering my intelligence" (p. 83). His isolation, and the unexpected and unintended respect and admiration which it accidentally breeds, are to be the very elements that plunge him into tragedy.

The theme of Razumov's empty solitude is struck throughout the novel. "He was as lonely in the world as a man swimming in the deep sea" (p. 10) .[7] ". . . Razumov's youth had no one in the world, as literally no one as it can be honestly affirmed of any human being" (p. 293). He walked through "the busy streets, isolated as if in a desert . . ." (p. 297). "His existence was a great cold blank . . ." (p. 303). When with others, he longed to be "in the middle of some field miles away from everywhere . . ." (p. 290). Significantly, the fate that he suffers at the end is to be rendered stone deaf, which gives his isolation a horrifying yet relevant sensory frame. Since Conrad had gone to some lengths to emphasize Razumov's fine ear and acute sense of hearing (p. 291), the loss of it is thereby made climactic.

Subtly reinforcing Razumov's isolation is his banishment from time. As Haldin, the student terrorist whom he betrayed to the police earlier that evening, leaves his room, the watch slips from Razumov's nervous fingers and breaks. It is midnight. Thereafter, he passes into another universe, timeless and terrifying. "Razumov looked wildly about as if for some means of seizing upon time which seemed to have escaped him altogether" (p. 65) . The next morning the watch is still stopped at twelve, and the hours drift by in oblivion. "The room grew dark swiftly though time had seemed to stand still. How was it that he had not noticed the passing of that day? Of course, it was the watch being stopped . . ." (p. 69). Long afterward, even when repaired, the watch keeps reminding him of the fatal evening, its movement seeming never to have progressed beyond it. And when he is ready to atone for the betrayal of Haldin, he—"the puppet of his past"—sits with the watch before him waiting for midnight to begin his final errand. The entire theme is introduced by the "mute clock" in the house of General T where the betrayal takes place. In murdering Haldin, Razumov also murders

[7] This image strikingly anticipates the plight of Leggatt, the fugitive in "The Secret Sharer," the celebrated story Conrad wrote in November, 1909, two months before finishing *Under Western Eyes.*

time, and the slain dimension cuts him off from the world as much
as the slain man.

Since he has no relationships with human beings, he is driven
to seek abstractions. In due course he identifies himself with the
greatest, the most impersonal, and at the same time the most immediate of abstractions—Russia. The novel is as much Conrad's
analysis of the country oppressing his own as of the life of Razumov.
The two—character and nation—are so coupled at the beginning that
neither appears without dramatizing the other.

Because Razumov feels himself blank and undefined, it is these
qualities in his native land that affect him: "Razumov received an
almost physical impression of endless space and of countless millions. . . . Under the sumptuous immensity of the sky, the snow
covered the endless forests, the frozen rivers, the plains of an immense country, obliterating the landmarks, the accidents of the
ground, levelling everything under its uniform whiteness, like a
monstrous blank page awaiting the record of an inconceivable history" (p. 33). The thought of this vastness fills him with "a sort
of sacred inertia" and a voice within him seems to cry, "Don't touch
it." At night he dreams of walking completely alone through drifts
of snow in the enormous expanse of immense, wintry Russia (p. 66).
The bomb-throwing of the revolutionists appears to him pitifully
ineffectual and, after a good deal of close reasoning reminiscent of
Raskolnikov, grossly immoral. "And what can you people do by scattering a few drops of blood on the snow?" he bursts out at Haldin.
"On this Immensity. On this unhappy Immensity!" (p. 61).

For that matter what can anyone do? Razumov thinks of himself as a liberal; he does not defend the oppressive bureaucracy. But
the wild outbursts of the revolutionists please him even less. He
embraces a vague *mystique* of change. Things will move somehow,
under their own momentum, and though this momentum is slow,
even glacierlike, it is suited to the soul of Russia, is indeed its expression. The very vagueness of Razumov's ecological attachment
reflects the amorphous void of his temperament. Within this void
there is only one recognizable impulse, a deeply grounded sense
of self-preservation. Razumov wants to succeed in his studies and
have a career—a future all the more desirable because it will enable him to merge concretely with the Russian stream. He is com-

peting at the university for a certain silver medal. The first painful thought that passes through his mind as Haldin declares himself the assassin is, "There goes my silver medal!" (p. 16). Any suspicion that he is involved will, of course, ruin his hopes. Thus goaded by his threatened and resentful egotism, Razumov plunges into the web of rationalization that finally persuades him to identify his own interests with the established Russian power.

When the coating of patriotism hardens sufficiently around Razumov's core of self-love, he betrays Haldin to the authorities, and soon afterward becomes a police spy.[8] Part One of the novel closes with Mikulin, spokesman for the regime, asking Razumov, "Where to?" Having taken the first step away from moral isolation, he must also take the second, and soon embraces the whole tangle of commitments that his new alignment involves. Our unfilled young man now begins to assume his first visible shape.

The Russia that encloses him has already been presented to us as an organism different from our own. It is everything Western Europe is not and when seen under Western eyes appears illogical, arbitrary, baffling, ruled by an uneasy despotism prostituting the noblest impulses of its oppressed subjects " to the lusts of hate and fear." The elderly Englishman who serves as the "Western eyes" of the novel is a professor of languages. It is his voice that we hear first. Appropriately, he is commenting on the nature of words which he regards as "the great foes of reality." And of all peoples it is the Russians, he finds, who love words most. So ardently do they speak, and often so aptly, that "one can't defend oneself from the suspicion that they really understand what they say" (p. 4). Such cynicism from a man who disavows cynicism stems from the pathology of a country that fascinates, mystifies, and disgusts him in about equal measure. The cruelties of the Czarist autocracy, applied by a police force that employs torture as a matter of course, breed in its victims a revolutionary sentiment of pure destruction that is just as monstrous. Oppressors and oppressed are morally alike. The unjust acts of the regime are well known, but the revolutionary movement can

---

8 He is the reluctant obverse of Verloc (protagonist of the immediately preceding novel, *The Secret Agent*), who goes comfortably underground as a means of making a living. Razumov becomes a secret agent against his real will, out of artificially induced conviction; it is not a role natural to him. Between them Conrad creates a composite portrait of the underground man.

breed a sadist like Nikita who loves killing for its own sake; and
even Haldin, whose motives are surely idealistic, throws a bomb at
M. de P, the tyrant, which kills at the same time a number of innocent bystanders, a dreadful result that he accepts in advance.
Yet Russia also breeds the noblest and purest hearts, capable of the
most exquisite feelings and unselfish acts. Our language professor
falls in love with Nathalie Haldin almost at once, though he regards her as no less Russian than the egotistical, falsely sentimental
Peter Ivanovich whom he detests.

Conrad himself, in an Author's Note published a decade after
the novel, sums up the feelings of his narrator. Russian life, he
remarks, can "be reduced to the formula of senseless desperation
provoked by senseless tyranny" (p. viii). Razumov is crushed by
the "sanguinary futility of the crimes and the sacrifices seething in
that amorphous mass . . ." (p. ix). Russia is an immense blind
alley begetting illusions that turn in upon themselves and lead
nowhere: "The ferocity and imbecility of an autocratic rule rejecting all legality and in fact basing itself upon complete moral
anarchism provokes the no less imbecile and atrocious answer of
a purely Utopian revolutionism encompassing destruction by the
first means at hand, in the strange conviction that a fundamental
change of hearts must follow the downfall of any given human institutions" (p. x). But it is "not so much the political state as the
psychology of Russia" that he hopes to render, and it is here that
Conrad transcends his feelings as an oppressed Pole to present with
a remarkable detachment and sympathy the soul of a nation for
which he could feel no love.

Inside the senselessness and the compulsion to suffering of the
Russian scene, the personal drama of Razumov unfolds with remorseless logic. His dream of pursuing his private life has been
shattered. Driven into the role of a government spy, he finds himself
worse off than before. He is now no longer isolated, but thrown
into the most intimate contact with others. Yet each relationship
is poisoned by duplicity. Befriended by the students in St. Petersburg,
he uses them shamefully as pawns to help his sham escape. Accepted by the revolutionary circle in Geneva, he betrays them in
long reports on their activities to their enemies at home. With
Nathalie Haldin, he poses as her brother's closest comrade though

he has in fact sent him to his death. Everything conspires to make this double role successful. The illusions that everyone nurtures about him are supported in each detail by a lucky arrangement of circumstances. But the easier the part he is called upon to play, the more tense and unhappy, the more nervously agitated he becomes.

At first this agitation is prompted by a fear of exposure. As this danger subsides, Razumov, falling in love with Miss Haldin, feels a growing revulsion for what he is doing and, almost immediately thereafter, for himself. The gap thus set up between his two selves slowly widens despite his frantic efforts to bridge it. The instant that he begins to love someone the foundations of his pure self-love are undermined, and he can no longer stand on his old ground. At the same time he makes the agonizing discovery that his attachment to Russia, deriving from self-interest, has been fed by betrayal and deception, and is therefore itself a deception. All these feelings come to a head during his long-delayed interview with Mrs. Haldin when, gazing at her hard, unbelieving, dying face, his rising sense of repugnance flings him into deepest despair.

Leaving Mrs. Haldin's room, he encounters Nathalie in the hall. Driven unendurably by the widening moral abyss that he can no longer straddle, he makes his first confession. He leaves her stunned while filling the professor of languages, the unheeded witness of the scene, with proper Western indignation. Razumov rushes back to his lodging, finishes the diary that he had begun to write in an attempt to relieve his anguished feelings, addresses it to Miss Haldin, then presents himself to the revolutionaries where he makes his second confession. Razumov's soul is now purged, and he meets without resistance the attack from the avenging roughs. They deliberately burst his eardrums, and by plunging him into eternal silence return him to an isolation even more profound than that which surrounded him at the start.

The name Razumov, in both Polish and Russian, means to understand. His journey through the novel is an exercise in understanding. He has come to understand what Jim, Nostromo, Captain Anthony, Charles Gould, Heyst, and other notable Conradian figures discover under different though no less difficult circumstances: excessive isolation leads to moral collapse; a purely egotistic attachment to society can be equally destructive; an unselfish response to the world is not a guarantee of sanity and endurance but an indispensable preliminary to them; this response does not destroy self-love but tempers and sophisticates it to the point where the tensions of living inside the ring of an inscrutable cosmos are made bearable. One of Conrad's uncommon achievements is his capacity to bring man and the universe into a coherent relationship.

He had come to grips with the cosmos in his earlier work and found that it had limits beyond which men could not penetrate. They could grapple with its manifestations but could not apprehend its nature. The explanations of Christianity and other organized religions Conrad rejected long before he began to write. The existence of a *primum mobile* he could find no evidence for. The operations of a supreme moral intelligence, fashionable among Transcendentalists and Unitarians, seemed to him grimly contradicted by the common experience of mankind. He was left with a view of the world as a dramatic spectacle rather than an ethical process,[9] whose essential character was mysterious, baffling, and inscrutable, which sometimes made sense and often did not, which was outside morality and theology, and which could not be overcome by the mere application of human intelligence or will. It was the basic fact about life that had to be accepted on these essentially unsatisfactory terms, and lived with as best one could.

From the start Conrad sought in his work physical embodiments of the psychological forces affecting his characters. The jungle of Borneo petrified Almayer in his dream of fortune and lured Willems to his final collapse. The sea was the agent that forced the crew of the *Narcissus* into its traumatic journey, thrust Jim into his great trial, taught the Marlow of "Youth" his crucial lesson, and imposed upon Captain Whalley the terms of his death. The silver mine played a parallel role in *Nostromo*, while in *The Secret Agent* the lives of the Verlocs and their anarchist circle were controlled and slowly suffocated by the iron darkness of London. Conrad searched for an equivalent arrangement in *Under Western Eyes* and found it in his conception of Russia. This served as the clamp that imposed itself on the lives of the characters.

So vast a country can be managed only by absolute force. This

[9] See his famous passage on the subject in *A Personal Record*, pp. 92–94.

simple principle animating the ruling bureaucracy is bluntly expressed by General T, whose hatred of any form of change is uncompromising. He even looks upon Razumov with suspicion, for
how can an informer retain the purity of his loyalty when living in
close contact with the traitors against whom he is informing. Such
rigidly ferocious logic fosters in the revolutionists a response equally
rigid and ferocious, a process that forces both sides to give up something of their humanity. Dehumanization here assumes the form
of betrayal, and the novel exploits the psychology of betrayal as
the atmosphere into which Russia ultimately thrusts its inhabitants.

Everyone is driven to betray. Haldin kills the innocent as well
as the guilty when he throws his bomb, then deliberately draws
Razumov into his dangerous affairs for no better reason than to
save his own skin. Razumov turns Haldin over to the police but
before doing so betrays his own avowed convictions by first trying
to help Haldin escape; when he finds the carriage driver Ziemianitch,
who was to have arranged the escape, dead drunk, Razumov flies
into a rage which leads him in the end to the police. En route, he
utters Conrad's well-known slogan, "All a man can betray is his conscience," perverting it to justify sending Haldin to his death. The
finality of the comment is ultimately brought home to him, but
not before he has used it to clothe his ignoblest act.

The other figures are caught up in the same moral smudge.
Prince K, out of sincere conviction, persuades his son to become a
police spy. Nikita, the avenging arm of the revolutionists, turns
out to be an agent of the dreaded regime. Ziemianitch proves *hors
de combat* at the very moment he is most urgently needed. Peter
Ivanovich is a rapacious, self-admiring sensualist who romanticizes
the oppression he had suffered heroically as a young man to exploit
everyone around him and particularly the revolutionary cause of
which he has made himself a leader. Sophia Antonovna is sickened
by the brutality employed by her fellow radicals, yet steels herself
and goes on. Even Nathalie, though with the best intentions, proves
treacherous; she delays in telling Mrs. Haldin of Razumov's arrival
in Geneva, and thus contributes to the final morbid seizure in which
her mother, rightly, believes herself betrayed and sinks stone-eyed
to her death. Nor is betrayal confined to persons; institutions are
contaminated as well. The most faithful figure in the novel, the
Czarist counterespionage chief Mikulin, is tried and convicted of

unspecified crimes which he did not commit by the government he has served loyally. He dies, his lips sealed, never disclosing any of the secrets in his possession that might conceivably embarrass his faithless masters.

The necessity to betray, endemic in the Russian psyche, is matched by the equally compulsive necessity to redeem. Razumov's violent confessions relieve his tortured soul and redeem his guilt. Tekla's suffering as a young girl converts her to the service of others with slavish and fanatical ardor. The good-natured student Kostia, who is ashamed of his wealth and stupidity, wishes to make up for both by plying Razumov with money and schemes for escaping from the country. Nathalie goes back to Russia in the end and devotes herself to helping the needy, moved in part by a desire to perpetuate the memory and especially the ideal purity of purpose which she is convinced animated her brother, in part to redeem the Russians from their own destructiveness.

The passions of the book are linked by correspondences that lie below the story surface. Razumov passes through the same stages as Haldin. He murders Haldin as Haldin murdered M. de P. The trust Haldin displays in him is analogous to the love Razumov later feels for Nathalie. Haldin is betrayed by this trust, and Razumov is "betrayed" by his love, which spurs his confession to the revolutionists. The assault he suffers at their hands is equivalent to the torture Haldin stoically endured at the hands of the police before his execution. The connection between them becomes absolute when the image of Haldin roots itself in Razumov's mind obsessionally, and he becomes a double man bearing the heavy and unshakable burden of this other self. ". . . Haldin, always Haldin—nothing but Haldin—everywhere Haldin: a moral spectre infinitely more effective than any visible apparition of the dead" (pp. 299–300). As he hurries home from his ugly mission to the police, he sees the phantom of Haldin stretched out in the snow. He walks over its chest, but it refuses to disappear. Much later, as he tells his lies to Mrs. Haldin in Geneva, the phantom continues clinging to him leechlike, splitting him away from the unity and purpose he has so uneasily achieved. ". . . the dark prestige of the Haldin mystery . . . clung to him like a poisoned robe it was impossible to fling off" (p. 299).

Another correspondence subtly links Razumov and the hapless Ziemianitch. Both are men who fail and are punished for their failure. Razumov yields to his capacity for self-deception and commits his crimes against humanity; Ziemianitch yields to his capacity for self-indulgence and is in an alcoholic stupor at the very moment Haldin needs him most desperately. Ziemianitch is thrashed by Razumov and mistakes him for a devil, which indeed he is on the point of becoming. Razumov is thrashed by Nikita, an actual devil. Both are thrown down flights of stairs. Ziemianitch hangs himself in despair; in despair, Razumov falls under a tram. Curiously, both have trouble with women. The carriage driver commits suicide out of frustrated love; so, in a sense, does Razumov. Both are referred to as "men of the people"; at one point, Razumov feels "a vague, remorseful tenderness" for the other. We are asked to regard them as typical Russians.

There are other suggestive images. The presence in the house of General T of Spontini's bronze figure "Flight of Youth" accents the grim nature of Razumov's mission there. Razumov writes both his diary and counterespionage reports on an islet in the Lake of Geneva where the statue of Jean Jacques Rousseau stands. In this way he composes his own confessions and carries out his own social contract with the state. During the sham escape, Razumov throws Kostia's bundle of money out the train window into the emptiness of Russia, a gesture that arrestingly underlines the hollowness and mockery of his new life. When Nathalie comes to the Château Borel, she sees no one at first, but hears a voice in the distance speaking a language she cannot make out; this eerie and unsettling experience somehow encapsulates the situation of a novel whose characters, in the midst of isolation, grope toward the sound of voices that are not quite intelligible.

This, too, is the problem for the professor of languages, the lone non-Russian in the book. He, too, hears voices, the voices of Russia, whose formal words he understands well enough but whose emotional significance lies outside both his sympathies and imagination. To him, the tragedy of life is the tragedy of language, and words, as he announces on the opening page, are a conspiracy to keep meanings and intentions from being communicated. He brings to his experience the conventional morality of the West. He is filled with "proper" indignation at the extravagant behavior of the Russians, chides them for their lack of democracy, their rudimentary

sense of law and order, their cruelty and violence. But these orthodox sentiments are of no use in enabling him to understand them,
and Conrad makes no effort to hide the obtuseness of his narrator
while exploiting the contrast his presence makes possible between
the competing systems of Eastern and Western Europe.

The emotional imperceptiveness of the West is reinforced by
Conrad's deliberately uncomplimentary references to Geneva and
the Swiss. The city is "the very desolation of slumbering respect-
ability," "the passionless abode of democratic liberty." The Swiss
who appear briefly in Part Second of the novel are inert and bovine,
"the man, colourlessly uncouth, was drinking beer . . . the woman,
rustic and placid . . . gazed idly around." Their fate "was made
secure from the cradle to the grave by the perfected mechanism of
democratic institutions . . ." (p. 175). If the Russians suffer from
an excess of feeling, the West Europeans are hobbled by a dearth
of it.

Himself a Polish Slav who later became (to some extent) both
Gallicized and Anglicized, Conrad was peculiarly equipped to penetrate the minds of both camps while dramatizing the failure of
each to comprehend the other. Only at the one point of his special
regard for Miss Haldin does our language professor, born though
he is in St. Petersburg and speaking Russian as fluently and often
more correctly than the Russians themselves, make any genuine
contact with their otherwise strange and hostile society. This is
the single emotion that he shares with Razumov, and he is trans-
figured by it in the same way.

Love is one of the sentiments in Conrad that releases men from
the suffocation of narcissism and the emptiness of noninvolvement.
It is by no means the only one: friendship, duty, honor, patriotism,
even a diffusely warmhearted generosity, feelings intricately dis-
sected in the other novels, have a similar humanizing effect. For an
instant, love draws the professor out of his restrictive sphere of
judgment.[10] It forces Razumov to examine himself as he is, free
from the obscuring effects of vanity and loneliness. It does not sepa-

[10] This restrictiveness comes out again in the way the professor discharges his
formal role as narrator. In introducing Razumov's diary, he fussily observes that
he is not a novelist writing a novel. This awkward pretense, common to the
fiction of Conrad's day and an archaic cliché in our own, is peculiarly irritating
to the contemporary reader. But Conrad intends it as an expression of the professor's character, as another sign of the fussiness and academicism that limit his
capacity for experience.

rate man from self, but humanizes the relationship between them, and by so doing redeems him from ignorance and betrayal. He cannot live within himself alone: "No human being could bear a steady view of moral solitude without going mad" (p. 39). He must move toward others: "A man's real life is that accorded for him in the thoughts of other men by reason of respect or natural love" (p. 14), an idea previously registered in Conrad by the French lieutenant in *Lord Jim*. But the search for acceptance and sanction by other minds leads back in the end to a reexamination of one's own —the classic process by which perspective is attained and the burden of living borne. This is the route followed in a limited fashion by our professor of languages, and in the widest possible arc by Razumov, a correspondence that establishes their common humanity [11] and, in effect, brings together the otherwise antipathetic civilizations they represent.

In no novel is Conrad more the European than in *Under Western Eyes*, and in none is there a more inclusive arrangement of his characteristic themes. The unfilled man, the morality of isolation, the cycle of betrayal and redemption, the narrator who is also a major actor, the interplay of men and their milieu with its necessities, risks, and complications, are given full-scale treatment. It is the last of the three political novels Conrad wrote in succession from 1903 to 1910, and superlatively concludes the fifteen years of unceasing and fruitful labor that formally began in 1894. Occasional heights appear during the last fifteen years of his life, but there is not the sustained and continuous achievement of the earlier period.

Among the longer works of that period, *Under Western Eyes* stands as the memorable finale, both in its prophetic account of the Russian temperament and its intrinsic power as a work of art.

---

[11] The link between them is suggested at the start of the novel by Haldin's references to Razumov as an Englishman (pp. 16, 22).

XII

Determined Women and Voyeuristic Men

WITH THE COMPLETION OF THE GREAT NOVELS ON POLITICS AND HIS-
tory, Conrad returned to the more traditional theme of personal
relations, which he pursued to the end of his life. This period, from
1911 to his death in 1924, is dominated by *Chance, Victory, The
Shadow-Line,* and *The Rescue,* and marks certain dramatic changes
both in his external fortune and the imaginative procedures of his
art.

The change in fortune came about almost overnight. *Under
Western Eyes,* when it appeared in 1911, aroused no more public
interest than *The Secret Agent.* The volume of short stories that
followed in 1912, *'Twixt Land and Sea,* containing "A Smile of
Fortune," "The Secret Sharer," and "Freya of the Seven Isles,"
brought no stampede of Conrad enthusiasts to the bookstalls. He
was now steadily at work on *Chance,* his next long novel. He had
begun it in 1905, put it aside, and resumed it intermittently. It was
proving just as painful, labored, and difficult an enterprise for him
as the others.

When finished, it did not seem to contain anything that threatened a sudden rush of popularity. Marlow had been dug out of the
mothballs where he had reposed for ten years and given a last tour
as narrator. On the surface he seems not to have changed. He is as
discursive, involuted, and touchy about moral issues as ever, though
perhaps a bit more crotchety than before and ever so faintly waspish;
the passage of the years would be enough to account for these slight,
almost imperceptible changes of tone. If anything, Marlow's narrative style in *Chance* is more complicated and concentric than before.
Often he will relate an incident which he heard from someone else
who heard it from someone else who heard it from someone else.

The action passes through two, three, sometimes even four chroniclers before reaching the reader. What this gains in density and refraction is paid for by a loss of immediacy; it deepens the movements of the story and muffles their sensory impact at the same time. This was scarcely designed to attract a large audience, though perfectly consistent and entirely within the spirit of Conrad's established tactics.

Nor did the cast of characters hold forth the promise of a sensational appeal: an unhappy young girl who feels herself persistently rejected; a sea captain so fantastically chivalrous that he is unwilling—or unable—to consummate his marriage for fear of taking advantage of his wife; a financial tycoon, given to promoting naïvely fraudulent enterprises, whose egotism, lurking under an air of diffident mediocrity, makes him peculiarly repulsive; an ardent feminist whose ideas and behavior jar so stridently on Conrad that he can scarcely conceal his dislike; a lovesick young sailor who moons about more or less idiotically through most of the book; and Marlow, roused from his long retirement and sounding occasionally as though he wished he had been left undisturbed.

But despite every augury to the contrary, despite the eighteen previous years of financial failure, the appearance of *Chance* in 1913 brought Conrad his first great public success. The reward he had longed for without any real hope had come round at last. Moved by some mysterious process unknown to him, the ordinary middle-class bookbuyer, with his unpredictable meanderings of taste, the very man who had passed the earlier novels by in blank indifference, now began buying copies of the new one by the thousands. *Chance* did not become by any means one of the best-sellers of the century, but it sold well enough to change Conrad's personal position radically. It helped reduce a large part of his debt to Pinker, the agent whose faith in Conrad as a marketable writer was now belatedly justified. The popularity of *Chance* stimulated interest in the other novels, prepared the way for a handsome reception to those still to come, and raised his royalties and his stock in general. Money, hitherto hard to come by, appearing in reluctant and niggardly driblets that seemed literally sweated from his brow, now began to flow in substantial quantities as though to make up in a single burst for its previous scarcity. Conrad did not become rich overnight, but within a few years he was comfortably well off, and the pressure under which he had labored from the moment he left the sea was lifted.

He showed no visible signs of relief at this highly surprising development. He had lived too long with anxiety to give it up easily. No alteration on the public's part, however much in his favor now, was going to lure him out of his disenchantment or persuade him to give up the luxury of complaining about the difficulties of life. These emotions had afforded him too great a release in the past to be readily abandoned. Besides, his present good fortune might reverse itself tomorrow, and he had no intention of bathing himself in euphoria when the approach of good times seemed all too evidently a matter of accident (or of chance, were he a man given to punning). Desperation breeds its own armature of tone and habit, and Conrad had grown altogether too accustomed to his to throw it aside lightly. As his debts melted away, so that he was able to move into larger, more attractive living quarters and to take his wife and sons on an extended trip to Poland in 1914, as he finally solidified into a public figure—Conrad the man of letters and not simply Conrad the writer living in the obscurity of a purely professional esteem—he nevertheless permitted no softening of the pessimistic countenance he presented to the world. The letters of the later years reveal few marks of change. They are perhaps a shade more oracular, probably because more of them are in response to admiring strangers asking his opinion on those sweeping questions inevitably directed to famous men. He refers to himself a bit more frequently in the third person, as though he were already a public monument. He accepts with alacrity the homage of worshipful young attendants like Richard Curle—a sign of his own consciousness of his changed position. But his personal correspondence remains caught up in that special combination of querulousness that just avoids being ill-humored, and high courtesy, that stops just short of becoming pompous, which was typical of it from the start.

The new role of the established and successful man of letters suited Conrad. For one thing he looked the part. Rather short of stature, with an aquiline profile dominated by a pair of narrow piercing eyes, tapering cheeks furrowed now by the years, and a small, well trimmed beard under a flaring mustache, he had a visible air of distinction. He bore himself with a touch of hauteur.

He had always appeared to be a personage, and now that in fact he was one, the appearance sharpened. In the old sailing days he had kept himself aloof from other seamen, dressing more fastidiously, and cultivating the small refinements of manner which, even more than differences of mind, set one off from others. He was a deliberately solitary man then, regarded as eccentric, plainly too educated for his station, and certainly apart from the ordinary run of mates and captains in the merchant marine. All these traits had intensified with time, only now they fitted his new *persona* of a literary celebrity without the effect of eccentricity at all. Add to them the monocle and the rich foreign accent striking off English words on the wrong syllable, and the result was impressive. In being out of the ordinary, he lived up to the highest expectations of his new role. Status had at last caught up with self. It was not a typically English status; in his last period Conrad seemed less an Englishman than ever. But it was a status in England, augmented by his spreading European reputation.

Accompanying this change of position came a shift in the thematic pattern of Conrad's art. He had begun in the 1890's with an account of individual lives against a background of politics and race. After the turn of the century, with *Nostromo,* this background invaded the foreground and became a protagonist equal in importance to the human figures. *Chance* is Conrad's first novel which has no background at all, either distant or immediate, not even the hitherto fixed background of physical nature, and is totally lacking in intellectual substance. There is, instead, a total concentration on the private lives, on the physical and emotional relationships of the characters projected only in terms of themselves. If in the reading the novel seems a little hollow, if its structure appears to exceed its substance, one can attribute the effect to the radical change in dimension which marks it off from the earlier work and inaugurates Conrad's third and final stage. As the scope of his interest narrows, the full-length novels of this stage seem increasingly filled with empty spaces. The one absolutely first-class work is *The Shadow-Line,* a novella considerably less than half the length of *Victory* or *The Rescue.*

One of the clues to the diminished effect of this later work is the widening gap between apparatus and theme, a gap of which Conrad seemed almost totally unaware. Douglas Hewitt reminds us that the narrative machinery of *Chance* is at least as complicated as *Nostromo's*. But the result is much less satisfactory. The later novel has no supporting frame of history, no organized social texture, and very little philosophical content.[1] The acclaim greeting the work may have helped obscure for Conrad the nature of the change that had come over him. The change, in any case, was not abrupt and climactic, but slight and at first imperceptible, the first, faint, scarcely recognizable step downward after reaching the peak of one's vital power. At first glance Marlow sounds like his old self; it takes a while to discover that, far from being involved in the particulars of an experience that draws from him some inward resonance, he is only commenting on things in general. At the start, characters and events are seen at a familiar Conradian distance. What is not immediately apparent is that keeping them there is no strain; they lack the emotional momentum to force their presence upon us, so that no very great narrative irony is needed to hold them back. Again, Conrad seems oblivious to this, for he brings the full weight of his irony and narrative machinery to bear quite as though he were in the presence of another *Lord Jim* or *The Secret Agent*. His firepower is disproportionate to the objective. He has his full orchestra playing a piece better suited to a string quartet.[2]

Chance is more occupied with the theme of love than any novel of Conrad's since *An Outcast of the Islands*. In his attempt to explain the decline of the later work, Thomas Moser has evolved a full-scale theory that love was an uncongenial and inhibiting subject to Conrad, that he failed whenever he came to grips with it, that his best writing either banished sex to a peripheral place or eliminated it altogether. There is evidence to support the theory, especially in Conrad's lengthy and unsuccessful wrestling in the late 1890's with *The Rescue* and its twenty-year postponement. In the

[1] There is an attempt to fill the philosophical void by having Marlow comment at length on women as a sex. All of it is wryly critical and most of it is extraneous to the novel. What happens has little or nothing to do with the intransigent or despotic nature of women as such. De Barral, decidedly not a woman, is as great an obstacle in the lives of the principals as Mrs. Fyne, the iron-plated feminist who is partial to women only to the degree that they behave like men.

[2] There is an analogy here with Henry James's last completed novel, *The Golden Bowl* (1904), where the relationships among the four principal characters are so removed from "life," so concentrated upon themselves, that they move from art toward mathematics. In an essay on the novel in his book *The Destructive Element*, Stephen Spender treats them, in fact, as equations.

final novels an access of love and a decline in narrative power seem to go hand in hand. But there is also evidence to the contrary. To the argument that Conrad did not understand love are the subtle accounts of the marriages of the Goulds and the Verlocs. In the treatment of sex, where Conrad is supposed to be inept, there is the great scene of sexual impact when Willems sets eyes on Aissa; indeed, the whole of *An Outcast of the Islands* is dramatic and convincing in its treatment of sex. It is true that none of Conrad's novels, late or early, is really about love in the sense that *Antony and Cleopatra* is about love. But his treatment of the theme has its magnificent as well as its unsuccessful moments. To ascribe his decline as a writer to a deep-seated incapacity here is a dubious procedure.[3]

More pertinent is Moser's comment on the sexual aggressiveness of Conrad's women and the impotence of his men. This has a special relevance to *Chance*, for the novel is dominated by two aggressive females, Mrs. Fyne and Flora de Barral, and contains two relatively passive men, de Barral and Captain Anthony, who for different reasons lapse into inertia and allow themselves to be manipulated. Mrs. Fyne is a feminist who manipulates men out of principle. Flora is a harried young woman who has had a series of unnerving experiences and takes an affirmative hand in her own affairs simply out of a need to stay alive. And on the outer edge of the novel, supporting these two in a peculiarly ferocious fashion, looms the figure of the malevolent governess who gave Flora her earliest shock, one of Conrad's great villainous personages, descended in a straight line from Schomberg and Sotillo.

Mrs. Fyne is a wholly unfeminine woman who has nevertheless

---

[3] The schematics of Freudianism lead Moser to many questionable judgments. Among his more debatable assertions are the following: The sentiments of Almayer and Captain Whalley for their daughters are incestuous. The jungle is "feminine" in *Almayer's Folly* and "masculine" in "Heart of Darkness." Jim is "possessed" by Patusan as Kurtz is by Africa, and leaves the place no better off than he found it. In "Youth" Marlow longs for death; the oar he holds in his hand is a phallic-shaped object. *The Shadow-Line*, a late work like *Chance* and *Victory*, is, like them, markedly inferior.

It is a bold attempt to discover some ultimate key. But Moser's use of psychoanalysis, like Morf's, leads him in the end to textual straining and doubtful aesthetic conclusions. Yet Moser is a model of restraint compared with Dr. Bernard Meyer, whose "psychoanalytic biography" (1967) reduces poor Conrad and his work to a tortured clinical mass of anxieties, fears, repressions, and inadequacies.

married and produced three children. Appropriately, they are all girls, as ill-mannered and unfeminine as their mother can make them. Mrs. Fyne is not without humanitarian impulses. She surrounds herself with "girl friends," usually young females down on their luck—Flora is one of them—but her interest in them is in direct ratio to their responsiveness to her convictions. She frowns on their marrying, for that is to accept woman's traditional role vis-à-vis men, and Mrs. Fyne is in icy revolt against all that. Her theory is that women ought not to be women but "unscrupulous sexual nuisances" (*Chance*, pp. 189–190). (In her own marriage Mr. Fyne does her bidding even when he disagrees with her.) Characteristically, her relations with her brother, Captain Anthony, are cold, formal, and loveless. The master of a sailing vessel, he looks upon people living on land as irritating and untrustworthy. With his sister as an example, one can scarcely blame him. Still, when Flora runs off with him, Mrs. Fyne is furious and does what she can—it proves to be a good deal—to spoil their marriage. By convincing her brother that Flora is an adventuress who wants to marry him only to escape from her own desperate position, Mrs. Fyne condemns him to the sexual and psychic impotence that descends over him like a blight. Her real motive, however, is to get rid of her brother. By objecting to the marriage in advance, while knowing all the while that she cannot prevent it, she is deliberately creating a quarrel with Captain Anthony that she hopes will be permanent.

Conrad has the outline here of a powerful study in modern psychology, but he mars it by supplying Mrs. Fyne with a ready-made dislike of Anthony. He does not, as in the earlier books, explore this crucial relationship between brother and sister or expose her motivation from within, but simply has Marlow assert it briefly and tenuously. This is a surprisingly superficial procedure for Conrad, especially since Mrs. Fyne's motivation is what determines so much of the later action. Conrad thus blurs the sharpness of a portrait otherwise effective and even of symbolic import in anticipating the unsexed female common after the First World War.

Flora is as pretty, feminine, and womanly as Mrs. Fyne is none of these, but she is no less determinedly aggressive, and no less successful in her aggressions with regard to men. We observe that she is always victimized by women. The governess humiliates her; later,

she is rejected by an elderly widow who finds her insufficiently
cheerful; her female relatives, who take her in after her father's
imprisonment, greet her with sneers, taunts, and scoldings, and reduce her to tears with their aggressive, mean-spirited vulgarity; she
is employed in a German household, but is driven out by the wife,
who is jealous of her husband's lecherous attraction to Flora. At
last, when she takes refuge with the Fynes, it is Mrs. Fyne who
poisons the start of her marriage with Anthony.

The men, however, are another matter, and with them Flora is
always in the ascendancy. The governess's young paramour sides
with her in his own way and responds to her plea for help when
she is being most violently attacked. Her male cousin and the German husband, and Marlow himself who saves her from an attempt
at suicide, are in one way or another partial to her, though the
cousin's protectiveness stems from his belief that her father has
money secretly cached away. She succeeds in arousing such powerful
and sacrificial feelings in Anthony that he is willing to have their
marriage unconsummated when he is led to believe (falsely, in this
novel of complicated misunderstandings) that she has married him
not out of love but from desperation. And when, after the discovery
of de Barral's attempt at murder, Anthony offers to give her up for
good and all, it is she who refuses, drapes her arms around his neck,
and virtually forces him to consummate their marriage then and
there.

She manages her father with equal dexterity. Convinced of his
innocence (though he is blatantly guilty), she persuades Anthony
to provide refuge for him aboard the ship. During the crucial carriage ride from the prison to the waterfront, she informs her father
of her marriage, forces him back to his seat when, in rage, he wants
to stop the carriage and get out, persuades him to accept, however
sullenly, the situation of living off the bounty of a son-in-law whom
he hates before even setting eyes on him, and bends him altogether
to her will. She reduces Powell, the young second mate and one of
the four narrators, to a lovesick state. He becomes her ardent defender against the combined hostility of the first mate, the ship's
steward, and the rest of the *Ferndale*'s company who dislike their
beloved captain's new connections. Mr. Franklin, the first mate,
whose eyes bulge like a lobster's, is acutely jealous of Flora; she has
plainly displaced him in the captain's affections. As for Marlow,

he sees her strong-willed mastery very clearly, but she is physically and personally attractive, and wins him over, too. His last act in *Chance* is to serve as a voluntary marriage-broker between Flora and Powell after Anthony's accidental death at sea.

Marlow, to be sure, verbalizes his hostility toward women throughout the book,[4] yet his actions make him as much the vassal of Flora as her father and husband. He saves her from suicide at their first meeting, does what he can to prevent Mrs. Fyne from stopping the marriage, encourages Flora in their long talk on the street near Anthony's hotel, and, still dripping misogynist sentiments, advances her second marriage at the end as he had supported her first from the beginning. What makes his hostile comments on women as a species irritating to start with and finally unconvincing is that they flatly contradict his actions. Where women are concerned, especially young and attractive ones, he turns out to be as softhearted as the next man, and his persistent misogyny is only a peppery seasoning designed to add flavor to the story. Since the story is romantically sentimental rather than philosophically cynical, the cynicism emerges as so much window dressing not to be taken seriously. Flora does not earn Marlow's sympathy. He gives it to her simply because she is a young woman in distress, a purely sentimental gesture since it is aroused by Flora not as an individual but as a member of a genre. Any other attractive young female in distress would arouse in him the same response. It is sentiment that ties him to her, not the genuine emotion that arises from an awareness, an acknowledgment of someone as a particular person. *Chance* has a great deal of sentiment but very little real feeling. If sentiment can be defined as simulated or camouflaged emotion, another source of the novel's hollowness is recognizable. It is rampant with elaborately structured situations that call for feeling, yet Marlow's response to them is entirely inadequate. This is concealed for a time, but only for a time, by the smoke screen of acid skepticism and antisentiment which he lays down throughout the tale.

Flora's impact on the other men is no less powerful. Her father, during his years in prison, had thought of her as a helpless, un-

---

[4] His misogyny is not a new development. Back in "Heart of Darkness," signs of it were already evident. "It's queer how out of touch with truth women are" (*Youth*, p. 59), he remarked, a comment that determined his attitude toward Kurtz's betrothed.

formed creature, but after his release, it is she who reduces him to such a complete helplessness of will that, in desperation, he commits suicide. The great de Barral, able to manipulate one of the great financial swindles of the day, mulcting thousands of gullible investors of their life savings, is unable to manage this young girl. Yet his condition is positively heroic compared to that of his son-in-law. Captain Anthony is ironically referred to as the Knight, just as Flora is referred to with equal irony as the Damsel. He has the chivalrous instincts of a knight but not the boldness or capacity for action. Flora has the demure helpless look of a damsel without the passivity. She has a far greater power of decision than he, and there is a subtle exchange of sexual roles between them as there is, more obviously, in the case of Fyne and Mrs. Fyne.

If Jim, during the crisis on the *Patna,* is Conrad's supreme example of psychic paralysis, Captain Anthony is his striking representation of sexual voyeurism. Before the object of his passion, he is helpless to act; he can only stare. He falls into the same immobilizing dream as does Jim, and it proves equally destructive. Just as Jim is a man ridden by an egoistic ideal, the ideal of being better, higher, more heroic than everybody else, so Anthony is ridden by a powerful sexual appetite that he can neither release nor control. This appetite, turned in upon itself, begins gnawing at him remorselessly from the moment that he marries Flora without possessing her. The study of his disintegration under the slow torture of an agonizing sexual blight is the most remarkable aspect of *Chance.* Mr. Franklin is the first to observe his sudden moodiness and abstraction, his growing indifference to the ship and its affairs, and this in a captain who had always prided himself on his professional competence. The new mate, Powell, unacquainted with the old Anthony, is struck by the captain's inattentiveness, his faraway look, the air of almost slack aloofness that marks his presence. The few direct glimpses we are allowed of the captain—Conrad's use of the outwardly observed as contrasted with the inwardly penetrated character is never more effectively displayed than here—show us his irritability and increasing exasperation, together with a whole complex of small signs and gestures of his enfeebled self. The only act of which he seems capable during the long months of his unfulfilled marriage journey is to stand on the bridge of the *Ferndale* and gaze with vacant, hungry hopelessness at his wife re-

clining in a chair on the deck below. Staring at her with hungry impotence, also, is her father (though there is nothing in the least
sexual about his glance), and the sight of these helpless men standing petrified day after day, week after week, before the image of a
motionless girl, like figures in a trance, becomes the central parable
of the whole novel.

Flora also suffers from enforced continence, but her personality
is not undermined as is Anthony's. At the critical point, he has become so impotent that his one wish is to give up the mock marriage
altogether and withdraw to his shattered privacy, but she summons
the energy necessary to throw herself upon him, rally his flagging
will, and force him to assert his masculinity. The determined
woman in Conrad is never more triumphantly determined than
here. It is psychologically if not dramatically appropriate to have
her outlive Anthony and prepare herself at the end for the advent
of a second husband.

Conrad studies the ravages of frustrated sexual desire upon his
hero with insight, but he accords him little sympathy. His "un-
selfishness" with regard to Flora is more destructive than self-
interest, not the first time that Conrad has been skeptical of humanitarian impulses. The split in Anthony between the man and
the gentleman is less a result of nobility than of overrefinement.
Anthony is, in short, not a hero really, but a fool, and Conrad uses
him with persistent irony as a whipping boy for the inhibited Victorian male. His father, the truculent poet Carleon Anthony, produced two children, a too masculine daughter and a too feminine
son. Neither of these unappetizing specimens of the Victorian age
arouses Conrad's admiration.

On the whole subject of love and sex, Marlow makes a final comment, no less shrewd for being self-evident.

Pairing off is the fate of mankind. And if two beings thrown together, mutually attracted, resist the necessity . . . and voluntarily
stop short of the—the embrace . . . then they are committing a sin
against life. . . . And the punishment of it is an invasion of complexity, a tormenting, forcibly tortuous involution of feelings, the
deepest form of suffering. . . . (pp. 426–427)

Conrad's tactful and deliberate hesitation before the word "embrace," a hesitation soon to be rendered obsolete by D. H. Lawrence,

a pause, as it were, to find the *mot juste* that would delicately suggest love-making without loss of accuracy while preserving the amenities of that more genteel time, does not obscure the nature of his feelings on the subject. He is all for love. One may take the statement as a companion piece to the better known one of Heyst's when, just before his suicide at the end of *Victory*, he remarks, "woe to the man whose heart has not learned while young to hope, to love—and to put its trust in life!" (p. 410). Jim is cut off from his ideal, Anthony from love, Heyst from life—they are Conrad's three portraits in immobility, in that mysterious inertia which, whatever the overt reasons, atrophies the capacity to act.

What reduces our responsiveness to *Chance* is that the characters, for all their psychological interest, do not seem to come from anywhere. They do not belong to any visible society and convey the disconcerting impression that they are the only human beings in the world. They emerge not out of life, not out of some organized or recognizable human context, but out of a formless void. Nothing about them is wholly real because nothing around or behind them exists, so that the very sound of their voices has a curiously empty ring. We grasp the full force of Marlow's observation, "You understand I am piecing here bits of disconnected statements" (*Chance*, p. 222). The people whose affairs he relates are equally disconnected. Marlow manages to piece their statements together, but they themselves remain unpieced to the end. Marlow himself stands on the sidelines chronicling, commenting, conjecturing, clearing up the numerous misunderstandings; but never becomes genuinely involved with either the characters or the events. *Chance* is a novel that dispenses with environment and is without milieu, the first such novel Conrad ever wrote (though not the last). It is remarkable as a triumph of style over substance, but in the history of art such triumphs are never of the first magnitude and do not commend themselves to posterity. The novel served Conrad as an exercise in craftsmanship—as well as a source of cash—between the ardors of Razumov and the struggles of Axel Heyst, but in itself gives off a tepid rather than a burning glow.

Variations on the sexual theme of *Chance* appear in two stories of the period, "A Smile of Fortune" and "Freya of the Seven Isles," which flanked the almost monastically nonsexual "The Secret

Sharer" [5] in the collection of three tales *'Twixt Land and Sea*. The young captain of the first story, a junior edition of Anthony, falls under the spell of a young woman who sits in her garden on an island in the Far East and greets his visits with sullen contempt. Like Anthony, he is powerless to act; he can only devour her with his eyes. "I loved to watch her slow changes of pose, to look at her long immobilities composed in the graceful lines of her body, to observe the mysterious narrow stare of her splendid black eyes" (*'Twixt Land and Sea*, pp. 58–59). His single capacity is to watch, look, observe, and not to consummate. His desire is "unrealizable." He feels himself "the slave of some depraved habit," and not even the awareness that her father is using her as bait can cure the captain of his emotional fever. On one desperate occasion he kisses her, and when she makes no move begins raining kisses upon her. After a moment she pushes him away, and this act of rejection shatters him so thoroughly that he is left with "a sudden and weary conviction of the emptiness of all things under Heaven" (pp. 78–79). He leaves the island with the father's cargo of potatoes whose decayed odor reminds him of the flowers and scents of the daughter's garden. He replaces his sexual disappointment with a sudden lust for money, and when this fails to fill his psychic emptiness, resigns his command and returns to Europe. His sexual ambivalence is subtly suggested at the outset when the father courts the captain with a fresh bouquet of flowers: "I assured him jocularly, as I took my place at the table, that he made me feel as if I were a pretty girl, and that he mustn't be surprised if I blushed" (pp. 22–23).

In "Freya," one of Conrad's hair-raisingly bad stories, we are presented not with one frustrated lover but two, rivals for the affection of a girl whose sole desire is to arouse their appetites while keeping them at arm's length. She shrivels one of them by continually postponing their marriage and destroys the other by making love to his rival when she is sure he is watching. After the two of them are annihilated, she herself, with no further victims in sight, withers and dies. This portrait of a female vampire and the men she

---

[5] Conrad himself was acutely conscious of this difference among the stories. On November 5, 1912, he wrote to Garnett: "I daresay Freya is pretty rotten. On the other hand the Secret Sharer, between you and me, is *it*. Eh? No damned tricks with girls there. Eh? Every word fits and there's not a single uncertain note. Luck my boy. Pure luck" (Garnett, p. 243).

feeds upon never rises above the level of a cartoon. The fantastic spread in quality of *'Twixt Land and Sea* testifies to the growing uncertainty of Conrad's talent. It contains one superlative tale, "The Secret Sharer," one tolerable piece, "A Smile of Fortune," and the dreadful lucubration of "Freya," and as a collection represents the most uneven range of all his short-story assemblages.

In Conrad's sexual arena, it is not always the woman who prevails. Jewel begs Jim to flee for their lives after Brown's ambush, but he brushes her aside and goes to his death at the hands of the tribal chief. She crumples as completely as Freya's male victims, and on the last page of *Lord Jim* we see her wandering, a lifeless ghost, through the corridors of Stein's house. Shortly afterward, in the story "Falk," Conrad deals with the florid conception of a man who has eaten his way out of the human race through cannibalism and wishes to win his way back to it through love.[6] The object of his affections is a buxom German fraulein who falls in love with him without ever uttering a word. Falk is fairly inarticulate himself, and their communication is further complicated by the fact that neither speaks the other's native language. It doesn't seem to matter. Falk tells his awful tale—it is necessary that he do so for his marriage proposal to be a true catharsis—and though it outrages the girl's uncle on whose ship she is living, it seems to make no difference to her. Falk marries her despite all the linguistic and moral obstacles that stand in the way. There is nothing impotent or voyeuristic about him, though in his early visits he never looks at anyone but stares fixedly at the capstan; this later emerges as his sense of being guilty and apart. There is never any question of his virility, and in the end his triumph is complete.

In the same genre but much more successful is "Amy Foster," which appeared with "Falk" in *Typhoon and Other Stories* (1903). Here Conrad carries incommunication between lovers to its absolute extreme. In "Falk" it was the girl who never spoke a word. In "Amy Foster" both hero and heroine are virtually mute. Once again love between two essentially inarticulate people is further complicated by language barriers. Yet Amy, a dim-witted, plain-faced servant girl, hopelessly unattractive to the young Englishmen of her neighborhood, can fall in love and be loved in turn only by a weird

---

[6] "Falk" is a striking eccentricity rather than a powerful tale because its emotions are altogether too large for its limited characters to assume.

refugee from Eastern Europe whose words she cannot understand but whose strange spontaneous gestures and painful disorientation in a country so different from his own arouse her pity and touch her simple heart. The great virtue of the story lies in its turning of natural barriers into avenues of entry and transforming the very act of alienation into an act of love. Beautifully rendered through Yanko's consciousness is the contrast between his native land back in the Carpathians and the England onto which he has been ship-wrecked. At home strangers were treated with hospitality and beggars with kindness; religion was an occasion for joy; singing and dancing were natural expressions of life. In England Yanko is greeted with savage hostility, stony disapproval, and cold indiffer-ence. Children pelt him with stones, adults think of him as a beast in the field. Even the couple whose granddaughter he saves from drowning show not a flicker of warmth though they give him food and lodging. Only Amy, scarcely more than a beast of burden her-self, responds to him as a human being and marries him despite the disapproval of the whole community. Even after Yanko learns English, his ways are too foreign for his neighbors to tolerate. He is thrown out of the local pub for dancing too violently and singing in too loud a voice. He suffers slights and humiliations on every hand. Conrad's sympathies and the sympathies of the local doctor who narrates the tale are plainly on the side of this warmhearted, spontaneous, bewildered man unhappily abandoned among this flinty race.

"Amy Foster" should put an end once and for all to the notion that Conrad was an uncritical Anglophile. The England that emerges here is as dour, unfeeling, and barren a society as any on earth. Yet even among these unlikely circumstances, love flares up between two unlikely creatures in a sudden, marvelously persuasive attraction, the man's quick spontaneous energy warming the lumpy clay of the woman. Not, alas, for long. His strangeness becomes too much even for her. After marriage, after motherhood, Amy re-lapses into the provincial stupidity from which he had briefly roused her, and their relationship collapses. Yanko dies brokenhearted and misunderstood. Their falling apart is not as convincing as their coming together. Conrad seems to lose interest in the tale toward the end, and hurries the dissolution of his lovers. But the story remains one of his absorbing studies in the psychology of human

attraction, and suggests once again that love was not perhaps so uncongenial a subject to him after all.

The success of *Chance* persuaded Conrad to plunge into another
version, this time more complex, of the knight rescuing a damsel
in distress. He spent 1913 and the first half of 1914 writing what
was to be the most controversial novel of his career. This novel,
Victory, was controversial not for any polemics or unorthodoxy of
theme but over the issue of aesthetic merit. For a long while after
its appearance it was not only immensely popular with the public
at large but greatly admired by discriminating readers who came
to regard it as one of Conrad's authentic masterpieces, embodying
his finest qualities and exhibiting his characteristic genius. Of all
the novels, it has been the one most frequently studied in schools
and colleges. But in recent years its claim to excellence has been
sharply questioned. Moser attacked its sexual crudities, and Albert
Guerard, scrutinizing in detail the procedures and rhetoric of the
novel, arrived at a devastatingly unfavorable judgment. *Victory*
has now visibly slipped from its once secure place among Conrad's
major works.

At first glance the book is as crowded in theme, tonality, and
personages as anything of Conrad's. The story contains not only
the romantic rescue of Lena, but also an account of an isolated man
maneuvering for some permanent *modus vivendi* with a world he
does not believe in. The novel offers definitions of good and evil,
explores relationships between the human, subhuman, and super-
human, presents a half-dozen varieties of sexual consciousness and
social stratification, and introduces Conrad's usual rich compost of
nationalities and races, including Swedes, English, Germans, Spaniards, Malays, and Chinese. For action-loving readers, *Victory* has
a rousing plot, with jealousy, love, vengeance, lust, greed, and pure
satanism released in a torrent of melodrama expressing itself in a
plummy mixture of ambushes, guns, knives, assaults, fusillades of
bullets, thunderstorms, and conflagrations. For the moralists, the
novel holds forth at length on right and wrong behavior, the egotism
of sentimental charity, the connections between life and nonlife,
and introduces a trio of villains so bluntly Gargantuan, so baldly
allegorical that they reduce even Schomberg—here given a full-
scale treatment—to almost minuscule proportions. For the sym-

bolists, the text is replete with magic circles, enchanted islands, purgative fires, hints of a struggle between God and Satan, and running references to the Garden of Eden myth complete with original sin, fertility rites, passion week, and judgment day. Conrad first thought of calling his hero Augustus Berg, which suggested nothing in particular. He then changed it to Axel Heyst, thereby opening up lines of agreeably oblique inquiry. The first name now pointed straight to Prince Axel, the aristocratic hero of Villiers de l'Isle Adam's novel who looked upon life with contemptuous disdain and whose famous remark, "Live? our servants will do that for us," served as an epigraph for the literature of the decadence. The last name, rhyming with Christ, is too rampant with obvious interpretive possibilities to need elaboration, though Conrad elaborates it further by specific reference to Lena as Magdalene (*Victory*, p. 364). However one looks at it, *Victory* is a teeming warehouse of materials, a kind of one-volume summary of Conrad's collected works.

The opening chapter is as fine as anything in Conrad. Written in a dry, severely underaccented tone, it fixes Heyst in a natural setting that sums up with exquisite indirection his position in life. He spends his days on the small island of Samburan surrounded by a tepid, shallow, passionless sea. Once the site of a thriving coal mine, the island is now deserted, its settlements abandoned, its boom days surviving only in a gigantic blackboard containing the initials of the mining company. Night after night, Heyst, the ex-manager of the mine, sits on his verandah smoking his cheroot, against the near background of an indolent volcano still smoking faintly "like the end of a gigantic cigar." The man and the volcano merge in one of Conrad's most brilliant ecological fusions. Like a male Brünnhilde, Heyst has withdrawn to the inner center of his magic circle away from the world that his father, a belligerently misanthropic philosopher, has taught him is meaningless and corrupting. There he sits, not waiting to be rescued by life, but to be kept safe from it. The double aspect of his situation is suggested by each of the physical details enframing him. The island is a small flat object, but it is also the top of a mountain reaching all the way down to the ocean floor. The sea around it may be tepid and shallow, yet is an "offshoot of the great waters which embrace the continents of this globe." The volcano is sleepy and spasmodic;

still, it is active and, in the mysterious fashion of its kind, may erupt violently at any time. The first sentence of the novel introduces us to the "very close chemical relation between coal and diamonds": one is a utilitarian element, the other an aesthetic. Each has its compelling fascination, and both are contained in Heyst. Appropriately, he has two nicknames, "Hard Facts" Heyst and "Enchanted" Heyst. The arresting question of *Victory*, arrestingly defined at the outset, is what kind of relationship will be set up between the coal and the diamond in the mind of the protagonist.

All of Heyst's troubles come from his inability to be definitely one or the other. He is lured from his isolation without being able to establish effective rapport with others. Even at Lena's deathbed he is unable to express his love for her and curses himself for his "fastidious soul" (p. 406). Despite his father's warnings, despite his conviction that "he who forms a tie is lost" (pp. 199–200), despite his announced purpose "to look on and never make a sound" (p. 176) in his deliberately assumed role of "an indifferent stroller going through the world's bustle" (p. 199), he allows himself, through a natural sweetness of temper, a vein of gallantry, a streak of Lingardism, to become involved as a benefactor and partner to Morrison and as a rescuer and lover of Lena. These involvements, the first dramatically conditioning and affecting the second, prove his undoing. The novel groans under a burden of contrivance, embarrassing dialogue, and grotesque melodrama, but its basic strategy of linking the final disasters to the unresolved duality of Heyst's own nature remains intact and provides the story with an underlying frame that somehow survives the many tactical disasters.

Lena, the London slum girl who plays Eve to Axel's Adam, is another of Conrad's "strong" females. Abused even more grossly than Flora de Barral, she too believes herself unlovable but is convinced that a sufficient effort on her part will change matters. If she can prove to Heyst that her love for him is out of the ordinary by, say, saving his life at the risk of her own, he will surely come round to loving her. This sublime self-confidence in her own role as an active agent of destiny carries her through the absurd heroics with Ricardo and succeeds in extracting from Heyst at least a posthumous expression of his love. This is a victory, indeed. It is a victory of character over social station, of action over inertia, of will over misanthropy. She shakes Heyst out of his accustomed mold and almost reconciles him to the world—a feat beside which her triumphs in the two grotesque encounters with Ricardo (she almost chokes him to death in the first, and in the second casts a mesmeric spell over him by a simple exudation of sexual magnetism) seem trivial. Of all the determined women in Conrad, she is the most instinctively so, but she is conceived in a simplicity too uninflected for conviction. There are no conflicts or confusions in her nature; she is ingenuously straightforward and resolved. Her problems are purely physical: to fend off Schomberg, disarm Ricardo, protect Heyst. This renders her relatively uninteresting as a person and places upon Conrad the burden of making her actions absorbing enough to take up the slack created by her undramatic character.

He fails in this, but not because Lena is a woman and Conrad is supposed not to be at home with women or because of any sudden inability to handle physical incident. His failure lies, instead, in the projection of melodrama divorced from character. At such times his writing loses its vigor and sinks to the routine level of popular fiction. Nor is his failure with character and the consequent relapse into melodrama limited to the novels at the end of his life. The tendency is endemically present in his art from the beginning. The five flabbily mediocre stories in *Tales of Unrest* (1898) cover a wide range of subjects, but in each either plot or setting drowns out the human figures. The drowning process occurs in the Malay moonshine of "The Lagoon" as it does in the weird frenetics of the overheated London couple in "The Return." Conrad's first African tale, "An Outpost of Progress," has a certain technical interest as a dry run for "Heart of Darkness," and "The Idiots," an account of a Breton peasant woman who kills herself rather than continue to beget defective children, is singularly interesting as a sign of Maupassant's influence; but internally, both are devoured by a spectacular reliance on the lurid. "Karain," the best of the five, has a guilt-ridden Malay at its center who is a bit more articulated than the others, but it too slides off into a highly synthetic though lively sequence of ghosts, amulets, superstitious charms, and a cloak-and-dagger chase *à la polynésienne*. Other outbreaks of second-rate Conradese occur in "To-Morrow" (1903), "Gaspar Ruiz" (1905), and, of course, the unforgettably horrendous "Freya of the Seven Isles" (written in 1910). Plainly, the lesion in Conrad's art, though more pronounced in his last years, was there from the start. There is never any slackening in the density of his plots. But his characters do not enjoy the same consistency; it is whenever they are thin or embryonic that his writing runs into trouble.

The three incredible villains of *Victory*, Mr. Jones, Ricardo, and Pedro, illustrate this trouble in its most virulent form. Mr. Jones—the very anonymity of the name suggests his abstract character—is a displaced gentleman-adventurer with a pathological horror of women. "If Conrad were not so unfailingly chaste a writer," wrote the late E. K. Brown, "Mr. Jones with his nervous disgust for women would have turned into an English M. de Charlus." [7] Brown flatters Conrad by the comparison. For, in truth, Mr. Jones, far from being a subtly developed Proustian figure, comes to us in bits and pieces. At certain moments he is an English gentleman kicked out of polite society for some violation of the rules and wandering about the world living off the countryside through gambling, blackmail, and outright robbery. At other times he is Satan displaced from Heaven by a fierce pride that does not allow him to take orders and now, after some years of ravaging ordinary men, he comes to his supreme test, the confrontation with his most formidable opponent in the particular shape of Axel Heyst. At still other times he is what Heyst calls an envoy of that outer world from which Heyst has withdrawn, an envoy allegorically embodying "evil intelligence," with Ricardo representing "instinctive savagery" and Pedro "brute force" (p. 329). Mr. Jones, then, appears to us in three distinct guises, as a man, a myth, and an allegory.

But in stretching Mr. Jones to cover all these *personae,* Conrad makes him satisfactory in none. As a menacing human being he is neutralized by the prolonged fits of languorous boredom into which he sinks. As the devil he is hoodwinked by his assistant Ricardo in the matter of the woman on Heyst's island and by Schomberg in the lie about the treasure. Can we believe seriously in a devil so easily deceived not simply by infernal subordinates but by mortal men? As an embodiment of "evil intelligence," he is undermined by his misogyny; it is hard to take as a serious threat any man so mortally afraid of women that he is reduced to a quivering jelly in their presence. The individual elements in Mr. Jones are arresting,

[7] *The Yale Review*, Winter, 1946.

but they do not cohere. As a last irritant, he lapses from time to time into an outlandish mode of speech. Watching Ricardo fawning at Lena's feet, he whispers to Heyst, "Behold the simple Acis kissing the sandals of the nymph, on the way to her lips, all forgetful, while the menacing fife of Polyphemus already sounds close at hand—" (p. 393). Long before Mr. Jones drowns in the water under the pier at Samburan, he drowns in his own yeasty gabble.

Ricardo, the Cockney killer attached to Mr. Jones as valet, companion, handyman, and executioner, suffers from a similar gap between what he is announced as and what he is. Conrad introduces him as a cunning, feral creature who kills as instinctively as he breathes. He is forever fingering his knife [8] and threatening to disembowel virtually everyone in the novel—Schomberg, Heyst, Lena, Pedro, Wang the Chinese houseman who deserts Number One (Heyst) when his position is menaced by the baleful trio, and finally Mr. Jones himself. He terrorizes Schomberg with tales of past murders, and prowls about like a jungle cat ready to spring. But on the one occasion when he does spring, Lena subdues him with almost childish ease in a scene which Guerard justly regards as one of the absurd sequences in *Victory*. And for all his sadistic mouthings about killing, he never does kill anyone. Schomberg tricks him into a wild-goose chase. Wang steals Heyst's revolver and retreats to safety. Lena overcomes him twice, and Heyst is never in real danger from him at all. As for Mr. Jones, it is he who attacks Ricardo. He fires at Ricardo, who turns and runs away; Mr. Jones pursues him, fires again, and kills him. Before his death, however, Ricardo seems to have frightened everyone, including Conrad himself—everyone but the reader. Were Conrad presenting Ricardo as a papier-mâché tiger, given to ridiculous pretensions, he might have been a triumph of ironic characterization. But we are asked to take him seriously. On these grounds, he is an outrageous and, in the

---

[8] Moser regards the knife as another phallic symbol and Ricardo's failure to use it as a sign of his impotence. The knife, however, is more than just the instrument Ricardo fails to plant in Lena. It is also the weapon he fails to plant in Mr. Jones. He conspires with Lena, whose origins are as plebeian as his own, to kill his patrician employer for strictly class reasons. Is he then a symbol of Marx? As plausible a case can be made out for this as for Freud. It is doubtful that Conrad intended all this sociopsychological baggage. In any event these interpretations clutter the portrait of Ricardo without enriching it. He is equally unconvincing as a tool of Marx and an illustration of Freud.

end, ludicrous fraud. He is further disqualified as a claimant for our serious attention by his weird mixture of high and low speech. His favorite word is " 'ypocrits," yet he can deliver formal declarations in the best pseudopoetic style: "We'll go wandering over the world, you and I, both free and both true. You are no cage bird. We'll rove together, for we are of them that have no homes. We are born rovers!" (p. 397). His love scenes with Lena, clotted with hoarse exclamations, foot-kissing, and florid transports of rhetoric, give off the tinniest sound of all.

As for the third villain, Pedro, he appears wholly superfluous, a shambling mindless creature on the periphery of the action, serving no visible function and performing no visible deed.

The one figure who emerges relatively whole from the weaknesses of *Victory* is Heyst himself, and it is he who redeems the novel in a way that *Chance* for all its moments of grace and interest, is never redeemed. He is a life symbol and a life conduit, pouring energy into everyone around him, quickening the tempo and heightening the consciousness of friends, enemies, and neutrals alike. It is he who saves the three brigands from death by directing the water into their parched mouths. Mr. Jones finds him stimulating enough to transform the proposed robbery into a supreme moral test. Schomberg is lifted by jealousy of Heyst to a pitch of emotion outside the ordinary range of his experience, and even Mrs. Schomberg, that waxwork figure with the sallow face and goggle eyes sitting like a joss behind the counter of her husband's hotel, is moved to help Heyst and save Schomberg from his infatuation for Lena. This action erases, in the eyes of Captain Davidson and the world, the impression of total stupidity in which she appears hopelessly encased. The real Mrs. Schomberg, concealed within her ugly immobile shell, emerges only through her conspiratorial intervention on behalf of Heyst, and would otherwise never have been known.

Heyst rescues Morrison at a critical point and makes possible his climactic adventure with the coal mine. What he does for Morrison financially he does for Lena emotionally, enabling her to live up to the richest possibilities of her nature. Even the neutrals in the novel, the group of sea captains and traders whose spokesman is the commonplace, well-intentioned Captain Davidson, whose function is less to participate than to comment, are affected by

Heyst. He exercises over them a steady fascination, the fascination of an exceptional man upon the ordinary, of an enigmatic existence upon lives bound and measured by common sense. They talk about him endlessly, speculate on his motives, dissect his intentions, and, as far as Conrad allows them to, chronicle his story. Davidson goes out of his way to steam past Samburan, not because he has any business there but simply to catch a glimpse of Heyst [9] and bring back tidbits with which to feed the eager curiosity of his friends. In this way, by his mere existence, Heyst adds color to their otherwise routine round and jogs their imaginations into life.

However beneficent his impact on others, his effect upon himself is almost wholly destructive. He bears all the stigmata of the Conradian consciousness: he is self-deprecatory, withdrawn, mordantly aware of the limitations of the world, quick to imagine it hostile. He suffers from a fastidious egotism that serves at once as an excuse for not taking part in life and a drag on successful performance when he does.[10] His refusal to kill his enemies is a sign of his civilized sensibilities, perhaps, but it is equally a sign of his shrinking from the hard necessities of action. His gentle contempt for the world may be a matter of rational conviction, reinforced by the abstract arguments of his father, yet he is painfully susceptible to its opinions. The calumnies spread by Schomberg about his relationship with Morrison cut into his inner fiber, and he is deeply wounded by what he takes to be Lena's belief in them. ". . . the power of calumny grows with time," he says to her. "It's insidious and penetrating. It can even destroy one's faith in oneself—dry-rot the soul" (p. 362). His temperamental pull toward life proves more powerful than the rational conviction that it is not worth bothering with. This is made evident in his behavior toward Morrison. It is not enough that he simply pay Morrison's fine. He has to go further and live aboard Morrison's ship, be drawn into his affairs, become his business partner, and in the end be victimized for his good

[9] His last appearance is jarringly improbable. It comes at the height of the thunderstorm a moment or two after Mr. Jones, aiming at Ricardo, shoots Lena by mistake. Davidson's sudden presence as she expires in Heyst's arms strains still further a scene already past belief.

[10] This was no doubt the basis of D. H. Lawrence's complaint about Conrad: ". . . why this giving in before you start, that pervades Conrad and such folks—the Writers among the Ruins. I can't forgive Conrad for being so sad and for giving in" (*The Letters of D. H. Lawrence,* New York, 1932, p. 68).

deeds—all because he secretly recognizes in Morrison—the trader who has not the heart to extract payment for the goods he heaps upon the impoverished natives—his own *alter ego*. Sentiment steals into him and undermines his rational judgment, just as later with Lena, sexual attraction appearing in the irresistible guise of chivalry causes him to renounce, for the second time, his vow never to form any ties.

Thus pulled in contrary directions, Heyst is unfitted for the crisis when it comes. He snatches Lena away from Schomberg, but Schomberg's revenge, in physical terms at any rate, is in the end complete. Heyst loses his revolver to Wang and cannot get it back. The very act of bringing his enemies back from death when they arrive at Samburan at death's door makes him ironically the agent of his own destruction. In the negotiations and maneuvers with Ricardo and Mr. Jones, Heyst preserves a startling nobility and unmistakable courage, but displays at the same time a monumental ineptness. He cannot even set up a series of simple signals to guide Lena's coming and going—his gaucherie here provides Guerard with an opportunity to make one of his most telling attacks on the novel's violation of elementary common sense. But the awkwardness is less a sign of Conrad's unintentional incompetence as of Heyst's quite natural fumbling with physical details that marks his conduct throughout and arises indeed from the split within his character. It all reaches a climax in the final scenes when Lena dies accidentally, the principal villains kill each other off, and Heyst takes his own life. He is a helpless bystander in the first two actions, and makes a decisive move with regard to himself only when all other alternatives have vanished.

The combination in Heyst of the power to transfigure others and the predisposition to undermine himself makes him one of the arresting figures in Conrad. He succeeds in keeping *Victory* alive despite its admitted defects in procedure and weaknesses of rhetoric.[11] With Heyst, too, Conrad succeeds in exploring another dimension in the psychology of voyeurism. For Heyst is a voyeur not

[11] This reinforces Somerset Maugham's observation that style is not an absolute prerequisite to first-class work. If it were, Willa Cather would no doubt be the greatest of American novelists and John Galsworthy the finest of the English. The example of Heyst indicates that in imaginative literature a fascinating personality can overcome defects in the supporting structure.

of sex but of life, and when he remarks that he has "refined every-thing away by this time—anger, indignation, scorn itself" (p. 329) he describes the process by which he has murdered the emotions most likely to interfere with his role of detached and indifferent observer. The man we see at the start, sitting in complete isolation on his island, smoking a cigar, gazing vaguely into the distance, is the perfect voyeur of existence. What follows is an assault upon this role, coming partly from the movements in his own nature he is unable to suppress and partly from outward circumstances. The transformation in Heyst from the withdrawn man to the involved, from a sleeping volcano to an active one (the funeral pyre in which he immolates Lena and himself symbolizes his final blazing-up), from coal to diamond, is the same process through which Captain Anthony moves and, in a more formidable way, Razumov and Decoud. None of them wholly succeeds. With Anthony not enough of the effort comes from within. With the others the price paid for their spectatorship proves too heavy to be overborne. Conrad is as interested in the movement away from inertia, passivity, and moral paralysis as he is, in the instances of Willems, Verloc, and others, in the movement toward it. Voyeurism is a fixed point in his psycho-logical landscape, but neither Conrad nor his characters are frozen there. Conrad's success with Heyst suggests that at a relatively late point in his career he still retained a large degree of mastery over an area so important in his art.

Two of the stories in the collection *Within the Tides* (1915), written while Conrad was laboring over *Victory*, further particu-larize his treatment of love. Neither "The Planter of Malata" nor "Because of the Dollars" is a distinguished tale, but the one intro-duces a young lady who is capable of feeling only for what is dead and the other supplies a polarized contrast between a woman who loves to excess and a woman who cannot love at all. Felicia Moor-som, in the first story, has every advantage but one. She is beautiful, educated, poised, well-bred, but burdened with an unresponsive heart. She becomes attached to her fiancé only after he disappears and never loves him so much as when she learns he is dead; in the meantime, she cannot react to the living man who pays court to her, for he suffers from the singular handicap of being alive. Moved by emotional necrophilia, Miss Moorsom subverts her numerous at-tractions and joins the company of Conrad's female monsters, together with Freya, Mrs. Fyne, the girl in "A Smile of Fortune," and the governess in *Chance*.

In the second story Captain Davidson appears once again, involved this time not with Heyst but with the two women tilted against each other. His wife is a cold egotistical creature with an "ungenerous mouth," a "mean little soul," and the heart of "a parched pea." She is inhospitable to his friends, unsympathetic to his profession which keeps him away for extended voyages, and locked up in a mold of gentility. While Mrs. Davidson is highly respectable, Laughing Anne has no social standing at all, but attaches herself to whatever man will live with her. She has an illegitimate son whom she loves very much and for whom she is willing to make any sacrifice. She saves Captain Davidson's life at the expense of her own. In gratitude, he looks after her young son whom he seeks to adopt. Mrs. Davidson coldly refuses, suspects her husband of the worst, and leaves him altogether to return to Europe. If Mrs. Davidson belongs to the chill world of Miss Moorsom, Anne is a blood relation of Lena. Between them, the extreme limits of the female temperament in Conrad are defined.

Within the extremes stand his two great portraits of women, Mrs. Gould and Nathalie Haldin, who combine—with their capacity for love—intelligence, sensibility, and grace of manner, and are in no way devourers of the male species. Different from them in design but no less bold and complex a figure is that iceberg of a woman Winnie Verloc, who conceals from her husband, from the reader, and from herself the depth of energy, the submerged violence of feeling that erupt at the end and cause her to be as much the secret agent emotionally as Verloc is politically. Ranging below these is a whole gamut of lesser heroines, from the clinging-vine girls of nineteenth century fiction to the aggressive and self-asserting females of twentieth.

It is from them that the heroines of Ernest Hemingway, Conrad's chief heir in our time, derive. Maria, Renata, and Catherine Barkley are variations on the Lena type while the vampire figures, Lady Brett and Margot Macomber, come in a straight line from Aissa,[12]

---

[12] Aissa, invading Willems's consciousness, becomes a disease that he succumbs to and struggles against simultaneously. At the point when he is about to throw her off altogether, she kills him. In Hemingway's "The Short Happy Life of Francis Macomber" Macomber passes through the same stages with Margot. When he is on the point of liberating himself, she, too, kills him.

Freya, and Mrs. Verloc. The slight air of unreality that surrounds Conrad's women is the product of the Polish chivalrous tradition [13] in which he grew up and which his later immersion in the cautious gentility of late Victorian England did nothing to dispel. He seems distinctly more at home with mature men and women in love than with lovers in the first flush of youth. But this does not diminish the scope of his gallery, proceeding at one end from the almost total silence of Amy Foster and Hermann's niece to the strident chatter of Mrs. Almayer and the cold pronouncements of Mrs. Fyne at the other.

His men, in their relationship to women, are no less varied. Congealed like Lingard in his dreamlike paralysis under the spell of Mrs. Travers or stimulated into abnormal activity like Decoud under the spur of love, they, too, embrace a wide range of attitudes, from voyeurism to impassioned consummation. Conrad's art may falter occasionally in its imaginative realization, but the psychology of his assembled men and women remains broadly and impressively focused.

[13] One of the terms of this tradition was the confining of women to an exclusive preoccupation with men. The relationship between Jewel and Jim is the matrix for all the others in Conrad. She loves him and wants him all to herself. He loves her well enough, but has other concerns and is in the end drawn off by them, leaving her to fade away—just as Charles Gould's other concerns leave Mrs. Gould to atrophy and Verloc's political activities cut him off irrevocably from Mrs. Verloc.

XIII

The Exhausted Self

"VICTORY" WAS FINISHED IN JUNE, 1914, AND THAT SUMMER CONRAD TOOK his wife and two sons on a journey to Poland. Despite attacks upon him from Polish quarters, chiefly on the grounds that he had betrayed his native country by writing in another language and selling his talent to foreigners, he had always planned to return someday. What Mrs. Conrad referred to as his "homing instinct" flared up in him as he aged, symptomatically accompanied by a marked increase in the foreignness of his accent. His changed position as a now popular writer made the trip possible, and the several months planned for the visit seemed well within his new means. It was typical of Conrad that while his pessimism about Poland's future had not altered in the least, his affection for her remained intact. To be emotionally involved with something one did not really believe in was an equation that recurred in his life as well as in his fiction. The Conrads crossed the North Sea and northern Germany, and at last reached Cracow. Shortly after they arrived, war was declared. Cut off by a Germany and Austria suddenly in conflict with England, Conrad, who had longed and planned for years to get into Poland, now tried frantically to get out.

After a number of increasingly anxious weeks in Poland, the Conrads finally managed to entrain for Vienna. There, with the help of the American ambassador, they secured exit visas and slipped across the Italian border to safety just before orders to intern all enemy aliens for the duration were issued by the Central Powers. In due course they got back to England where Conrad, in grateful acknowledgment, was to dedicate *The Rescue* to Ambassador Penfield. The whole experience was something of an ordeal for a man in his fifty-seventh year, suffering from neuresthenia, accompanied by an ailing wife, in the grip of emotions complicated by a special sort of home-coming. After forty years, this was the second of his painful exits from Poland.

The Great War brought to an end the liberal hopes of the nineteenth century. It also marked the end of Conrad's significant work. In 1915 he wrote *The Shadow-Line,* the last of his major efforts, which he dedicated to his older son Borys, then a combat soldier in France, and to Borys's generation going through its dreadful trial. During the last six years of his life after the war was over, he wrote two full-length novels, *The Arrow of Gold* (1919) and *The Rover* (1923), at long last completed *The Rescue* (1920), moldering in his desk since its abortive beginnings in the late 90's, and began *Suspense,* a novel with a Napoleonic background, left unfinished at his death in 1924 and published posthumously. These works are large in design, full of plots and passions, but so awkwardly executed and unevenly written that they stand as a painful record of Conrad's failing powers. The old will is there, the urge to create remains, enough to flare up in an occasional finely turned moment of action or a descriptive swatch filled with the earlier magic. The energy, however, is largely gone, condemning these last novels to reading like curiously empty husks or shells of the former work. At first Conrad seems like the same writer. It is not immediately apparent that his story is not flowing forward, does not proceed from some organic base, but, gradually, it freezes into immobile scenes, into characters who strike attitudes and assume poses, into a moribund art, from which the last gestures and flickers of life are ebbing. This is the art of old age, the last expostulations of the exhausted self.

The advancing pressures of gout compelled Conrad to dictate the whole of *The Arrow of Gold,* the first of his novels to be composed in this way. Begun in the autumn of 1917 and finished in the summer of 1918, it represented an expansion of the *Tremolino* chapter in *The Mirror of the Sea.* Both dealt, Conrad announced in his Author's Note, with "the quality of initiation . . . into the life of passion" (*The Arrow of Gold,* p. ix). Subtitled "A Story Between Two Notes," the story seems hardly to need the notes, the account of Monsieur George being entirely able to stand by itself. But Conrad, perhaps out of sheer habit, proceeds with this sort of double narration anyway.

The novel never gets off the ground. The first two-thirds of the book is altogether static, a series of genre descriptions and inflated dialogue. Such action as does take place (mainly the sea adventures of George and Dominic gunrunning for the Carlist cause in which George risks his neck not out of any passion for Don Carlos but out of love for Doña Rita) takes place offstage. We are simply told that George is in love with the sea without any direct account of him *at* sea.

We are, instead, confronted with a love affair. Here Rita appears as a symbolic apotheosis of all women, her beauty and magnetism beyond compare. Stiff as a statue, she walks down staircases or sits cross-legged on divans while the men in the book goggle at her calf-eyed. The writing itself is puffed up and frequently banal, an effect heightened by the caricature of Captain Blunt (*américain, catholique, gentilhomme,* who lives by his sword), an anachronistic survival from the age of chivalry who marches through the novel with a severe look on his thin, mustached mouth, and by the total failure to characterize Mills, the bookish Englishman whom George admires so much. Monsieur George, telling the story, is a bit more animated, but for long stretches he, too, suffers from posed rigidity.

A quick glance at the prose reveals that it is not vintage Conrad. One figure expresses "surprise in his keen glance" and looks about "with a faint smile as attractive as the rest of his rustic but well-bred personality" (p. 11), the adjectives *keen, faint, rustic, well-bred* cutting off the evocation of anything concrete by their clichéd generality. Stationed at the center of the daguerrotypes that make up the book stands Rita, an ex-goatherd from the Basque country, but now rich and celebrated.

. . . the delicate carnation of that face . . . drew irresistibly your gaze to itself in an indefinable quality of charm beyond all analysis and made you think of remote seas, of strange generations, of the faces of women sculptured on immemorial monuments and of those lying unsung in their tombs . . . there being in her "something of the women of all time." (*The Arrow of Gold,* pp. 66–67)

And again: "She was rosy like some impassive statue in a desert in the flush of the dawn" (p. 101). She remains conveniently still while Monsieur George gazes at her fixedly: "The last of the light gleamed in her long enigmatic eyes as if they were precious enamel in that shadowy head which in its immobility suggested a creation of a dis-

tant past: immortal art, not transient life" (p. 93). The more immobile she remains the more he warms to her: ". . . the finer
immobility, almost sacred, of a fateful figure seated at the very source
of the passions that have moved men from the dawn of ages" (p.
146). She hardly seems to be a woman at all but rather a motionless
image: "She paused with an inscrutable smile that a painter might
have put on the face of some symbolic figure for the speculation and
wonder of generations" (p. 218). Rita is a study not in life but in
still life. Conrad yearns to animate this Galatea. He succeeds only in
paralyzing her with his rhetorical straining after universals.

Now and again he rouses himself from his imaginative lethargy.
The scene with Ortega pounding at the locked door, screaming love
exclamations and curses at Rita and George crouched within, is a
well managed piece of melodrama. Mrs. Blunt, though preposterous,
is not unimpressive as the *grande dame* without scruples but with
manners and taste, seeking to marry her impoverished son to the
wealthy Rita. George and Rita become lovers at the end; the symbol
of his youthful romance is the arrow of gold that she wears in her
hair and gives him before leaving, and which he finally loses at sea.
But even when the novel moves forward instead of remaining static
and transfixed, it functions on a purely external level. Feelings are
announced but not unfolded. Characters are described but not developed. Situations follow but do not emerge from one another. The
structure of the novel is mechanical, not organic. Rita's desertion of
George after nursing him back to health is a purely arbitrary act; it
would make just as much sense for her to stay.

Conrad himself thought otherwise. In a letter to an inquiring
reader, he explained: "A connection of that kind would have spelt
ruin for a young fellow of 19 without fortune or position. . . . Had
R. been merely sensual and selfish she could have kept George
chained to her by his passion. . . . By going away beyond his reach
she gives him the supreme proof of her love. . . ." [1] But why the
affair would spell ruin for George and how her leaving is proof of
her love are not evident from the text. They seem arranged to give
the novel a final touch of romantic pathos.

For a long time *The Arrow of Gold* was taken as Conrad's one
authentically autobiographical novel. He indicated as much in his

---

[1] Letter of September 5, 1922, LL, II, 271.

Author's Note. But with the doubt now cast on Conrad having fought a duel like the one between Monsieur George and Captain Blunt and the equal uncertainty about the existence of Rita's prototype, *The Arrow of Gold* has lost most of its meaning as a source document of Conrad's life. About all that can be said for it in the personal sense is that its Marseilles background was based on Conrad's recollections of the city during his four-year stay there as a youth. But autobiographical or not, the novel does not seem quite real. It exists in the mind of the writer without passing into the mind of the reader. The vital process of transfer now seems beyond Conrad's powers. The novels of his old age, though tenanted and occupied, are not really lived in.

The largest and most ambitious of them, *The Rescue*, begins solidly enough. Tom Lingard, at thirty-five, is at the height of his powers. It will be some years before he sets eyes on Almayer and Willems, but he appears to be the same bold, adventurous, aggressive man who will penetrate secret rivers, establish trading posts in remote Malay country where no white men had appeared before, rescue Mrs. Almayer as a small girl from the hands of pirates, set up Almayer in another station, and free Willems from his impasse on the mainland. The quixotic egotism that makes him an almost professional meddler in the lives of others moves him here to take up the cause of a pair of noble Malays, Hassim and his sister Immada, and seek to put them back on their lost throne. The complications of Malay politics, tangled and treacherous enough to deter ordinary men, only stimulate him, as tribal warfare on Patusan did Jim. He is a trader to start with, but trade is only an excuse for adventure. Having worked in the Australian gold fields and on the Malay Sea after leaving England as a boy, Lingard is now embarked upon that bold maneuvering in business, exploration, and tribal politics that gives him a heady sense of climax. He apears a masterful figure, a small-scale Sir Francis Drake with a strain of Sir Galahad.

The tool that makes his enterprises possible is his brig, the object that he cherishes above all else in the world. It is the fastest craft of its size in the shallow waters of the Archipelago, and Lingard gives it the kind of meticulous care bestowed on a thoroughbred being primed for a great race. Both man and vessel are in supreme physical condition, ready for any hazard, a pair of remarkable machines poised for some ultimate action. And the setting befits them: the narrow Malay Sea punctuated by scores of islands, dotted with hidden reefs ready to snag unwary ships (the Travers yacht is grounded on one of them), the sky overhead alight with Conrad's full complement of stars, sun, sudden squalls, winds of varying velocity and warmth, clouds in constant metamorphosis, and the perpetual play of light and shadow in its endless mutations. Equally ramified is the suety tangle of Malay intrigue into which Lingard joyfully springs: established chiefs maneuvering for power, free-lance upstarts jockeying for position, brigands feeding wolfishly on the spoils dropped by contending factions, with the warships of the Dutch, who control Indonesia, hovering menacingly in the background—exactly the situation of Conrad's first two Malay novels and already detailed in the first draft of *The Rescue* going back to that early time. But where the fallen Almayer thrashes helplessly in the tangle and the falling Willems drowns in it, Lingard, neither fallen nor falling, stands on the edge confidently prepared to make his way through it in pursuit of his particular purpose.

His purpose in *The Rescue* has no ethical or intellectual content, and nothing more clearly establishes Lingard as the mindless hero of romantic fiction than his indifference to meaning. He espouses Hassim's cause not because he is convinced that Hassim is a better man or a better ruler than the revolutionary clique that overthrew him, not primarily out of gratitude for his help in a village scrape when they first met, but simply out of a categorical imperative to action: "There was something to be done, and he felt he would have to do it. It was expected of him. The seas expected it; the land expected it" (p. 87). It is only in action, in trade, in politics, in sheer movement from place to place, that he feels alive, and he draws no distinctions in quality between one action and another; any will do. He spends two feverish years stealthily accumulating ammunition and amassing allies to put Hassim back on his lost throne, while the traders and seamen of the Archipelago begin referring to him as Mad Tom. Such energy, power of concentration, physical strength, and dogged tenacity are qualities large enough to accomplish some great end. Here they are devoted to no purpose at all; it could not matter less in the general scheme of things whether Hassim or his rivals rule the remote Malay principality of Wajo.

Lingard is a large man; he is handsome and heroic; and altogether empty. He is a parody of Nostromo, also a man of action but subtly bound to his heroic vanity as Jim is to his perverted ideal, Kurtz to his liberal imperialism, and Captain Whalley to that sense of professional honor so cruelly betrayed by his one affection. These figures, variants on the Lingard type, have human content; they are capable of creating values and distinguishing between one category of behavior and another; this is what makes them interesting and, in supreme moments, fascinating. Lingard has no supreme moments; his moments are all alike. At long last Conrad reverts to his early reading of Cooper and Marryat, and creates in the hero of *The Rescue* a figure like theirs, long on pragmatic energy, short on both brains and moral intention. In one of his despairing moments during the struggle to complete the novel, Conrad referred to it as a book for boys. Lingard is, in truth, a juvenile hero.

There is room in his head for only one maneuver at a time. As long as things move along a single track, all is well, and Lingard is every inch the triumphant man. But at the first serious complication, his imposing façade gives way. The accidental stranding of the yacht with its white passengers near Lingard's ammunition cache threatens his plans. If the Dutch are summoned to the scene for salvage operations, the game will be up. The Malays are, in any case, bound to be disturbed by the intrusion and to suspect Lingard of partiality to his own race if he goes to the aid of the Europeans. The yacht creates a bad situation all around, yet surely not so bad as to chill our intrepid adventurer.

But chilled he is. He clambers aboard the stranded vessel, has his first brief unfriendly conversation with Travers, the owner, and is at once struck dumb: "Their coming at this moment, when he had wandered beyond that circle which race, memories, early associations, all the essential conditions of one's origin, trace round every man's life, deprived him in a manner of the power of speech. He was confounded. It was like meeting exacting spectres in a desert" (pp. 121–122). The racial conflict between the whites, to whom he belongs, and the Malays, to whom he is attached, immobilizes him at a single stroke. Though three hundred and fifty pages of densely detailed plot are yet to come, Lingard is already a dead man. He passes through the intrigues that follow, the shootings, kidnapings, pourparlers, shifting alliances, procedural disputes like a traveler in a strange country groping his way through a thick fog, rubbing his

eyes in a vain effort to see clearly. Conrad seeks to supply him with
a specific reason for failure by involving him in a love affair with
Mrs. Travers which paralyzes him still further. But he is disoriented
before he sets eyes on her.

What he lacks is an interior self. He has plenty of courage in
terms of nerves and muscles, but no visible character. He is made to
withstand any physical blow, but a psychological thrust completely
unnerves him. He is, in short, a man-boy, and when confronted with
an adult situation he can offer no resistance; he simply crumbles.
Lingard is not just another of Conrad's unfilled men; emotionally
arrested as he is in both conception and development, there is
nothing in him to be filled. Since he lacks substance, there is no
possibility in him of growth. *The Rescue,* so active in plot, is
doomed to a static psychology. But the psychology, though unde-
veloped, is also intrusive and, with the appearance of the racial
choice that atrophies Lingard's will, dominates the plot and forces
it along its own fixed line. It is this intrusion that spoils the balance
of the novel, and makes it satisfactory neither for boys nor for men.
The presence of the moral complication prevents it from being
another *Ivanhoe* or *Treasure Island,* masterpieces perfectly geared to
younger readers; they are not barren of moral dilemmas, but these
are nicely subordinated to the action. The inwardly empty personality of Lingard, the unfinished man, prevents the moral complication
from being dealt with at all. Conrad is intent on constructing a novel
that will round out his Malay trilogy and succeeds reasonably well in
all ways but one. His Pacific stage setting is effectively projected, his
plot is animated, his minor characters clearly if not subtly drawn.
But his imaginative failure to realize Lingard as a human being is
fatally compounded by the ambitious act of plunging him into a
situation too large for him to cope with. He gives up at the start and
thereafter only goes through the motions, dooming the novel to
fragmentation.

As a mélange of occasionally attractive parts, *The Rescue* is a
better book than *The Arrow of Gold,* but with the arrival of the
Travers party, it sinks into the same deep freeze. Lingard is exposed
as a no-man after the first brush with his fellow whites, and Conrad
proceeds to demonstrate it at length in his marshmallowy love affair
with Mrs. Travers. The terms of their mutual attraction are rudimentary. She chafes at the tepid conventionality of her marriage and

the querulous self-importance of her husband. The sight of Lingard, brawny, primitive, living under the spur of powerful feelings, draws her at once. What he sees in her, aside from the initial impression of fair-haired good looks, is not evident. She is the first woman ever to have attracted him; perhaps that is reason enough. Once under way, their relationship deepens the psychic fog that already muffles Lingard. They converse at great length about their earlier lives. Lingard briefs her on his Malay involvement, takes her back and forth among the several camps, and enlists her as his special assistant. But at no point do they ever make contact. There is no exchange of identities, no awareness of each other as distinct persons, no annihilation of spiritual distance. They are the two most solipsistic lovers in Conrad since the Verlocs.

Yet they embrace, exchange confidences, and spend a night together on the beach when presumably they become lovers. Lingard assigns to her a decisive role in his plans. But however intimate their physical relationship, their psychological contact is nil. Nothing seems real to them, least of all themselves. Mrs. Travers compares herself and Lingard to characters in an opera. An opera may be a gorgeous show, she admits, but too artificial and unreal to be taken hold of. Lingard, who has seen only one opera, during his gold-digging days in Melbourne, surprises her by remarking that he found it "more real than anything in life" (p. 301). It is hard to say which attitude suggests more acutely the abstract remoteness of their love affair, the woman who compares it with the operatic form which she finds fatally inane, or the man who thinks opera more real than life itself.

What goes on in her heart is even more opaque than what transpires in his. Aside from a mechanical responsiveness to a "romantic" situation, apparently nothing does go on. Because they feel so little, what they do is reduced in consequence. When at the decisive moment Mrs. Travers betrays him by keeping silent about Hassim's ring, he says that it would have made no difference. He was incapable of going to Hassim's aid anyway. Lingard is perfectly right. Their actions, like their emotions, have no relevance, and though the two of them are passing through a strong if nebulous personal experience, it remains unrelated to and outside the current of the novel. It belongs to the same category of nonexistence as Lingard's own self. Their last scene together, on the sandbank after Lingard's plans have been blown sky-high, has them bidding each other farewell with the insubstantiality of two bodiless ghosts. Shortly afterward she throws Hassim's undelivered ring into the sea, a gesture that underlines the meaninglessness of what has happened. The ring, key to the unfolding events, fails to draw her into them before they come to a head and leaves her blankly unconcerned after. To the end, Mrs. Travers remains an ornamental appendage. The indifferent woman and the empty man—an appropriate pair of lovers for a narrative that strains beyond its emotional means.

But if *The Rescue* fails at the center, it has its peripheral triumphs. Virtually all the description of sea movements, from the dead calm of the opening chapter to the violent thunder squall that strikes the brig (pp. 44–46), is firmly textured. The plot has its spurts of excitement, climaxed by the ten pages when Lingard, with Mrs. Travers by his side, negotiates for the release of the two kidnaped white men (pp. 289–298). The Malays may not be "real," but aside from Hassim and Jaffir who are a bit too stiflingly noble, they are an interesting lot; Daman, Belarab, and Tengga stand comparison, in effective definition, with the Abdullas and Babalatchis who brought down Almayer. And in Mr. Travers, Conrad introduces a pompous, stiff-necked, apoplectically conceited man who lends great weight to the supporting cast.

The story itself is brought to a rousing finish by another of those jumps that recur in Conrad's life and work. This time it is not Conrad jumping out of his racial surroundings or Willems frightened by his dream of falling into a deep pit or Jim jumping into the everlasting black hole of the lifeboat or Brierly jumping to his death by drowning or Falk falling out of the human race altogether, but old Jorgenson deliberately blowing up the ammunition ship, and himself with it, by jumping down the hatchway with a lighted cigar in his mouth. This act of naked courage is muffled somewhat by being told in flash-back. Since it is a straight physical event without psychological overtones, it deserves to be told as it occurs instead of recapitulated after it is over.

Jorgenson's jump is the first such event in Conrad that brings matters to a close. The earlier ones initiated the jumpers, or their survivors, into a life of moral action. This one finishes off an affair whose consequences and characteristics are almost purely mechanical. As such, it bares the fabric of *The Rescue* more incisively than any other single event. For in its melodramatic excitement lies the novel's principal appeal, as in its emotional blankness lies the work's chief shortcoming. In these illuminations, it underlines the falling-off of the late novels from Conrad's earlier work. In his recurrently Sisyphean task Conrad is still struggling to reach the top of the hill, but his diminishing supply of imaginative energy dooms him to failure.

The Rescue is a braver try than The Arrow of Gold, yet it too falls painfully short. Its real trouble is suggested by Lingard himself. When told of the disastrous slaying of Daman's Malays by his own men, he feels that the cause lies "in the unexplored depths of his own nature" and mutters "I am not a lucky man" (p. 329). He is convinced, however vaguely, that some secret enemy, some subtle traitor lies within himself, and this robs him of his sense of mastery. Instead of reacting in some visible way to the shock of this suspicion, Lingard sinks for the umpteenth time into emptiness. "A sort of blankness fell on his mind," Conrad observes. If the Lingard trilogy had followed the life of its hero in chronological order, the Lingard who performs so decisively in Folly and Outcast would have been inconceivable after the shattered man of The Rescue. The blankness which seizes him now settles upon Conrad at the same moment of decision, the moment when action is transformed into emotion, when figures become characters, melodrama drama, when the physical is invested with the metaphysical, and a rousing novel turns into a purposive work of art. These transformations, which were still taking place as late as The Shadow-Line, occur no longer. Conrad's mind is no less clear than before. His sense of structure is as powerful, as conceptually rich as ever. His will to create remains unflagging. But his aesthetic reflexes have slowed. He is still able to formulate a blueprint, set the scene, and get through the preliminaries. But at the catalytic instant, the power fades. Just when he should rise to the final effort, Conrad slumps back into his exhausted self.

The last of the three late novels, The Rover, brings into focus the range of Conrad's plan governing all three. The passage through the three stages of life in Youth and Two Other Stories is once again chronicled, at however slackened a tempo. Monsieur George is a youth still in his teens. Lingard, at thirty-five, is in his prime. Peyrol, the aging central figure of The Rover, has retired from a long career as a pirate and freebooter to spend his remaining years in rural obscurity near Toulon. A quick comparison with Captain Whalley, however, indicates the attenuation of Conrad's art. Both old men are still physically vigorous and strong-willed. But Whalley has an interior nature intricately compounded of honor, professional pride, parental affection, and instinctive judgment, which defines him as a particular person without diminishing his heroic energy. Peyrol is little more than an image of an elderly seaman with white hair and muscular arms. The stock virtues of courage, intrepidity, serenity of spirit are slapped on him like labels but do not emerge from any action of his mind. On the few occasions when Conrad visits his mind, he finds nothing there: ". . . Peyrol discovered that his own mind was a perfect blank. . . . His head feeling strangely empty, he felt the pressing necessity of furnishing it with some thought without loss of time" (p. 121).

He searches hard for a thought, but to no avail. "But still he could not find an idea for his head. Not what one could call a real idea. It wouldn't come" (p. 122). Finding ideas elusive, Peyrol falls back on recollections. Of these he has an abundant supply, most of them from his years in the Far East as a member of the Brotherhood of the Coast, a trade association of pirates raiding the shipping lanes off China. The only event of any consequence since his return to France has happened a few hours before, when he knocked unconscious an English sailor landed from one of Lord Nelson's hovering warships to spy out the coastline. The memory of the blow, delivered with neatness and force, fills the chafing void of his mind and rescues him for the moment from the vacuum of idleness. The incident is characteristic of Peyrol. He functions only within the frame of simple sensory experience, undisturbed by refinements of feeling, intellectual agitations, or emotional conflicts. Whatever course his story will take, it will be free of serious issue.

The tone is quiet, deliberately subdued, almost matter-of-fact, in contrast with the formidable size of the historical and geographic properties surrounding the tale on all sides. The French Revolution, from the Reign of Terror to Napoleon, is present. So is Lord Nelson not long before Trafalgar. The intimate communion of the English and French, enemies but with an elaborate respect for each other, is a persistent leitmotif. In the offing, yet audible and visible in every chapter, is the Mediterranean, bearing Peyrol home at the beginning from his long exile and cradling him in death at the end as he ventures forth upon it for the last time. Its glistening surge moves Conrad to brief descriptive rhapsodies that enamel *The Rover* throughout.

The characters make their appearance as the nineteenth century dawns and take on something of the melodramatic inflation of the period. The heroine, Arlette, has been shellshocked by her bloody experiences during the Terror. The villain, Scevola, is a dimwitted, brutish fellow who rose from obscurity during the Revolution like scum to a bubbling surface, sent Arlette's parents, among others, to their deaths, and is now master of their farm, maneuvering avidly to be master of their daughter as well. Conrad describes this gloomy Jacobin as "a creature of the universal blood-lust of the time" (p. 48)—the French Revolution, like all other political upheavals, appeared to him a physically violent, morally meaningless transfer of power from one group of incompetents to another. The young hero, Lieutenant Réal, is an agent of Napoleon dispatched by the French navy to lure Nelson's blockading fleet off on a false scent, at the expense of his own life if need be. This sacrificial gesture seems not to disturb him; he is a dry, bureaucratic, humorless young man who does not sweat. Even when he falls in love with Arlette and suddenly wants to live, he remains curiously matter-of-fact. " 'I have my duty,' said Lieutenant Réal in measured tones" (p. 226), experiencing little difficulty in pulling himself together. A phlegmatic temperament is in his case not just a screen cutting off a view of his inward self but a substitute for it. The role of duenna is filled by Arlette's old Aunt Catherine, who fell in love with a priest when a young woman and never got over it, an exotic emotion attached to a figure whose experiences are otherwise ordinary.

Presiding over this cast is Peyrol, whose own adventurous life has left little visible mark upon him, and who, in the role of *deus ex machina*, removes Scevola from the scene and sacrificially substitutes himself for Lieutenant Réal with a single bold maneuver. He draws off Nelson, dies under British musket fire, paves the way for the lovers to embrace unimpeded, and permits the warring sides to exchange compliments on each other's gallantry as he is buried by the British in his beloved tartan, the French flag flying on it, with full military honors. The gold pieces he leaves behind, his life savings, are found by the happily married Réals who turn them over to the state. The novel closes on a note of sentimental reverence and hushed finality as the man "of large heart," now asleep in the Mediterranean, is remembered by the living in terms of the mulberry tree "standing like a sentinel" (p. 286) at the head of the peninsula under whose shade Peyrol used to sleep at noon.

In this last completed novel of Conrad's, Peyrol had returned home after a lifetime of voluntary exile, and with a deliberate act of devoted heroism, partly personal, partly patriotic, was received back and restored to high esteem by his native land. No psychological complexities in him or in the figures grouped about him interrupt the even flow of his requiem, which serves in retrospect as Conrad's farewell not alone to Peyrol but to his own art and perhaps even to the stresses of his own life. The lines from Spenser on Conrad's tombstone at Canterbury apply to Peyrol as well:

> Sleep after toyle, port after stormie seas,
> Ease after warre, death after life, does greatly please.

These assuaging words were painfully earned by Conrad. In Peyrol's case, they are merely assumed. The novel is filled with sleep, port, ease, and death, but the more difficult antitheses of toyle, stormie seas, warre, and life appear for the most part offstage, when they appear at all.

For many chapters nothing happens; except for the brief sea chase at the end, when Peyrol maneuvers to be overtaken while pretending to make every effort to escape, the narrative is almost totally static. The characters stand about musing or observing one another's movements with scarcely any progression, and the noonday nap that Peyrol takes under the mulberry tree is taken by Conrad as well. There are prolonged stretches when Conrad does not appear interested in what he is doing, an indifference reflected in the blankness of mind that overtakes Peyrol at frequent intervals and causes him, as we have already observed, to go forth in search of an idea. He almost welcomes the opportunity to die to some purpose at the end, for it at least signals a relief from the tedium of retirement. After his death, the exact commemorative note is struck by the survivors. The most significant thing Réal can say about him is that "he was not a bad Frenchman" (p. 286), his public role overshadowing the private to the very last. Peyrol has, in fact, no private side in terms of a distinctive and articulated inner consciousness. His motivations and activities are purely external, making him faithful to the tradition of the final trio of novels. We are fenced off from Monsieur George's inner life by the stylized gestures and emblematic rigidity of *The Arrow of Gold*. Lingard bows out in paralyzed confusion the minute his inner self is summoned. With Peyrol, Conrad no longer bothers even to make the effort. The rover is a man who lives in things rather than in consciousness. He manages to function through almost three hundred pages without venturing an opinion, registering an emotion, or expressing a thought that is not strictly limited to an immediate pragmatic situation. This is an achievement of sorts, but the achievement of a man palpably writing at half steam.

Aside from its consistently effective tone of elegiac quietude, a tone unmarred by issues or complications of any real kind, the novel relies heavily on its re-creations of sky and sea. These indicate that, however far Conrad has faltered in other directions, he has lost little of his natural skill as a scene painter. His color sense is still active: "Far below him the roadstead, with its play of grey and bright gleams, looked like a plaque of mother-of-pearl in a frame of yellow rocks and dark green ravines . . . while above his head the sun, behind a cloud-veil, hung like a silver disc" (p. 144). His sentences dealing with nature still retain their voluptuous beat: "The blue level of the Mediterranean, the charmer and the deceiver of audacious men, kept the secret of its fascination—hugged to its calm breast the victims of all the wars, calamities and tempests of its history, under the marvellous purity of the sunset sky" (p. 286). Flashes of the old metaphorical power are still in evidence: "The whole neck of land was so low that it seemed to have no more thickness than a sheet of paper laid on the sea" (p. 15). And at climactic moments his landscape widens to encompass a large tableau without loss of boldness or vigor:

Astern of the tartane, the sun, about to set, kindled a streak of dull crimson glow between the darkening sea and the overcast sky. The peninsula of Giens and the islands of Hyères formed one mass of land detaching itself very black against the fiery girdle of the horizon; but to the north the long stretch of the Alpine coast continued beyond sight its endless sinuosities under the stooping clouds.
The tartane seemed to be rushing together with the run of the waves into the arms of the oncoming night. (*The Rover*, p. 261)

All this treatment of nature, however effective in itself, has as little to do with the narrative as the nature in *Almayer's Folly,* when Conrad was first learning to fuse the dissociated elements in his writing. Here it matters less, for the narrative is itself largely inorganic and therefore hard to fuse with. *The Rover* is as amorphous in its main course as its two predecessors and, like them, is successful chiefly in its secondary qualities. The tone of the book, with its muted threnody, is appropriate to the farewell appearance of Conrad's last formulated hero. The waters of the great inland sea that finally engulf him supply the tale with an eloquent format. In the end we read *The Rover* less as a story with a cast of characters and a progression of plot than as an ode, formal, dignified, elegiac, a commemorative farewell to life rather than life itself.

The separation of Conrad from his art, ominously announced in *The Arrow of Gold,* was now in full swing. The ebb of his creative energies was not, however, a steady process. *The Rescue* and *The Rover* are better books than *The Arrow of Gold,* yet they too bear the marks of a dwindling power: a failure to relate emotion to character, an inability to link thought and action, a faltering at the point of crisis when plot and psychology, fusing, pass into a more complex dimension; these are all mirrored in a slackened prose that now struggles for effects once achieved sustainedly, and succeeds only in intermittent flashes. The steady erosion by long years of gout and neuresthenia had at last affected Conrad's vital energies. He could no longer write by hand. Dictation to a secretary thrust a wedge between himself and the flow of language, which became visibly stiffened and formalized.

But as the pressure of bad health increased, financial pressure eased. His success with the reading public was now assured, following at long last the critical success he had enjoyed from the beginning. He had driven himself without letup through disheartening obstacles so that he might make his way in a profession for which he was ill-suited by temperament, however gifted by natural genius. The act of writing had always come hard to him. Now the relaxation of external obstacles seemed to produce a corresponding relaxation in his imaginative efforts. He was no longer descending to the deepest sources of his consciousness, to that "lonely region of stress and strife" that he had invoked in the Preface to *The Nigger.* His last narratives emerged from the top of his mind rather than the bottom.

They leaned more heavily on memory and less on imagination. And as Conrad ascended from the depths toward the surface, his work relied increasingly on plot and on externals, drawing the characters away from the ambiguities of their moral selves to the certainties of physical action. The fineness of balance between the psychic and sensory dimensions shifted, destroying the harmony between them which had been one of his supreme achievements. Removed from its inner frame, his work began sliding toward melodrama with its extravagant emphasis on action. It was all too easy to yield to this process after the enervating struggles of a long lifetime. His aching nerves, his gouty hands, the sudden assault of old age, accelerated the loosening and unhinging of his art. "He was very tired toward the end," Galsworthy recalled; "he wore himself clean out." [2]

Nor was he the first great writer to suffer a decline. Shakespeare's last plays—begun when he was fifteen years younger than Conrad at a similar point in his career—*The Winter's Tale, Cymbeline,* and even *The Tempest,* recede sharply from the height of *Lear, Othello,* and *Macbeth.* Shakespeare retreated in better order than Conrad, but he unmistakably retreated. Conrad's syndrome of decline, like the other largely baffling operations of the creative process, made its appearance irresistibly. His last three novels, stretched over the last six years of life, bear the encroaching symptoms of decay. They are portents of the approaching end, the exhausted products of his fading power. By this margin Conrad outlived his own greatness.

[2] *Castles in Spain,* p. 110.

XIV

The Inscrutable Universe

MEANWHILE HE CONTINUED TO WRITE. "THE ROVER" HAD REVERTED TO Napoleonic times, a period that had fascinated Conrad for many years as it did the nineteenth century as a whole. In 1906 he had written a lengthy but thin-blooded story, "The Duel," dealing with a feud between two French officers in Napoleon's army. He now began reading books on the period in the British Museum, and in 1921, on a vacation in Corsica, cast about for local color. All this research went into the novel *Suspense*, worked at off and on from 1920, more than two hundred pages of which were written when Conrad died.

The published fragment flows as viscously as the other late novels, introducing the characters with elaborate flourishes and in densely circumstantial detail. There is little in it to arouse our interest, for the figures do not emerge from their historical cocoons and the intrigue centering around Napoleon at Elba unfolds slowly and without enough *brio* to capture our attention. The young protagonist, Cosmo Latham, is an English version of Monsieur George, about the same age and equally impressionable. Having made a sweep through the three ages of man in the stories of *Youth,* and repeated the course a second time in his last trio of novels, Conrad appears ready to start the same circuit still a third time with *Suspense*.

The formal resemblance to *The Arrow of Gold* is striking. The central figure is again a susceptible youth whose only vocation is to have adventures (though neither Cosmo nor George impresses us as being adventurous by nature). The scene is not Marseilles but Genoa, another large port on the same sea. Cosmo is on the verge of falling in love with a French girl just slightly older than himself, lovelessly married to a much older man, not unlike Rita in her liaison with Allègre. The Don Carlos figure in *Suspense* is Napoleon, himself in exile but gathering his forces to return to power. And Dominic Cervoni reappears in the person of Attilio, the stalwart Italian sailor involved in deeply secretive ways with the maneuvers in Elba. The tone of this book is not quite so rigidly lofty, the rhetoric not quite so portentous as in *The Arrow of Gold,* but the sight of Conrad following in his own track with so little psychological variation is another sign of his depleted inventive powers.

In 1920, before starting serious work on *Suspense,* he wrote the Author's Notes and assembled the volumes for his first collected edition, perhaps the most satisfying single climax available to a professional writer. During that same year he also turned *The Secret Agent* into a play. It was produced in 1922, but was unenthusiastically received and had only a brief run. In 1923 he made a trip to the United States as house guest of the Doubledays, his American publishers. He gave a public reading before a specially invited audience, the only such occasion in his career; he was pleased with it, but remained too self-conscious about his heavy accent to try another.

He continued to be beset by familiar difficulties, his own ailments, his wife's, the usual despair about the progress of his work. But in the light of his continuing prosperity, these difficulties did not seem quite so burdensome or at any rate his lamentations about them were expressed in accents not nearly so heart-rending as before. The sense of having reached a professional height sustained him amid his persisting woes. If he needed any final proof of this, it was supplied in 1923 by the celebrated auction in New York of the John Quinn library. The numerous Conrad manuscripts bought by Quinn over the years for modest sums were sold to dealers and collectors at staggering prices.[1] Though Conrad enjoyed no direct cash benefit from the occasion, the public accolade was bracing to his self-esteem.

No special events marked the year of his death. If anything, he spent 1924 more quietly than usual. There were no trips abroad. Conrad worked intermittently on *Suspense,* his main project at the moment. He refused invitations from editors to contribute articles on the state of Europe, a subject he used to put forth strong opinions about but in which he had now lost interest. He kept up his usual

---

[1] After Conrad's death their value in the speculative market fell sharply, as part of the general decline of interest in him. Conrad, however, was spared the pain of this reversal.

barrage of letters, though Curle and Aubry had succeeded Garnett, Galsworthy, and Cunninghame Graham as his chief correspondents. Perhaps his most striking gesture of 1924 was to refuse the offer of a knighthood from the government, of a piece with his earlier refusals to accept honorary degrees from universities. [2] Since he never indicated his reasons for declining, one can only guess at them. He may have felt that academic and political distinctions of this kind might symbolically encroach on his independence as an artist—which was Galsworthy's reason for rejecting an offer of knighthood from Lloyd George in 1917.[3] It is more likely, however, that his sense of being an intruder in England blocked him off from accepting these peculiarly English honors.

The final months and weeks passed by with no great alteration in the routine of his life at home. He was often tired but not more so than in recent years. His doctors found nothing unusually wrong with him, nor did he complain unaccustomedly. He spent a good part of August 2 at his desk working. Yet at eight-thirty the following morning he was taken by a sudden fatal heart seizure, and died within minutes. In four months to the day he would have been sixty-seven.

At the end of his life he was an honored and eminent man. He had had two careers and succeeded in each. If his uncle was the gadfly spurring him on from crewman to captain, he was his own goad in the riskier, more ambiguous pursuit of letters. The pressures he endured in this, the difficulties surmounted, the fortitude displayed are among the remarkable human records of the age.

In what is perhaps Conrad's greatest and most moving single letter, written on May 31, 1902, to William Blackwood, the Edinburgh publisher who had printed a number of his celebrated stories, he declared: "Now my character is formed; it has been tried by experience. I have looked upon the worst life can do—and I am sure of myself, even against the demoralising effect of straitened circumstances." [4] And farther on in the same letter, in response to Blackwood's assertion that he had been a loss to the firm, Conrad launched into an impassioned estimate of his own achievement. He made the

[2] LL, II, 297–298.
[3] H. V. Marrot, *The Life and Letters of John Galsworthy* (New York, 1936), pp. 435–438.
[4] *Letters of Joseph Conrad to William Blackwood and David S. Meldrum*, p. 154.

following ringing affirmation of his work, his most significant statement on the subject aside from the Preface to *The Nigger:*

My work shall not be an utter failure because it has the solid base of a definite intention—first: and next because it is not an endless analysis of affected sentiments but in its essence it is action . . . nothing but action—action observed, felt and interpreted with an absolute truth to my sensations (which are the basis of art in literature) —action of human beings that will bleed to a prick, and are moving in a visible world.[5]

His novels express his fascination with the workings of the atrophied will, but his own life and career is a continual affirmation of a persistent, self-rousing, and triumphant will. Triumphant over what? Over the most difficult of antagonists: nothingness. The world was a void whose emptiness could be filled only by the creation of experience. As a boy, Conrad, oppressed by the iron blankness of Poland, instinctively broke free of it in search of a meaningful universe that would draw from him the responses that alone could testify to his being alive. For twenty years, as a volatile youth in France, as an able-bodied seaman advancing in the British merchant marine, and as an officer aboard trading vessels in the Far East and the Congo, he pursued sensations and actions that he hoped would give his existence purpose and substance. In the end the pursuit failed. The French interlude wound up in the despair signaled by the probable attempt at suicide. The years as a seaman were accompanied by growing boredom, a sense of personal isolation, and disaffection with the sea. His Far Eastern and African passages were punctuated by spasms of gnawing ennui or acrid disillusionment often unrelated to the particularities of time and place. One of the chief reasons for Conrad's turning away from the sea to literature was that the psychic props of his sea life had collapsed and it had become a matter of personal survival for him to try his hand at something else.

For years his uncle had urged him to write for the Polish newspapers; hence, the idea of literature as a subsidiary or secondary profession was by no means something that turned up out of nowhere; it was in his mind as a possibility long before he quit the sea (or the sea quit him, considering the difficulty he had getting

5 *Ibid.*, pp. 155–156.

berths). The writing of "The Black Mate" as far back as 1886 and the commencement in 1889 of *Almayer's Folly* as a time-filler suggest how early the process had been present in his consciousness. Though he entertained various schemes in the 80's of other employment, when he and the merchant marine came to a parting of the ways in 1894 he went straight and undeflected into literature. He had, after all, written plays as a boy in Poland, almost as though he intended to follow in his father's footsteps. His becoming a sailor was the really surprising development, unlikely, unprepared for, and unpredictable from any angle.

Although in many ways the profession of letters was particularly trying for a man of Conrad's temperament, it nevertheless had two attributes that held a special appeal for him. One was its aloneness as a natural condition of work. A writer is in a room by himself, cut off from others. To a man like Conrad, fastidious, highly temperamental, with rackety nerves and enduring one kind of physical pain or another most of the time, a craft which he could pursue in solitude, without the multitude of constant adjustments which working with others entailed, must have been peculiarly attractive.

Its other inherent condition was the blank page. That unfilled rectangle symbolized the meaning of Conrad's universe. By itself it was nothing, but leaped to life when filled by the images of his brain. Moreover, it demanded to be filled, and nothing was quite so intoxicating to him as the creation of meaning. The stream of inchoate sensory experience exerted a perpetual challenge, crying out to be shaped. The call of the world was as strong to Conrad as to Browning, though he did not believe for a moment that God was in his Heaven or that the world meant intensely and meant good. Though he held to order as tenaciously as Alexander Pope, he did not accept the conviction that whatever is, is right. Whatever is, is in all probability wrong. What may be—there was some hope, though not very much, for that. The power of man to create form out of a formless world was the cornerstone of Conrad's metaphysics, and of his art. It was a lure that drew him to literature not simply as a means of earning his bread but of fulfilling himself.

There was nothing Godlike about his act of creation. On the contrary, it was always painful, spasmodic, and prey to stretches of sterility. It frightened Conrad and made him wish himself free of the whole wretched business. He became conscious all over again of finiteness and limitation. Every man might create his own moral universe by an act of will, as the existentialists claim, but even when the will is strong and unflagging nothing meaningful necessarily emerges. The nature of human creativity is as uncertain and finally as inscrutable as the world men inhabit. Through a persistent display of character, by dogged endurance, Conrad hung on through the sterile times until the fertile ones came. These he fell upon greedily, knowing they would not last. Locked in an eternal cycle of fullness and emptiness, he was equally conscious of how much men could do and how little, of how far the darkness of an enigmatic cosmos could be penetrated and of how difficult was the effort required, and how finally limited. Sören Kierkegaard, eyes popping, veins bursting, in a supreme straining to subdue his rational self in order to release the energy of faith which alone would lead him to God, recalls Conrad in a similar posture. Conrad also addresses what he conceives to be the creative principle, working not through the outside order of things but in his imagination. It proves as recalcitrant and elusive as Kierkegaard's Deity, and Conrad's struggle to seize it taxed him to the utmost as it did the gloomy Danish theologian. The blank page was eventually filled, but with travail. Conrad's books got written, yet the birth of each was an ordeal.

Marlow's last sight of Jim verbalizes Conrad's view of man's position in the world. As the boat taking Marlow away from Patusan moves from shore, Jim recedes in the distance, and Marlow describes him in the fading twilight just before darkness falls.

For me that white figure in the stillness of coast and sea seemed to stand at the heart of a vast enigma. The twilight was ebbing fast from the sky above his head, the strip of sand had sunk already under his feet, he himself appeared no bigger than . . . a tiny white speck, that seemed to catch all the light left in a darkened world. . . . (*Lord Jim*, p. 336)

The blob of white in a gathering dusk is an image central to Conrad's imagination. Unlike D. H. Lawrence who felt the darkness was somehow sacred and must not be eliminated, Conrad was all for expanding the area of light. But he had little hope that it could be expanded far. And whatever penetrations could be made were piecemeal and minuscule compared to the immense belt of mystery that ringed the human horizon and rendered the cosmos ultimately inscrutable. Conrad embraced this as a metaphysical certainty. He was equally certain of the drive in men to wrest meaning from life despite any rational conviction that it would avail them little. "Droll thing life is—" observed Marlow in "Heart of Darkness," "that mysterious arrangement of merciless logic for a futile purpose. The most you can hope from it is some knowledge of yourself . . ." (*Youth*, p. 150). The paradox of the categorical imperative from within ceaselessly assaulting a resistant, opaque, and, in its final reaches, impervious universe armed Conrad's novels with their philosophical tension.

On both sides of this paradox Conrad was outside the format of the nineteenth century in which he grew up. His experiences in Eastern Europe made it impossible for him to accept the optimistic affirmations of society, with the accompanying faith in the possibilities of a millenium, that marked the West. The idea of progress was to Conrad the least durable of illusions. Among his contemporaries in England, the one man he was least in sympathy with, whom he detested most, was George Bernard Shaw. Shaw was the final manifestation of the liberalized, Western, nineteenth century mind, and everything about him irritated Conrad: [6] his passionate preoccupation with social and political reform, his energetic summoning of men to transform themselves into supermen, the rationalistic premise of his unending reliance on argument, and his unforgivable cheerfulness. The conception of life as a debate in which problems could be argued out and settled grated on Conrad's conviction, confirmed by his earliest reading of Shakespeare, that life was a dream whose reality, fleeting at best, had to be constantly reformulated by the imagination. The moment the effort was relaxed one sank, like Decoud, into the nothingness of things. Experience was a formless element in which, nevertheless, one had to immerse in order to survive on human terms. Conrad took the world in its harshest possible aspect: it was neither good nor bad; it was, of itself, without meaning or ethical energy; this did not

[6] H. G. Wells reported that Conrad on one occasion, feeling himself insulted by Shaw's attack on his work, wanted to challenge him to a duel. Wells cooled him off by saying it was just Shaw's humor. "One could always baffle Conrad by saying 'humour.' It was one of our damned English tricks he had never learned to tackle" (*Experiment in Autobiography*, p. 530).

make it meaningless, but only kept it from creating its own meaning; its meaning could be fashioned only by the creative principle rooted in human nature, and since this principle was uncertain, it too functioned in a perpetual abyss of uncertainty. To the Western temper of the last century, and particularly to the English, this was a treacherously abhorrent, perhaps even irresponsible doctrine. E. M. Forster, an exquisite product of that temper, believed in the objective existence of a moral element in the universe. It was inevitable that he should have found Conrad distressingly ambiguous and suspected that at the bottom of his work, underneath the verbal ornament, there was probably nothing at all. Forster's hostile verdict was the reasoned judgment of his age, and of his England, which Conrad entered from the Polish labyrinth and where, despite his long residence, he remained a stranger.

But if he did not subscribe to the tenets of the nineteenth century, he prefigured the twentieth. T. S. Eliot and Eugene O'Neill, born thirty years after Conrad, came under his influence. The figures in Eliot's early poetry, from Prufrock to the enervated cosmopolitans of *The Waste Land* and "The Hollow Men," suffer from the same atrophied will that immobilized Almayer, Willems, and Jim. The lonely men aboard the *Narcissus,* adrift on an unknown sea, are the matrix of O'Neill's sailors aboard the S. S. *Glencairn;* the dramatist's deepening plunge into the psyches of his characters in the later plays, with the almost total elimination of society and the obsessive concentration on the climate of their subrational selves, is a variant on Conrad's definition of the struggle for identity in a faceless universe. Ernest Hemingway, born forty years after Conrad, takes over from him the bleakness of that universe, from which he produces the test situations that raise his characters, like Conrad's, to their maximum pitch.

The First World War stripped the world of its intentionality and men of their psychic confidence. A sense of drift, bordering on helplessness, replaced the old feeling of purposiveness. The confidence in human nature as essentially good, which animated the romantic writers and their Victorian successors, was driven out by an ominous awareness of men ridden by forces within themselves too destructive to control. All these ideas are present in the work of Conrad and lend his thought its essential coloration. In the aesthetic mold of his fiction, he helped train the modern sensibility.

On the psychological side, he was a creator of the modern consciousness. Well before our own appearance on the historical scene, he was already "one of us."

The skepticism which he brought with him to the West did not affect his lifelong insistence that Poland was a Westernized country of Latin origin and in the humane tradition. But it freed him to examine Western assumptions in ways not easily admissible to the native-born. The prosperity and success of the age seemed to him temporary counters in a game of historical chance, based as much on the exploitation of the poor and the depredations of imperialism as on virtues of character or triumphs of technology. Society, history, the world of external nature were shifting, treacherous, protean elements that men relied on to their peril, supporting men, then withdrawing their support with quicksand instability. In the end the individual had to discover in himself the resources to withstand misfortune, a process which the novels of Conrad defined with exquisite precision. Misfortune consisted not only of pressure from the outside, but of private snares and demons from within. Conrad had a lively sense of the evil in man. Honor, fidelity, courage, communal spirit, and professional skill may have been the ideal values which he formally cherished, but they were at best only tempting ideals standing above the battle. His characters had to learn, like Marlow, to live with the Kurtz inside themselves, with the devils, murderers, cowards, betrayers lying in wait within. And at the bottom of the heap lurked the deadliest of the seven medieval sins—sloth—slowing the reflexes, eating into the will, paralyzing the moral sense, spreading its deadly inertia with muffled tread.

Conrad did not allow himself to be dragged under by these perilous visions. The trancelike dream, chill, opalescent, for long stretches empty, was, in fact, his normal mode of operation; from it, his scenes and rhetoric emerged. In the procedures of art, he succeeded not in eliminating his enemies but in forcing them to do his bidding. Far more the Manichean than the Christian, Conrad embraced the permanent coexistence of energy and sloth, his special form of the struggle between good and evil, but put this abrasive conviction to creative use. His ability to exploit his own philosophical pessimism to productive ends, to ride the tiger of his own treacherous temperament, led finally to his being fascinated by the very process of life he did not really believe in. The fascination became an act of belief. The universe may be ultimately inexplicable, but it supplies men with every opportunity to develop their powers. It may lack a moral intention, but it is charged with psychological and emotional energy. Though the cosmos may be beyond philosophical or theological speculation, it is not lacking in drama. And Conrad takes it on the dramatic side. If Henry James was, as Conrad called him, "a historian of fine consciences," Conrad is the historian of lost causes, somehow redeemed by the manner in which they are lost. He records the price men pay for having brains, conscience, and imagination, which is also the price of their humanness.

Disbelief in his case led to affirmation, the affirmation of existence as a self-producing, self-nourishing, and self-sustaining process that carried its own reason for being. He filled the blank cosmic stream with the assertions of his art. The destructive terrors of human nature made the plunge into experience more dangerous but did not make it insurmountable, so that even figures like Decoud and Willems assert their personalities and establish their identities before they vanish into their respective oblivions. Conrad's function was to peel life down to the essential core and then ask if it made sense. All the stereotyped classifications of Conrad as a romantic realist, an Elizabethan adventurer adrift in modern times, a *puissant rêveur* (the striking epithet of Gustave Kahn), an ambitious storyteller at his best when dealing with stalwart virtues and simple hearts, England's Polish genius, an exotic writer with a flair for realistic detail, suggest the ambivalence of his position without suggesting that this ambivalence became the deliberately accepted, deliberately exploited source of his career, his outlook, and his art.

To accept the worst and still go on functioning began as an instinct with him and wound up as a creed. He had plenty of opportunity to display it, for his difficult and arduous life produced an unfailing sequence of painful crises: the slow obliteration of his parents before his eyes in childhood, the entombment of his country, the corrosive monotony and loneliness of the years at sea, and the psychic perils of the changeover to a new profession, perils all too radically confirmed by the eighteen years of hardship that followed. These pressures and misfortunes he managed at first to endure, then organized them later in the objectifications, exorcisms, and penetrations of his novels. By testing his observation of others in the crucible of his own emotions, he forged the instrument by which his art was structured, and cast light on the mysterious relationship that prevails between the writer and his work.

If Conrad's life, through its persistent fortitude, is a triumph of character, his art, in its prolonged examination of spellbound men stirring from their trances toward the fullness of passion and energy, is a complex marvel of imaginative insight. Between them he made the universe he inhabited less forbidding, while extracting from it, on its spectacular side, a full dramatic account.

His first great work came at the beginning of our century, whose signs and portents he read so prophetically. He was, to be sure, a master of modern fiction, and for this reason his name will endure in the history of letters. In a more personal sense, he transcends the confines of his time and speaks to us in terms that seem immediately relevant and in accents that are surprisingly contemporary.

Perhaps the ultimate tribute to Conrad is our consciousness that he made us his inheritors.

A Selected Bibliography

BY CONRAD:

Complete Works. Canterbury Edition. 26 vols. Doubleday, Page, 1924–26.

Conrad's Polish Background: Letters to and from Polish Friends, ed. Zdzislaw Najder, tr. Halina Carroll. Oxford, 1964.

Conrad to a Friend; 150 Selected Letters from Conrad to Richard Curle, ed. Richard Curle. Doubleday, Doran, 1928.

Joseph Conrad's Letters to His Wife. London, Privately Printed, 1927.

Joseph Conrad: Letters to R. B. Cunningham Grahame, ed. C. T. Watts. Cambridge, 1969.

Letters from Joseph Conrad, 1895–1924, ed. Edward Garnett. Bobbs-Merrill, 1928.

Letters of Joseph Conrad to Marguerite Poradowska, 1890–1920, tr. and ed. John A. Gee and Paul J. Sturm. Yale, 1940.

Letters of Joseph Conrad to William Blackwood and David S. Meldrum, ed William Blackburn. Duke, 1958.

ON CONRAD:

Baines, Jocelyn. *Joseph Conrad.* McGraw-Hill, 1960.

Berthoud, Jacques A. *Joseph Conrad: The Major Phase.* Cambridge, 1978.

Conrad, Borys. *My Father: Joseph Conrad.* London, Calder & Boyars, 1970.

Conrad, Jessie. *Joseph Conrad and His Circle.* Dutton, 1935.

———. *Joseph Conrad As I Knew Him.* Doubleday, Page, 1926.

Cooper, Christopher. *Conrad and the Human Dilemma.* Chatto & Windus, 1970.

Cox, C. B. *Joseph Conrad, The Modern Imagination.* Dent, 1974.

Crankshaw, Edward. *Joseph Conrad: Some Aspects of the Art of the Novel.* 2d. ed. Macmillan, 1976.

Fleishman, Avrom C. *Conrad's Politics: Community and Anarchy in the Fiction of Joseph Conrad.* Johns Hopkins, 1967.

Ford, Ford Madox. *Joseph Conrad, A Personal Remembrance*. Little, Brown, 1924.

Glassman, Peter J. *Language and Being: Joseph Conrad and the Literature of Personality*. Columbia, 1976.

Gordan, John Dozier. *Joseph Conrad, The Making of a Novelist*. Harvard, 1940.

Graver, Lawrence. *Conrad's Short Fiction*. U. of California Press, 1968.

Guerard, Albert J. *Conrad the Novelist*. Harvard, 1958.

Hay, Eloise Knapp. *The Political Novels of Joseph Conrad*. U. of Chicago Press, 1963.

Jean-Aubry, G. *Joseph Conrad: Life and Letters*. 2 vols. Doubleday, Doran, 1927.

Keating, George T. *A Conrad Memorial Library*. Doubleday, Doran, 1929.

Lohf, Kenneth A. and Eugene P. Sheehy. *Joseph Conrad at Mid-Century: Editions and Studies, 1895–1955*. U. of Minnesota Press, 1957.

Meyer, Bernard C., M.D. *Joseph Conrad, a Psychoanalytic Biography*. Princeton, 1967.

Modern Fiction Studies. Special Number devoted to Conrad. Spring 1964.

Morf, Gustav. *The Polish Heritage of Joseph Conrad*. London, Sampson Low, Marston, 1930.

Moser, Thomas. *Joseph Conrad, Achievement and Decline*. Harvard, 1957.

Mudrick, Marvin, ed. *Conrad: A Collection of Critical Essays*. Prentice-Hall, 1967.

Palmer, John A. *Joseph Conrad's Fiction: A Study in Literary Growth*. Cornell, 1968.

Randall, Dale B. J. *Joseph Conrad and Warrington Dawson: The Record of a Friendship*. Duke, 1969.

Sherry, Norman. *Conrad's Eastern World*. Oxford, 1966.

———. *Conrad's Western World*. Cambridge, 1971.

Symons, Arthur. *Notes on Joseph Conrad*, with some unpublished letters. London, Myers, 1925.

Teets, Bruce E. and Helmut E. Gerber, eds. *Joseph Conrad: An Annotated Bibliography of Writings about Him*. Northern Illinois U. Press, 1971.

Index